FRIENDLY ENEMIES

MAXIMIZING THE
DIRECTOR-ACTOR RELATIONSHIP

Delia Salvi

FRIENDLY ENEMIES

MAXIMIZING THE DIRECTOR-ACTOR RELATIONSHIP

Delia Salvi

BILLBOARD BOOKS
An imprint of Watson-Guptill Publications

Senior Acquisitions Editor: Bob Nirkind
Edited by Elizabeth Wright
Cover designed by Cooley Design Lab
Interior designed by Cheryl Viker
Graphic production by Ellen Greene

Copyright © 2003 by Delia Salvi
First published in 2003 by Billboard Books,
An imprint of Watson-Guptill Publications
A division of VNU Business Media, Inc.
770 Broadway
New York, NY 10003
www.watsonguptill.com

LIBRARY OF CONGRESS CATALOGING IN PUBLICATION DATA
The CIP data for this title is on file with the Library of Congress.
Library of Congress Control Number: 2002109299
ISBN: 0-8230-7944-9

Excerpt from *On the Waterfront* reprinted by permission of the Miriam Altshuler Literary Agency,
on behalf of Budd Schulberg. © 1988, by Budd Schulberg

Manufactured in the U.S.

1 2 3 4 5 6 7 8 9 / 09 08 07 06 05 04 03

I dedicate this book to my beautiful and talented mother, Renata Vanni, for having had the courage to pursue her dreams and making it possible for me to pursue mine. I love you very much, Mommy, and I'm so grateful for all you've given me.

ACKNOWLEDGEMENTS

First and foremost, I owe it all to the students, past and present, of UCLA's Department of Film, Television, and Digital Media. Their openness to exploration has allowed me to push them into mysterious areas and adopt a new way of thinking. Their hunger for a way to communicate with and direct actors was my impetus and inspiration for writing about this previously ignored subject. And to the actors — without your trust, this would not have been accomplished. It's been a long road and I have many to thank for their time, encouragement, and input.

I want to thank Professor Ray Goodlass of Charles Sturt University in Australia for his diligence in helping me organize my material and seeing me through the early chapters; George Gary for encouraging me to write in my own voice; Hal Ackerman for his valuable and inspirational comments on my first draft; Elaine Madsen for her painstaking, honest, detailed and encouraging notes on each chapter; Dean Robert Rosen for his endless support over the years and for always being there when I needed him; Professors Vivian Sobchack and Peter Wollen for their support and guidance; our staff for their assistance, especially Martin Terrones, my heartfelt thanks; Elizabeth Wright for her valuable editorial assistance; Steven Stein of Ramer and Prestia for making me feel safe; Myrl Schreibman for keeping me laughing all the way; and Dr. Theodore Mitrani for holding my hand and sharing his wisdom. To my fellow artists: Alexander, Anthony, Audrey, Barry, Brand, Burt, Geena, Mark and Todd, for generously sharing your experiences and wisdom. I offer you a big hug.

To the faculty of UCLA's Department of Film, Television and Digital Media, my gratitude for introducing me to the rewards of teaching, for being such a joy to work with, and for always believing in and supporting my work.

Not to be forgotten are my professional friends in Holland, Paris, Italy, Israel, Canada, Seattle and Portland who had me return year after year to share my work with them, while at the same time sharing their culture, values and talents with me.

I must also thank the Actors' Studio, my creative home, whose high standards always inspire me to reach for the stars. It's a place that nourishes my talent, challenges me to take risks and gives me a safe haven to pursue the "art" of acting and directing.

Finally to my editor, Bob Nirkind: I am deeply indebted. Your support, patience, guidance, demands, warmth, humor, and wonderful comments made it possible for me to complete this book. Where would I have been without you?

CONTENTS

FOREWORD

What really happens between the director and actor? How do they communicate with one another? Where can one learn that special and private language? The answer lies in Delia Salvi's insightful new book, *Friendly Enemies: Maximizing the Director-Actor Relationship.*

I first met the author in 1979 when I directed her in a scene for *The Last Married Couple in America,* which starred Natalie Wood and George Segal and featured Valerie Harper, Dom DeLouise, Bob Dishy, and Delia Salvi. The scene required Delia to play a wistful spouse who is awakened by the police while they are investigating a young married couple (Natalie and George) making out in a car parked in front of their home. Delia's character, instead of being annoyed by the ruckus, is actually jealous of the fun the "necking" couple is having. It was a funny moment.

Behind the scenes, Delia was clear and direct. She actively engaged in the desire to have the set be a good workplace. Delia believed, as I do, that good acting is more easily achieved in an atmosphere of respect and professionalism. Stress, anxiety, and panic serve neither the actor's nor director's best interest. Remember that actors are playing a role. The operative word is "play." While it is hard work to "play" a role, there must be a sense of pleasure in its achievement.

It is essential to allow for failure in the thousands of choices that an actor and director make. No one is 100 percent right all of the time. And what is "right"? It is simply extending a vision with appropriate instinct and intelligence. Frequently, it is necessary to stretch and try things that are outrageous in order to understand their limits. Curiosity and trial and error are important parts of the director-actor craft. Boundaries must first be pushed before they are set.

This is what makes *Friendly Enemies* such an excellent book. Delia not only encourages directors and actors to explore their world more deeply, but also offers the ways, means, and vocabulary with which each artist can communicate efficiently with the other.

The question young film directors most frequently ask is, "How do I talk with the actor? Do I demand, insist, provoke, beg, and plead?" The question most frequently asked by young actors concerning their directors is, "What do I say if I don't like the director's views or suggestions?" Fair questions. Salvi deals with them directly and with a clear, concise style. Chapter 9, "Conversations with Directors and Actors" amplifies — with professional grace — how seasoned artists deal with their colleagues.

Actually I am surprised this book was not written years ago, because the need is great. It took an actress/educator of great accomplishment and experience to write it properly. I enthusiastically endorse *Friendly Enemies: Maximizing the Director-Actor Relationship* for use by both students and professionals alike.

— Gil Cates, July 2002

PREFACE

The best-kept secret in the entertainment industry is how much actors, including award-winning performers, distrust directors, and how directors often fear or dislike actors. Why should this be? Is it ego? Could it be a lack of knowledge? After years of addressing this problem, I've found that the answer is: both.

The job of an actor is to open up the most fragile areas of one's being. But exposing oneself like this requires trust and most actors find it impossible to trust someone who may not understand how to effectively communicate ideas to them. Directors sensing distrust protect themselves by becoming immersed in the technical issues of "the shot." The actor may be ignored completely. The reason for this is that directors often don't understand what actors want and need from them.

In a marriage, this lack of communication is grounds for divorce. In the world of film, television, and theater, millions of dollars are at stake and both parties have to tough it out with the hope that the project won't be a disaster. What should have been a mutually exciting endeavor is reduced to an uncomfortable situation. Why? Because there is no common language or understanding of each other's process.

It's no accident that the best actors' directors are either actors themselves or from the theater. The typical director has never been taught that understanding the actor's process can be learned just as precisely as learning about the mechanics of filmmaking.

With this in mind, I developed a system and structure based upon my training and continuous exploration as an actor *and* director. It's based on existing ideas, personal experiences, and a lifetime of study. This book's intention is to provide the tools necessary for fostering a creative collaboration between directors and actors as well as to make each aware of what it's like on the other side of the fence.

My hope, with this book, is to open your eyes to a new world and that it will inspire you to keep searching for the links that unite humankind.

INTRODUCTION

Friendly Enemies: Maximizing the Director-Actor Relationship is intended for film, television, and theater directors—whether they are already working in the business or are on the journey to becoming practicing professionals. It is intended for anyone who has to direct actors and is unsure how best to do so. It is for those who may know how to move actors around but do not understand how they function or how best to talk with them in order to achieve outstanding performances.

This book addresses the general dilemma faced by many directors. The problem is best described as a limited understanding of the actor as one of the instruments through which directors tell their stories. Directors are often encouraged to take an acting class in order to learn about the acting process. Good advice, but few actually follow it and those that take the plunge don't attend long enough to gain a craft. They do profit from experiencing what it's like to act and what actors go through but, usually due to time and finances, they don't develop a workable technique.

Film and television directors, as well as students, will benefit from this book. Their backgrounds and educations have stressed all other elements of filmmaking, but have left no room for mastering — if that's even possible — the art of working with actors. Directors with a theater background have a distinct advantage, as they often started out as theater majors with the intent of becoming actors or, at the very least, took some acting classes. Yet, even with such a background, there are still many shortcomings. Most theater productions I attend appear more concerned with the mise-en-scène, leaving the actors to their own bad habits. Since this book is specifically geared to the creative interaction between directors and actors, theater directors will benefit from the focus placed on working with an actor as an instrument to create an organic truth behind every directional choice.

Friendly Enemies will also be helpful to writers. The writers who took my classes at UCLA were astounded to discover how little they understood about characters and behavior. Their previous focus had always been on plot, structure, and dialogue. But as a result of incorporating this new way of looking at stories, they found that their writing became deeper, grounded, and more satisfying.

Actors will benefit from this book by discovering how directors perceive them. Little do most actors realize how important they are and how much they can bring to their directors. Here they will learn how complex a director's process is and how much responsibility rests on their shoulders. And, hopefully, actors will learn more about their own craft.

In the early 1970s, I developed and structured my original class at UCLA, "Directing the Actor," on the basic principle that it was not necessary for a director to go through all the minutiae of actor training in order to understand the acting process. My workshops and master classes have borne out this idea: that by learning and understanding the essential techniques and principles of acting, a director would have all the tools required to guide the actor's instrument into its full potential. My intention in this book is not to turn you into an acting teacher, nor to tell you more than you need to know. Too much detailed information can be counter-productive. Instead, I have endeavored to keep the various techniques and principles as simple as possible in order to demystify "acting."

WHAT THIS BOOK IS ABOUT

There are a plethora of books on the market about stagecraft, directing, pre-production, acting, the aesthetics of camera work, cinematography, lighting, sound, editing, and so on. However, there are practically none devoted solely to how directors work with actors: their human instruments. It is through the actors that stories are told. They are the ones to whom the audience relates. Therefore, it is essential for directors and writers to understand this complex entity, as well as understand human nature itself. Knowing how to effectively work with actors furthers your interpretation of the material.

My objective in this book is to give you a basic understanding of the acting process and offer practical tools to use in pre-production rehearsals and on the set. It is also to stimulate creative problem solving, because once you understand how the actor's instrument works and apply the basic principles put forth in this book, everything else will fall into place. Equally important is my goal to sharpen your instincts so you can trust them.

Conventional wisdom supports the idea that a director either understands actors or doesn't, and that's the end of the matter. This is not so. Like most elements necessary for success in any endeavor, the processes needed to elicit good performances can be learned. Although this is all well and good, no director is going to succeed solely by applying techniques without an understanding of how and why they work, what to look for, and when to use them. Consequently, in order to give you a solid and clear foundation upon which to build, this book begins with chapters that address how directors and actors regard each other.

Oftentimes, directors sense something is wrong with a performance or a scene but cannot identify the problem, let alone fix it. My intent is to help identify problems that mystify you and give you the tools to solve them. I want to develop your confidence so that you can create your own solutions once you understand this process and its basic principles.

By failing to understand the acting process, directors are often at the mercy of the actor's background. By learning the actor's language, however, you gain their trust — and nothing could be more important. By using this common language, you have the means to trigger all manner of appropriate responses.

Many acting terms — whether they are for stage, film, or television — are now part of the mainstream acting terminology. These words, including preparation, theme, objectives, actions, sense memory, affective memory, personalization, substitution, adjustments, and tasks, may be familiar but are often misunderstood. It's not enough to just know the language. It is necessary to know how and when to use it in order to guide your actors. By acquiring a certain fluency and ease with the actor's language, you will be able to create a positive environment, avoid clichés, and direct — not simply for results — but for human behavior.

WHAT THIS BOOK CONTAINS

Too many directors fear or misunderstand actors. Not enough attention, if any, is paid to understanding them as human beings. Chapter 1, "Understanding the Actor," sheds some light on the actor's psychology, their daily existence, what they need, and what they are afraid of. It also examines the various types of actors and focuses on the difference between organic acting and conventional acting, what each approach can contribute, and how collaboration between directors and actors may be fostered.

Some directors are loath to admit to themselves that they feel helpless in their ability to direct actors. As a result, they ignore them, bully them, talk them to death, or accept any sort of performance as long as the actors hit their marks and know their lines. This creates tension and a distrust of the director resulting in unnecessary fear and pain. Chapter 2, "Director: Know Thyself," explains how directors can inadvertently create problems on a set. As with most people, directors are not aware of their own bad habits or the counterproductive effect they may have on their cast. By making you conscious of these habits and suggesting what you can do to counter them, I hope to improve your interaction with your cast.

As previously mentioned, there is an actor's language that has become part of the mainstream of how we talk about acting. Most directors are not familiar with the actor's language, but those who are fluent in its use are more productive. That's because they are able to use terms that trigger appropriate responses in their actors. Chapter 3, "The Actor's Language," teaches you the terminology, the acting tools, the concepts, and explains when and how to use them.

This vocabulary was developed by Constantin Stanislavski and came to dominate the way most people speak about acting. It was later strengthened by Lee Strasberg at the Actors Studio and become known as the Method (the term most associated with him) but I, for one, never heard him use it. The New York press originated the term "method." This approach is merely a continuation of Stanislavski's work as practiced by leading actors and directors in New York. It was, and is, the development of a process that enables actors and directors to transcend mannered and predictable performances, and which guarantees consistent results.

Chapter 4, "The Director's Preparation," deals with how to analyze a script in a specific manner and create director's notes. By doing this you gain more insight into the material. This, in turn, will stimulate your imagination. This process enhances communication between you and your cast and enables you to achieve the performance that best serves your interpretation.

Another important issue for directors is the casting of a production. Much stress is placed on the importance of casting because, in truth, actors can add or detract from the quality of a production. Chapter 5, "Casting the Production," covers the standards and procedures needed to choose the right casting director. It also focuses on the proper analysis of your script and characters to support what you need to be looking for during the audition process. Suggestions are offered for setting up and conducting your auditions. I also point out common, but easily avoidable, casting traps.

Actors crave rehearsals and generally get several weeks of them when working in the theater. In film productions, however, most directors and producers resist such a notion, citing a lack of time and money. Too often, they wouldn't know how to use the time anyway. Directors who understand the acting process, on the other hand, always manage to have pre-production rehearsals despite budget concerns. The benefits of rehearsal are numerous, but if you are not skilled in directing actors, you may be hard put to understand that notion. Chapter 6, "Rehearsing the Cast," explores why and how rehearsals will serve you. This chapter explains how to schedule your sessions, how to proceed during a rehearsal, and what to strive for.

The repeated performances of a stage play and the technical aspects of filmmaking create equal problems for the actor's ability to sustain reality. Actors tend to dry up due to the repetition caused by multiple shots, long waits in between takes, or long runs in the theater. Chapter 7, "Resolving Problems on the Set," addresses these issues and proposes solutions to revive the instrument by stimulating the actor's imagination.

Chapter 8, "Director's Notes: *On the Waterfront,*" is a working model of what is outlined in Chapter 4, "The Director's Preparation." It illustrates what a script and character analysis should contain. This chapter also includes a scene from the screenplay to further demonstrate the use of objectives, beats, and actions.

Finally, Chapter 9, "Conversations with Directors and Actors," contains comments from: Alexander Payne, writer/director of *About Schmidt* starring Jack Nicholson and *Election,* which won numerous awards for writing and directing; Brad Silberling, director of *City of Angels, Casper, Moonlight Mile,* and many episodes of the critically acclaimed television series *NYPD Blue;* Todd Holland, director of *The Larry Sanders Show* and *Malcolm in the Middle,* for which he has been honored with three Emmys and the 2002 Directors Guild of America award for best director of a comedy series; Burt Brinckerhoff, producer and director of the successful television show *7th Heaven;* Mark Rydell, director and executive producer of the recent TNT production, *James Dean,* and director of *On Golden Pond* and *The Rose;* and Audrey Wells, the much-produced screenwriter of *The Truth About Cats and Dogs* and *George of the Jungle,* who directed her most recent script, *Guinevere.* In these conversations, they share their experiences and discuss what they feel is their role in directing actors. Approaches to casting, creating characters, communicating with different actors' personalities, viewing dailies, and giving actors freedom are covered, along with what they believe to be the best way to work with actors.

Also included in this chapter are conversations with a few highly respected actors: Geena Davis, Oscar winner for *The Accidental Tourist* and Oscar nominee for the highly acclaimed, groundbreaking *Thelma and Louise;* Anthony Franciosa, noted Broadway and film actor whose acting garnered critical praise in *City Hall* and a Golden Globe award for *Career;* and Barry Primus, Broadway and film actor and director of the movie *Mistress,* talk about being directed by Elia Kazan.

The Appendix includes a character analysis, sample of active verbs, and a list of books on directing and acting that will point the way to further exploration.

PROBLEMS FACING DIRECTORS AND ACTORS

The content and structure of this book is the result of a lifetime's observation of the problems facing directors and actors. Although, these days, many directors have a superstar public image, the reality is often quite different. Even well known directors must contend with many problems built into the medium and the industry. To get their films made, directors are often forced to compromise their vision of the script because of pressure from producers and distributors. In order to protect their investment, these producers and distributors inevitably want control over which star gets cast, even if the star is unsuitable for the role. This decision often results in the script being rewritten so often that the original concept is lost.

The pressure of a shooting schedule can also force compromises. But on a set, at least, it is possible for a director to have control of the cast. This is what my teaching has always been about and it is the purpose of this book: to help directors find the way to direct actors in the most productive and creative manner possible. To accomplish this, directors have to identify what they feel is an unsatisfactory performance, to be able to diagnose the root of the problem, and to then employ various tools to remedy the situation.

In film, theater, and television, producers, writers, designers, directors, the production crew, and post-production personnel all make important contributions to the finished product. But it is the actors whom the viewing public primarily pays to see. Actors provide the basic audience connection to the film, television show, or play. The actors who drive the story forward and provide its human face and heart.

Yet, despite the significance of the actor, the director-actor relationship is one of the most problematic in the creative process. This is certainly true in film and television and, to a degree, in theater. Though there can be communication problems between the director and other members of the creative team, no one group is as misunderstood and misused as actors.

Problems in the director-actor relationship are universal. I discovered this during the past 20 years of conducting "Directing the Actor" master classes for professionals throughout Europe and the United States. Most film and television directors come from behind the camera. Therefore, while they have an extensive technical background, they know little about acting. Unfortunately, they rarely come to terms with this lack of knowledge. For them, the emphasis has long been focused on telling the story through technical means that often overshadow the performances. Most screen directors, in contrast to stage directors, come from film school or through the industry itself (which means the writer, the producer, or technical staff). These directors usually have little experience working with actors and no experience in acting. You don't have to be an actor to be a good director, although if you have done some performing you will at least understand the actor's experience and be better able to solve particular problems. In part, this book is intended to help redress a director's lack of acting experience.

As we see in detail in Chapter 2, "Director: Know Thyself," the very nature of filmmaking can create enormous problems for the director. Casting an actor who looks the part, for example, can result in stereotyped behavior at best — or simply bad acting. Looking the part, not falling over the furniture, and getting the lines right are not enough. Similarly, the mechanics of the medium can be problematic. If the actors, with little rehearsal, are concentrating on remembering the blocking or hitting their marks, it can make a difference because their focus is on mechanical concerns instead of being emotionally connected to the material. You need to go beyond giving the actor basic blocking and business; you shouldn't expect actors to "will" the performance you want into being.

Many performance problems can be directly related to a director's lack of perception. If a final performance is flat or exaggerated, to use two obvious extremes, directors must be held responsible. If the flaws aren't recognized, the director is not exercising responsibility. Being able to discern who is acting truthfully, who is overacting, or just flat is an important part of a director's role.

By now, it's probably clear that the director needs to work on more than one level. My approach is based on the three levels that you need to be conscious of:

- human level: trust your instincts if you feel dissatisfied with what the actor is doing.
- diagnostic level: diagnose the symptoms, such as physical tension, monotonous delivery, lack of active behavior, etc., in order to understand what is causing the problem.
- prescriptive level: create an instant solution to the problem.

All of this is covered in Chapter 6, "Rehearsing the Cast," and Chapter 7, "Resolving Problems on the Set."

There are many pressures on directors that make it difficult to focus fully on the actors. Special effects, for example, tend to swamp a story. The film industry's tendency to produce imitative movies and television's reliance on copying successful formulas similarly encourages directors to avoid working on an original, human level. Chapter 5, "Casting the Production" discusses ways to avoid some of these common pitfalls.

The marketplace can also pose problems for the director. Due to ever increasing doses of violence, action, and special effects, it seems that audiences have become desensitized. There may well be a connection between the emphasis on effects, action, and violence and the state of contemporary society, but that is outside the scope of this book. What I do pay attention to, though, is the consequences of this state of affairs on the work of directors. Audiences are preconditioned to accept what is dished out to them in lieu of the truths of life and genuine excitement. They have come to believe they are experiencing emotional excitement because their senses are assaulted. But it's as authentic as a drug-induced high and even shorter lived. Consequently, directors are dealing with audiences that don't have the opportunity to compare this kind of manipulative film with those that reflect their lives. These professionals often end up directing for the desensitized market. It's a vicious cycle. In contrast, there are films that deal with the heart, mind, dreams, and struggles of real people and they need to be characterized by organic and truthful acting.

It is important for both directors and actors to look beyond their own special interests and recognize their role as artists in society. When they begin to explore and experience the world, they find themselves tapping deeper and deeper into human issues, thereby getting in touch with a sense of universality.

Understanding the nature of theater, film, and television can benefit the work of directors. Like other art forms, their nature lies in the reflection of the human condition. This is why it is important to maintain high standards. If you're going to do something, do it better than you think you can. Otherwise, don't bother. As artists, we share our humanity with the rest of the world. We give the audience a vicarious experience. We can make them laugh and cry. We can fill them with awe and we can make them experience another person's inner life and discover unifying bonds. I believe that when we watch television, go to films, or the theater and experience other people's lives, we see our own lives and reconnect with the common bond that helps us resolve the isolation we all suffer from.

As an actor working in the theater, it is possible to reach a deep sense of truth within oneself, that, when freely expressed, creates an intense communion between actor and audience. It is extraordinary and astounding because it transcends everything else. It is so immediate in the theater; the experience happening here and now. You feel as if you could fly. All you have to do is open your arms and soar. It's an amazing experience and it can really hook you. I've also experienced this feeling as a director, but not with the same intensity. Unfortunately, films do not offer the director or the actor this instant gratification, although this doesn't mean one's standards should be different.

I never feel a sense of futility when teaching talented directors and actors and then turning them over to the world of commerce that often characterizes American film and theater today. Rather, I say to my students and to you, "The competition is fierce. The only way you are going to stand above the crowd is if you remain true to your vision of the world and express it in your unique way. To be an artist takes awareness, empathy, a point of view, and the tools with which to express it."

Beyond this, I encourage students to reflect upon the world around them, to be sensitive and patient, to trust their human instincts, and to get out of their heads and into their hearts. Easier said than done and easier in a workshop than in a book, but I want to encourage this in everyone.

Ultimately, my intention in *Friendly Enemies* is to offer you tools to help translate your vision of the world into artistic expression through organic means.

THE ORIGINS OF THE STANISLAVSKI SYSTEM

I would be remiss in my duties as the author of a book on the director-actor relationship if I did not briefly discuss the Stanislavski System. The origins of the sort of acting you want from your actors dates back to the late nineteenth century when Constantin Stanislavski began his work in Russia to help actors at the Moscow Art Theater create real and truthful performances, as opposed to the artificial and stylized work that dominated most of the stages at the time. Though subsequent interpreters of his work have found different aspects of it to champion, it is acknowledged that one of his greatest contributions to acting was to establish a system that the actor could use at all times. With this, actors did not have to rely on the chance moments of inspiration or mannerisms. Essentially, Stanislavski codified his knowledge of human behavior into a system that allowed the actor to re-create human behavior truthfully.

Stanislavski and his Moscow Art Theater first popularized the Stanislavski System in the United States through a visit in the 1920s. Subsequently, some of his disciples, notably Richard Boleslavski and Maria Ouspenskaya, stayed in New York City and taught Stanislavski's principles by forming the American Laboratory Theater. Many American actors were inspired by these principles, including Harold Clurman, Cheryl Crawford, and Lee Strasberg, who went on to form the groundbreaking Group Theater in 1928. By putting Stanislavski's ideas into practice, they changed the face of acting in the United States.

It was in the late 1940s, with the establishment of the Actors Studio in New York by Elia Kazan and Cheryl Crawford, when a particularly potent version of the Stanislavski System came into being. Ultimately, it dominated American acting. Known as "the Method" and used principally by Lee Strasberg who had been brought in by Kazan to take over the acting sessions, it extended the actors' tools by focusing on how they could draw the character's behavior from their own internal resources — to find the inner common denominator between the characters and themselves. The two most famous (or infamous, if you will) tools to come out of the Method are "sense memory" and "affective" or "emotional memory." These, as well as many other useful tools, are explored in Chapter 3, "The Actor's Language."

These twentieth century developments have done much to create what we recognize as powerfully moving acting today: acting based on characters motivated by an internal, psychological truth rather than externally applied mannerisms. When directors understand this, and more actors are skilled in the process, the stories will be told in a way that will move audiences.

A BRIEF BIOGRAPHY

I'd like to end my introduction to this book by sharing with you those aspects of my personal and professional life that set the stage for my search for artistic truth. What I have learned, after a lifetime of work in the theater, film, and television as an actor, director, and teacher, has been distilled in these pages to make the book practical to directors today.

Though I was to major in theater in college, take professional acting classes, earn my living as an actor in New York, Rome, and Los Angeles, gain my doctorate, and, ultimately, become a professor of film and theater at UCLA, my first exposure to acting and the business of theater was close to home. It came via my mother, who was a star in the Italian theater in New York and who was later brought to Hollywood to work in films and television.

At the time, the Italian theater was as commercial as Broadway. In fact, they often used the same theaters. Occasionally, a child's role would appear and I would be used, but one very unique experience stands out for me: I played a child whose father had just died. At rehearsal, I recall thinking that if I imagined my own father dying it would help me. Even though I didn't have a strong relationship with my father (my parents separated early on), I used this fantasy and shed genuine tears. Looking back on it now, I am amazed and gratified. Using my father as an object of personalization was purely intuitive and validates the Method principles, for I'd never heard of Stanislavski or the Method — I was 9 years old! This first experience foreshadowed what I would devote my life to as an actor, director, and teacher. What came to me intuitively affirms the Method's premise that all acting should be rooted in basic human behavior. It is not something mystical, but a conscious and systematic process that aids in creating a character's reality.

After moving to Hollywood where my mother continued acting in film and television, I went to college where once again it was the accidental discoveries that contributed most to my development. Because I wanted to be a well-trained actor, I chose to attend a college with a strong theater program. Sad to say, college started me very much in the wrong direction. The emphasis was solely on technical matters. Though I don't want to undermine the importance of knowing your way around a stage, learning timing, creating characterizations, et al, my experience was, unfortunately, at the exclusion of any inner process.

At its best, the technical education led to polished behavior on stage. At its worst, it led to bad habits. Although gifted at creating physical characterization, I had no guidance as to how to find and sustain an emotional connection to the character. When it came, it was by inspiration and it was very exciting. When it didn't, I pushed for it, which is the worst thing an actor can do. Not only does this result in physical tension, it also encourages the false idea that the desire will make it a reality, or that knowledge of the character and the event will do the trick. Unfortunately, it doesn't. That is where the craft of organic technique comes in.

Inspiration can produce wonderful results, but how reliable is it? Not very. An actor's art includes having to repeat the performance over and over again, while keeping it fresh and alive at all times. Unfortunately, when inspiration doesn't come, the actor who doesn't have the tools to produce the desired results ends up forcing or resorting to using various facial and body muscles to "illustrate" the effect of the required emotional result. This is known as "indicating." Instructing the director how to recognize this and how to help the actor at this critical point is one of the major aims of this book.

However, here I must add that the opposite is equally true. I see actors today who have studied only internal work and find that they don't know how to work with their fellow actors, how to create characters, how to channel their feelings through active choices, or how to create behavior. The performance of the role is then reduced to how much the actor is "feeling" and becomes terribly self-indulgent. This problem occurs with people who have only a very limited understanding of the Method, which then leads to a painful misapplication of this process. If a technique is used correctly, it never shows. The Method is a process, not an end in itself. Nor is it a style. Those who insist that it is are not only misinformed, but also run the risk of hurting others through their ignorance.

Style comes from the material — its structure, language, events — that makes varying demands on actors but does not and should not preclude a foundation of truth. Shakespeare's characters dealt with larger-than-life issues derived from human flaws and it is incumbent upon actors to reach these heights. Contemporary plays deal with issues stemming from human and social flaws as well, but actors are not expected to play modern dramas as you would Shakespeare, or Shakespeare in the style of *Death of a Salesman*.

My first formal training in the Stanislavski System was with Jeff Corey, who had trained primarily with the Group Theater's offshoot classes for younger actors in New York. In Jeff's classes we did exercises, scenes, and improvisations; learned how to break down a script; and how to play objectives and actions. It was undeniably exciting. I no longer needed to rely on inspiration, because I had found a way to encourage my instincts and to find truth in every role. At the same time, I developed a very organized system of analysis.

Later on, I did further work on the sensory process with Lee Strasberg at the Actors Studio. This emphasis became my rock-bottom foundation. It taught me that if I trusted the process, it would serve me beyond by my wildest hopes. This made for a well-rounded system that is always reliable and effective when applied correctly. I am still working on it and am continuously amazed by the flawlessness of the process.

After years of acting and directing, I decided that teaching what I'd spent my life working to achieve would be a "mature" way to go, since having only an actor's life was no longer for me. I enrolled in UCLA's Theater Arts department and while earning my Ph.D. in Theater History and Dramatic Criticism, I was drawn to the other half of the department: Film and Television.

It was immediately and painfully apparent to me that the acting seriously marred the films of these very talented and innovative film students. The directors hadn't a clue as to what was good or bad acting, and they knew even less about how to direct the performances. The thinking through the 1970s was that everything directors needed to know about performance could be learned in a ten-week acting class. Any deficiencies could be tackled in the editing room. And so, after a couple of years of discussion, I was asked to design a course dealing with directing actors. This was unheard of at that time. It was not until the mid-1980s, when a few more film schools came into existence, that the subject was given some consideration as having any value as part of a film student's curriculum. By that time, I had already been teaching master classes to professional directors and actors in the Northwest

United States, the Netherlands, Israel, Belgium, Italy, France, and Canada. Much to my surprise, the hunger for such knowledge was universal.

Thus began my teaching career at UCLA's prestigious School of Theater, Film, and Television. It never ceases to be exciting and fun. I'm still directing and acting professionally, of course, but my greatest thrill is watching former students make wonderful films with wonderful performances and seeing them secure in their knowledge.

My major goal has always been to make directors and actors more independent — to give them something they can call their own. The real judgment isn't what they do under my tutorship, but how much they are able to make it their own and function independently of me. This, to me, is the criterion upon which I've judged my work as a teacher and, subsequently, upon which I've written this book.

UNDERSTANDING THE ACTOR

The Actor's Cycle:
Who is Bob Brown?
Get me Bob Brown.
Get me a Bob Brown type.
Get me a young Bob Brown.
Who is Bob Brown?

Directors don't always understand how actors create a role, and what they either need or don't need in order to do so. A director's resentment, fear, or awe of actors can be just as debilitating to his work as regarding them as mechanical tools that are as lifeless as filmmaking equipment.

A director's ability to understand all aspects of the complex entity that is an actor is important not only because it helps establish a positive working relationship, but also because it provides a recognition of how much actors bring to the process of creating a role. The director who recognizes this establishes an atmosphere that encourages actors to use their special skills in the interpretation of the role.

THE ACTOR'S LIFE

Acting seems to attract people who have a desperate desire to be loved and accepted. That desire has to be desperate in order to withstand all the guaranteed rejection of the profession. At the same time, however, acting provides individuals with the opportunity to express themselves in many different ways, to release feelings that society may deem inappropriate, and to have the luxury of using various aspects of their personalities.

Many people go into acting because they want to be "stars" and give nary a thought to the talent or skill the job requires. Fortunately, they don't stay in the business long. Most actors, however, have chosen acting because they love the process of creating a role and, of course, the affirmation and validation they receive for a job well done. These factors, combined with most actors' powerful need to be loved, share their humanity, feel creative and free, and connect with audiences on a deep level by moving them to laughter and tears explain why they will sacrifice anything to keep experiencing the incredible high their work (particularly for a live audience) gives them.

This drive, however, can never be fully satisfied because the profession offers no security. Consequently, actors have to prove themselves over and over again, which leaves them in a perpetual state of insecurity and makes them vulnerable and sensitive to criticism. It behooves directors to be conscious of how they provide feedback. For example, if the piece of direction you give an actor doesn't deliver the result you want, don't make the actor feel he or she is at fault. Take responsibility for having made the wrong choice or acknowledge to yourself that the choice you explored didn't fulfill your expectations. Then, tell the actor, "I don't think we should do that at all. I was wrong," or, "That leads us in the wrong direction." In this way, you free actors of self-blame and nourish their confidence. It is also important that you involve actors in your choices and try out their suggestions as often as possible.

The Actor's Life and Its Effects

Directors who have never pursued acting as a career or been close to an actor have no way of knowing what an actor's life is all about. It may, therefore, be difficult for such a director to understand the many conditions that can erode an actor's self-confidence and self-esteem. Such an awareness goes a long way toward understanding what and whom you're dealing with; the following thumbnail sketch may help provide some valuable insight into the life of an actor.

Everyone knows how painful rejection can be. Can you imagine it as a constant in your life? That is what actors live with on a daily basis. But when they do get that job, they are ecstatic. They gave a good audition . . . they've been accepted . . . maybe this will lead to more work . . . maybe they finally have that important break! And then, back to reality. The phone doesn't ring, and who knows if they'll ever get a job again. Their confidence, self-esteem, and hope are at an all-time low.

They go back to their part-time jobs tending bar or waiting tables to pay the rent, and many spend hundreds of dollars on showcases in order to present audition scenes to casting directors — who are often out of work themselves. Actors often spend a lot of their hard-earned dollars on cold-reading classes in the hopes of meeting the casting directors who teach them. When they do meet them, they are seldom called in for an audition. Actors pay for acting classes (some of which are useless) and work in 99-seat equity-waiver theaters where the owners and producers are not required to pay salaries. They do all of this anticipating that agents, casting people, and producers — anyone who can help them get a job — might show up. They rarely do. Everyone but the actor profits.

Actors also spend hundreds of dollars on headshots and videotapes to land the representation of an agent, but, usually, they do so to no avail. Reputable agents rarely see anyone without a good referral. Actors submit dozens and dozens of 8 x 10 photos, résumés, and tapes, only to be ignored. Or, if they are lucky enough to get an interview, they are, most likely, rejected again. The relationship between actors and agents is both difficult and complex. They need each other, but because there are many more actors than there are jobs, the agents have the upper hand.

In theory, the actor hires the agent, but in practice, it doesn't always work that way. Actors often feel the agent is doing them a favor by even interviewing them. Even when contracts are signed, there is no guarantee of work. Actors hang on, but rarely get sent to auditions. In frustration, they either drop their agent or their agent drops them, and the search begins anew. More time lost, more dollars spent, more fear, and more rejection. It becomes an endless merry-go-round of disappointment.

The casting process is another element that can be frustrating and disappointing. Every director and casting director has a different standard for a lead, a character type, an ethnic type, etc. One casting director may see one actor as a perfect leading woman, while another may see her as a character type because she is not pretty enough. One casting director may think an actor is too short for a part, while another may consider him too young for the same role. An actor may be considered too ethnic for certain roles and not ethnic enough for others.

Hungry for a job, many actors will try to become what they are told makes them more commercial or they will try to change what keeps them from certain roles. "Oh, if only I were prettier, taller, had a better nose . . . then I could get work." But, there is only so much they can do (cosmetic surgery notwithstanding). It is mind-boggling and destructive to the actor's identity and to his acceptance of his true self. Instead of appreciating their uniqueness, actors end up hating themselves. At the same time, actors also question their talent and ability. In other words, nothing they do is good enough. Of course, if they get the job, then they are reassured of their worth — until the next time.

Unfortunately, the "business" of acting is a difficult beast and devours more actors than it nourishes. Many hang on despite their disillusionment. Some lower their expectations until acting becomes "just a job." For others, typecasting feels like a straightjacket. The lucky ones earn a living doing commercials and playing the same type of role over and over again, but miss the creative experience. Last but not least are the actors who garner two or three days of work a year and spend the rest of their time working at unrelated jobs. Too many lives are spent waiting for a break that will open doors to a career and to a reasonable living, until, one day they wake up to find they are over forty and still working part-time jobs in order to be available for that elusive audition.

This perpetual state of insecurity erodes the human spirit, confidence, and self-esteem, so that if or when that job does come along, the actor's sense of joy in the creative process has been so dampened that the performance may suffer. The actor is so afraid of not doing well that an inhibiting tension results, and all those classes, all those part-time jobs, and all that waiting and hoping is to no avail.

Yet there is something heroic about actors. They pick themselves up and try again and again, with no guarantees.

Actors can be resistant, patronizing, argumentative, insecure, arrogant, desperate, and challenging. They may even try to take over. Just remember that the actor's fear, frustration, and lack of trust are behind it all. When you encounter these attitudes, keep in mind who actors are and what their lives are about so you can see beyond the surface and perhaps uncover a gem. Being a director is about more than just being creative. You have to be a psychologist, diplomat, and best friend.

ACTOR TYPES

There are many types of actors whose characteristics aren't determined by a style of acting but, rather, by personality, drive, professional history, and the way they utilize whatever training they may have.

The Difficult Actor

As a director, you will meet difficult or temperamental actors. Most often, such behavior has little do to with their acting ability or even their psychological makeup, but is instead the result of the place of the actor today in the theater, film, and television industries. While actors attract publicity and seem to enjoy a certain level of status in our society, in reality (unless the actor is a star) they are not in an enviable position at all. The economics and structure of the business mean that, at best, they are only guns for hire. There are countless other equally attractive, talented, and well-connected actors out there, so the competition is fierce.

The circumstances of producing stage plays, movies, or television can be equally demeaning. Casting is usually the last part of the production to be addressed and actors, once on board, are not included in any creative decision-making. They are often simply moved around with little consultation. In fact, those who don't know any better sometimes refer to them as "warm props." Actors certainly don't get much of a say in what their characters actually do. And though their work is complex and emotionally demanding, they are expected to perform instantly on cue, to jump straight in without any preparation, and to repeat the scene over and over again. The stakes are high, the tension is higher, and the actor feels like a pawn in a game totally controlled by other, more powerful people. All of these conditions can explain, but not justify, an actor's temperamental behavior. You can avoid this problem by casting well and making the actors feel like an integral part of the production. Treat the actor with courtesy, but, perhaps more importantly, regard the actor as a creative partner with his or her own professional and artistic skills and dignity. You won't change the industry — let alone an actor's lifelong habit of defensiveness — overnight. Nonetheless, you will have made a start.

Remember that fear, frustration, and lack of trust are usually behind difficult behavior. Actors, like children, need a safe place where they can be entirely free. The truly gifted actor (a rarity) can more easily tolerate the confusion and chaos that often permeates the working environment. Average actors, on the other hand, pick up the cues given to them; they notice if directors don't know what they want from the actors, don't respect them, take them for granted, or ignore them altogether. The actors' consequent fear and resentment creates a lack of confidence and respect that can lead to difficult behavior. Actors, like children, need guidance and parameters. They need to know where you are leading them and what you expect from them. They need to feel encouraged rather than judged. Again, like children, if you don't give actors guidelines, they will respond with either tantrums, blocked emotions, or a loss of respect for you. Many will even try to take the reins into their hands and will often succeed.

Conversely, actors will eat out of your hand if they feel you can guide them clearly, be honest with them, and take full responsibility while remaining open to their ideas and feelings. Actors want to give you their best and they hope that you can help them surprise even themselves.

Marlon Brando has often been described as being extremely difficult to work with. As a result of this behavior, he costs the studios hundreds of thousands of dollars — as he notes in his autobiography, *Songs My Mother Taught Me.* He writes that he has absolutely no respect for the majority of directors, except perhaps Elia Kazan and Francis Ford Coppola, and, as a result, he makes working with him hell for them. But Brando, for all his genius, rebels like a child and, consciously or unconsciously, tests and punishes the authority figure. Recently, Marlon Brando's working relationship with a director was all over the news. It appears that while shooting *The Score,* he and director Frank Oz had so many disagreements that Brando finally refused to shoot any more scenes if Oz was even on the set. To keep production going, Robert DeNiro, Brando's co-star, had to direct the scenes.

I wondered what could have happened to escalate the conflict to such an extreme until I heard Oz on the nightly news: "I should have been more supportive." I was stunned! Didn't he know this before? True, Marlon Brando is an actor of genius and a living legend, but when you have a brilliant actor working for you, count your blessings and stay out of the way. In the end, they'll make your direction look very good. This event serves as a glaring example of the attitude too many directors have toward actors.

Your compassion and humanity will serve you extremely well if you keep in mind that when actors are difficult it is usually a symptom of miscommunication or an underlying problem with the work. Actors appreciate knowing if they are heading in the right direction, and unless this is constantly reinforced, their confidence begins to wither and confusion sets in.

It also helps if you are honest with them about moments or choices in a scene that don't work. Believe me, they will respect you for it. You must be honest and specific, both in criticism and praise. Don't judge. Don't fawn. Just be simple, direct, specific, and constructive. Actors need productive guidance, with a firm but supportive hand.

The Actor's Persona

An important consideration facing a director is whether or not to cast a star (an already famous actor) in a role. I will not discuss stars of the theater here — audiences tend to equate the persona a film actor creates with that actor as a person, but this is rarely the case in theater. There are many myths surrounding movie and television stars. Not all of them have validity, and those that are valid do not necessarily pose problems for the director. For example, one movie-acting myth purports that stars only "play themselves." This does not necessarily equal bad acting, nor does it mean that all stars are good actors. Far from it. In my opinion, John Wayne was hardly an actor, even though he was a big star. Indeed, he became an iconic figure of the quiet, strong, tough American hero. Ironically, his limitations as an actor were turned into assets.

When I refer to an actor's persona, I'm referring to a strong personal presence. When someone walks into a room and everyone is drawn to that person, we call that "star quality." There's just something magnetic about them; they emanate an attractive energy.

Many actors — Marilyn Monroe is an excellent example — have capitalized on this quality and developed it into an entire persona. Her vulnerability and sense of play were enlarged to the degree that the audience believed her to be exactly the same off screen as she was on screen, which was not the case at all.

There are other legendary film stars whose personas dominated every role they played — every role they were given seemed to exacerbate their magnetic qualities. James Dean is one of those stars. Although long deceased, he is still alive through his films because of his powerful persona. He never disappeared into any role; on the contrary, he had the courage to share his deepest feelings of loneliness, hunger, despair, and tenderness with us. His every thought and feeling — deep or shallow — was projected to his audience and still resonate years later.

Some stars deliberately seek roles that break their "mold." Bruce Willis is a prime example of a star who doesn't want to play it safe. He went from playing a cocky, brash character in the television series *Moonlighting,* to a bigger-than-life hero in *Die Hard,* then on to a caring and sensitive psychiatrist in *The Sixth Sense.* Willis has also played minor roles in films like *Pulp Fiction* and each time has exercised the freedom to create a unique character. He has conducted himself as a true actor — experimenting with his talent and not hiding behind the film persona with which he has become identified.

Tom Hanks, a fine actor with a sympathetic, likeable personality, also recently attempted to stretch his abilities in the film *The Road to Perdition* by playing a cold-blooded professional killer with strong feelings of family and loyalty. Hanks portrayed the latter elements strongly, but the hardened ruthless killer his character had grown into was nowhere to be found. Consequently, we were deprived of an extremely dynamic inner conflict and some intense character development. Hanks' essence dominated the role to such a degree that the complexities of the individual he played were lost. He was still just a nice guy facing a different moral dilemma.

Conversely, we have wonderful actors such as Al Pacino and Jack Nicholson who have such strong, unique personas that they would overshadow mild characters more suited to an actor like Tom Hanks. And, can you imagine fearing Julia Roberts? Not a chance!

Other actors draw upon every aspect of themselves. There are some, for instance Meryl Streep, Dustin Hoffman, Vanessa Redgrave, and Russell Crowe, who totally disappear into their roles. They use their deepest emotional resources while meshing into the character physically and emotionally. Sean Penn is a prime example of such an actor. We are not drawn to his personality so much as we are taken in by the intensity and rawness of his feelings. He exposes every nerve within his being and dares to show us his humanity. The result may not always be pleasant, but it is always real. This sort of acting takes courage — Penn doesn't seem to care whether we like him or not. His only concern is to explore and reveal the inner truth of his character.

Of course, Marlon Brando is the absolute prototype of an actor that becomes his character. He brings his raw power and sensitivity to every role he plays, even though each character he creates is totally different. His extraordinary range of characters and his total submersion into the physical and emotional characteristics of each role is awe-inspiring. Such extraordinarily gifted actors are in a class by themselves.

For the director, then, it is essential to be totally aware of what will serve the production best. Do you need an actor with "star quality" and a distinctive, unique persona? Or do you need an actor with a major life-force who is willing and able to go beyond any "persona," to plumb the depths of his existence and immerse himself completely in the role? The bottom line, unfortunately, is usually what actor's "name" will ensure funding and distribution for the film. Under such circumstances, the leading role is rewritten to fit the personality of the star and, as a consequence, the integrity of the director's project may be violated. Nevertheless, forewarned is forearmed. Being aware of these differences in actors' personas will serve you well.

The Self-Indulgent Actor

In life, feelings are often overwhelming and difficult to get rid of. Since actors have to consciously create those overwhelming feelings, they may be afraid to trust letting go of them out of fear they will dissipate entirely. That's why we see some actors wallowing in their own pain when in life they would do just the opposite.

These actors presume, or are encouraged to believe, that opening their instrument is all that their training requires of them. They lose sight of the fact that the training of their instrument is only the beginning. It is necessary for them to play their instrument well in order to bring life to their characters and the story. It isn't enough to be in touch with your feelings and to be able to express them. All these feelings must be generated according to the logic of the characters and the given circumstances of the script. Unfortunately, actors can sometimes focus solely on their feelings and ignore their fellow actors and the environment. This is usually considered self indulgent, and rightly so. The effect on the audience — especially a theater audience — can be devastating. Fortunately, in film, an editor can sometimes salvage a scene. But the result, however, can be jarring because the edited portion may be out of sync with the rest of the scene. Understanding the tendencies of a self-indulgent actor will save you from many problems.

The Intuitive Actor

Intuitive actors trust themselves and follow their impulses. This can become a problem if every impulse they follow creates confusion by taking you away from the logic of the characters and the event. Such actors should be allowed freedom, but they should also be made aware of the parameters and logic of the character and the event. The primary problem with these actors is inconsistent performance. At the same time, the beauty of this type of actor is that their work is always exciting and surprising.

The Intellectual Actor

These actors have astute minds and ideas galore. They are precise and logical in their analysis of character and scene and are very reliable, although perhaps a bit too predictable. They will fit the bill but rarely surprise or move you because they operate using their heads, not their hearts. Such actors are afraid of the unknown and feel safe only when they are following clear guidelines. I recommend encouraging these actors to be daring — to let go and have fun — until they feel absolutely safe being free.

The Mail-It-In Actor

These actors suffer from years of being typecast and working with unimaginative directors. Their previous directors have been perfectly satisfied with the bare minimum — that the actors look the part and read lines well — and have never asked for more. These actors, who must have once had creative aspirations, gave up along the way and no longer try. I can assure you, however, that once encouraged and stimulated, their imaginations will return.

The Insecure Actor

These actors are their own worst enemies. They are talented and bright, but since they don't trust themselves, they end up third-eyeing themselves (checking their performance at every moment). By being their own judge and jury, they lose touch with any emotional connection to the role, or they have too many impulses that are scattered, disconnected, and that cause confusion. Such actors need to be relaxed — physically and emotionally — and allowed to release their feelings of fear (off stage). Once they become centered, the problem usually disappears. They also need constant reassurance, but don't let that turn into their unconscious way of getting attention or a ploy they use to avoid the plunge into uncharted waters.

The Narcissistic Actor

These actors single out an aspect of their body, voice, or movement upon which they have always been complimented. This focus forces us, unknowingly, to become acutely aware of their voice, their legs, or hands — whatever part of their bodies they are singling out to use and draw our attention. This, of course, creates artifice, which detracts from the scene. Fortunately, we rarely see this in film, although it is quite prevalent in theater.

You can deal with the different "actor types" outlined here in a reasonably successful manner by using the techniques that are presented in detail in forthcoming chapters.

TALENT, TECHNIQUE, AND ORGANIC ACTING

At this point, it is necessary to recognize what good acting is, and, specifically, what I mean by organic acting. When we speak of acting, we are referring to the practice of individuals portraying characters other than themselves. The characters were created by a playwright or a screenwriter, and they all play a part in a fictional narrative. The actor's primary task is to create a believable character. No matter what the genre (tragedy, drama, comedy, film noir, etc.) or style (epic, absurdist, Shakespearean, etc.) of the written piece, actors still have to portray authentic characters. Performance styles may differ, but nonetheless the actors are still portraying characters and aiming for truth in their performances.

Directors need audiences to believe that the actors *are* the characters they are playing. Even though viewers may know the actor, those viewers will suspend their disbelief and accept a character as real if the actor is doing his job properly.

Truth in Acting

Directors who want their audiences to be truly moved by what they see must know how to achieve verisimilitude — they must know how to give a performance the appearance of truth. I believe there is a spiritual connection between an actor and an audience when absolute truth emanates from that actor. People aren't usually deeply emotionally affected by what they are witnessing unless it is something they, too, have experienced in some way. They can be manipulated into feeling something through the use of music, editing, and lighting, but the effect of these elements alone is not particularly moving or long lasting.

Watch a range of contemporary feature films, across all genres; do the same with television programs. You will find that most of the performances are banal. How often do you sit in the cinema or in front of your television and become totally absorbed by the characters? Not very often. Most of the material we see today is formula-driven and, consequently, much more difficult for actors and directors to humanize. When we are really moved, it usually because of a performance that is not predictable and that we can identify with. We often find such performances in independent films and, very occasionally, in a TV movie-of-the-week or an outstanding dramatic series on television.

The impact of such performances is not usually achieved through language. The actual words themselves don't carry all the authenticity of the moment. It's the impulse and the energy with which the language is delivered and used. As I jokingly say to my directing students, "Those who say that the word came first are usually writers. The impulse came first, then the grunt/sound which eventually became a word." Noted director Sydney Pollack put it well when he said that, "language is the last thing that comes between people. You have responses and reactions to things, and then you have impulses, and then, maybe you'll say something, and maybe you won't. But whether you do or don't say anything, language is the last thing to emerge."

An example: You are walking down the street and you hear loud voices. You can't hear what they are saying, but you know whether those people are having a good time or having an argument. This isn't because you understand the words, but because you hear the speaker's tone. It's the tone we respond to, not the words alone. Words merely give us information. Tone appeals to us. Accordingly, an actor has to create that realistic tone behind the words. You can't rely only on words to play the moment. Otherwise, the audience might as well stay home and read the script.

Talent and Technique

Though many have tried to define "talent," no one definition is satisfactory. For our purposes, let's say that talent in acting is a conglomeration of many elements. Talented actors have the following qualities: they are in touch with their own feelings and perceptions; they are very much in tune with their environment; they are receptive to the effect people, places, and all sensory stimuli have on them; and they have rich imaginations and the willingness to express them. They have the ability to project a life-force without effort. They are people who emanate a great deal of what they are feeling; the energy that comes from them makes them special.

Talented actors have the ability to empathize with other living creatures, put themselves in another's shoes, and feel the experience. Acting talent is the ability to penetrate the truth behind a person's mask, to imitate other living creatures. It is the ability to reveal one's deepest feelings through one's physical instrument and to be able to use one's intuitive powers. Last, but not least, talent requires the ability and willingness to be a child — to believe in the make-believe. Lee Strasberg once defined "talent" as the ability to respond to imaginary circumstances. I'd like to elaborate on that by adding "the ability to respond to the imaginary *as if it were real.*"

The components of raw talent are unreliable and will be wasted unless the actor develops a conscious awareness of how to selectively arouse them during the creative process. This is "technique." Artists cannot fully utilize their talents without complete mastery of their instrument. With actors, that instrument is their bodies, minds, and souls. Mastering those is not an easy task.

Talent without technique is unreliable and frustrating. Likewise, technique without talent creates journeymen actors who are knowledgeable, reliable, and safe but not inspiring. These technical actors will be in perfect command of their vocal and physical appearance, adept at creating characterizations vocally and physically; they will move about the stage with the greatest of ease, be very adept at timing, give intelligent line readings, and will rarely deviate from them. Essentially, such a performance will be mechanically perfect but without soul, leaving an audience empty.

The magical component of the actor-audience relationship occurs when an actor conveys a character's internal life (as well as technique); the audience then has a vicarious experience through the actor. When an actor is empty, the audience's experience is also empty. It's up to the director to catch and sustain the moments of truth.

Organic Acting Defined

One of the most important aspects of believable, truthful acting is a quality we call "organic." By that we mean an actor's ability to be free with his feelings and express what he is feeling openly and freely through his body and voice; it's an actor's way of using his physical and vocal instruments to convey information about a character and what it going on with that character internally — details that are not necessarily written in the script. The audience always knows what that actor is thinking. Great actors, such as Brando and De Niro, possess this organic quality. Organic acting leaves no room for clichés. In real life, people are both unique and complex, whereas clichés are generalized and simplistic. The beauty of organic acting and directing is that it helps actors find the truth of a character, which is then expressed spontaneously through the actor's physical instrument — there are no false notes.

Which Comes First: Emotion or Physical Activity?

Acting that stems from psychological impulses is preferable to external acting that relies heavily on a set of choreographed vocal inflections, facial expressions, gestures, and body language that are, in essence, mechanical and imitative.

This raises the question of which comes first: emotion or physical activity? This is an issue that has fascinated acting scholars for centuries. Stanislavski, who developed an organic approach, clearly showed that truth in acting can only come from internal sources and that physical activity unmotivated by psychological impulses leads to false and empty work. Others championed the notion that physical activity *can* generate emotions. Here we reach a fascinating but complex stage of our understanding of the mechanics of acting. It is not that one approach is right and the other wrong. Physical activity can indeed generate emotions and is a useful approach for actors when used judiciously and with expertise. But you must know what you are looking for before you use this approach.

Generally, behavior comes after or follows an impulse or emotion. However, there is also validity in an opposing theory that suggests that emotion can follow muscular activity rather than being the cause that provokes it. Let's take the emotion of fear. There are various processes the actor can use to create an inner state of fear, but some theories suggest that if the actor adopts the *posture* of fear, he or she will be able to get in touch with the *feeling* of fear. This idea is related to the concept of "psychological gesture" developed by Michael Chekhov, who was a pupil of Stanislavski's before coming to the United States and developing his own methods. This approach argues that, for example, if you hit the arm of a chair often enough and strongly enough, you will start to feel the emotion of anger. Then, when you immediately switch to stroking the chair, you notice a strong shift from anger to calm, loving, comforting feelings. Thus, physical action or behavior can trigger emotion.

While there is value in this approach, directors have to be sure that the external behavior genuinely does stimulate an inner life. Actors using Chekhov's psychological gesture have to allow themselves to be *affected internally* by what they are doing externally. It's not enough to simply say that muscular activity generates emotion. You need to know what your actors achieve when you suggest various physical moves or gestures and note if your direction provokes the appropriate inner state of consciousness or whether it merely maintains a level of superficial behavior. Such physical behavior — and this is very, very important — can sometimes free blocked actors and liberate their impulses. It is a useful tool for helping actors who are locked into an intellectual approach. In other words, it can help them get out of their heads and into their bodies.

Imagination

Imagination plays a large part in acting because it taps into the unconscious, which is the reservoir of all our experiences. Asking actors to connect with and bring to life the experiences their characters are having by imagining details and dimensions of that experience (emotions, memories, smells, sounds, sights, etc.) that aren't spelled out in the script can be very useful. However, one must be aware that it may work very well the first time one tries it, but then dry up. Don't panic. By focusing on a new stimulus, imagination can be reawakened. Frankly, I prefer to start by imagining a real personal experience or situation because I find it reliable and repeatable.

Intuition and Inspiration

The actor's instrument includes a sixth sense: intuition (sometimes referred to as inspiration). The problem is that so little is known about this sixth sense. It is not understood or defined and it's a very hit-and-miss affair. We see it work in acting when an actor has a deep and spontaneous connection to the character's overall spine and identifies with the character so completely that the usual technique of personalization seems unnecessary. (Personalization is the substitution of a parallel object from the actor's personal life that has the same emotional value to him that the character's object has to him. This term is covered in Chapter 3, "The Actor's Language.") Some connection is unconsciously made, through "intuition," between the text and the actor's instrument. Those moments are golden and they do happen. It's what I call intuition or inspiration and sometimes it does stick. At other times, it starts to fade away and then it becomes the actor's job, as well as the director's, to find the road back to the connection. That's when a process (like Stanislavski's system) that links the actor with their personal reality will provide you with the safety net you need.

The Method as a Means to Re-creating Organic Behavior

Despite how wonderful inspired acting can be, there is a real risk that it will die out when faced with the repetition involved in filmmaking or with the number of weekly performances in the long run of a play. Inspired acting is repeatable if there is a technique behind it. Actors get used to the situation they are playing when doing repeated takes or a large number of performances.

When the instrument becomes accustomed to something, it tends to become numb. That's when you have to find some way to reignite the actor's instrument to get it to respond in a spontaneous way. That's what Stanislavski aimed for — to create a process by which the actor could, at will, re-create truthful behavior. His approach accomplishes that by emphasizing the actor's need to explore and connect with the *emotional* and *psychological* life of the character and identify with dimensions of the character beyond those written in their lines.

The Actor-Audience Connection

Directors need to be aware that good acting allows the audience to identify with the characters and their circumstances. Steven Spielberg demonstrated that in *E. T.,* in which he had the sense to make *E. T.* and the children very human. They weren't just cute, lovable, open, and adorable characters — they did unpredictable things. This enabled us to identify with them and as a result, their loss becomes our loss. We cry at the end of *E. T.* — not because we have been manipulated, not because the music has worked on us, but because we feel empathy.

Empathy leads to what the Greek philosopher Aristotle called catharsis, which is also known as purgation. Though it's unusual to find such issues discussed in a book on directing actors (instead you will find it in theater history and dramatic theory books), understanding empathy and catharsis is important because they have a great deal to do with truth, or verisimilitude, in acting. Aristotle, who theorized about and documented the golden age of drama in classical Greece, argued that the purpose of tragedy was to move the audience to pity and tears through a process of identification and empathy. This is what happens in the best of movies and television dramas. It doesn't happen when a character is one dimensional or stereotypical. No one identifies or empathizes with a cliché.

If a character's behavior strikes a chord of universality within viewers, it becomes easy for viewers to identify with that character. That's because certain emotions are universal; we've all experienced the same emotions — love, rage, sadness, joy — though in different situations. At times, we are well behaved and at times we are petty or outrageous. Sometimes we are very decisive and at other times weak as babies. When we relate to a character in a play or film, we do so because we see something in that character that strikes a familiar chord within us. This opens the door to identification; our key to this door is the actor. In the theater, actors are given common advice: grab the viewer with the first line. But that is only possible if the actors are realistic as soon as they hit the stage. That is what makes the spectator sit up and take notice. Many times I've gone to the theater, heard the actors' words clearly, but still didn't know what the actors were talking about because there was no thought or emotional reality behind their words. Making a connection between the actors and the audience is a major concern that directors must recognize and address.

ACTORS' NEEDS AND FEARS

Actors, like the rest of us, have the deep desire to please others. While some may see this as a character flaw, for actors, internal needs and fears are a fountain of inspiration for their work. Understanding the root of actors' needs and fears will allow you to work more closely with them and be cognizant of their unique requirements.

The Will to Succeed

Actors, like everyone else, have a need to prove themselves and succeed. They care very much about their profession and want to exceed their own expectations. This means that they bring professional skills to their work and expect those skills to be respected. If they are treated like puppets and are not encouraged to "reach," they close up and give a one-dimensional, conventional, predictable performance. Such performances don't move audiences and they are not the sort for which you should settle.

The Need for Direction

Actors long for real communication with their directors. They need you to be their mirror . . . to reflect back. They are not always in a position to demand such communication, though. All actors are desperate to work with someone who understands their medium and who will help them give the best performance of their lives. Actors try to get what they need by asking questions or offering their own ideas. But if the director is insecure, afraid of the actor, or has not given any thought to the characters and their place in the script, the actor remains unheard. When put on the spot, directors in this situation usually respond by saying something like, "Let me see it. Just do it." At this point, the actor knows he or she is dealing with a director who hasn't a clue and, as a result, will immediately lose respect for that director. Then you're in trouble. If actors start constantly questioning themselves, they lose their involvement in the scene; they are outside it, not *in* it, because they are directing and observing themselves. In effect, they are doing your job.

This need for direction is prevalent in all actors, stars included. In 1999, Dustin Hoffman came to the School of Theater, Film, and Television at UCLA to speak to the student body, which was primarily filled with young actors and directors. When the issue of working with directors came up, he shared his own experiences and described how, after a shot, he and the other actors often turn to each other for feedback because it is abundantly clear that the director is useless to them. Actors trust the eye of other actors because they share the same goals — to give the best performance they can. Nevertheless, actors keep hoping the next director will help them. Mark Rydell, one of our finest "actor's directors," tells of his first rehearsal with two film legends, Katherine Hepburn and Henry Fonda. He approached the awesome responsibility of working with these major stars in *On Golden Pond* with trepidation. Much to his surprise, after the first reading, they both turned to him, seeking his approval. In that moment, he relaxed because, legends or not, they were like all actors. For this film, Hepburn and Fonda won Oscars for their leading roles. It was, actually, Fonda's one and only Oscar.

The Effect of Technical Realities

Technical realities can adversely affect an actor's performance. Repetition is one such problem. In film and television, this problem is caused by the number of shots needed to get the required coverage and by the number of takes needed to get the best possible material in the can. In the theater, the problem results from the number of performances in a long-running season. As a consequence of all this repetition, actors tend to lose the impulse that made the scene successful in the first place. They dry up.

Another problem that film and television create for the actor is the need to match each shot — not just repeating the basic physical activities in each, which are usually easy enough to replicate shot by shot, but the need to repeat and match the actor's emotional state in each shot. You can be helpful by giving actors enough time to prepare emotionally, by suggesting new actions to play, and by suggesting simple tasks to reinvigorate their instrument. Chapter 6, "Rehearsing the Cast," deals with this in greater detail.

Spare Time on the Set

Like most other people, actors don't like having their time wasted. Yet, in a business notorious for the "hurry-up-and-wait" syndrome, it certainly happens. True, setting up lights, sets, camera positions, and so forth take up a great deal of time, but few directors take advantage of this time to work with their actors. Experienced actors will use this break to help themselves, but others are unlikely to do so unless you encourage them. If actors don't use that time on their own, the director who understands the actor's instrument will suggest things to think about or try during the next take. This not only saves time but also increases the quality of the actor's performance.

Camera Rehearsals

Acting in front of a camera places heavy technical demands on actors. They have to hit their marks, remain in the frame, stay in their key light, avoid casting shadows on their fellow actors, and still deliver a truthful performance.

One or two run-throughs of a scene are usually done to familiarize both actors and camera crew with the moves and the marks, and they are often the only rehearsal there will be of that particular scene. Only the highly experienced actor will know to save his performance for the take and just walk though the rehearsal. Relative newcomers should be reminded to save the performance for the actual shot.

Energy on the Set

The energy on a set — the pace at which the crew has to function — can be a distraction for actors. Many years ago, I had to do a scene for a television series in which I visited my young son in a hospital. Children are only allowed to work so many hours on the set, and by the time we came to shooting the scene, it was near the end of the day and everyone on the crew was rushing. Naturally, I picked up the crew's energy, and by the time we got to my scene with the boy, I was racing. Though I consciously tried to slow down, it was difficult to do so. It's hard to take your time with that kind of energy surrounding you. Directors can help their actors by understanding that the atmosphere on a set has a definite effect on their work.

It's also good to keep in mind that most actors only get to work every so often. Only a small percentage of Screen Actors Guild (SAG) members, 5 percent at most, work regularly. As a result, each time an actor goes to work, it's like starting and learning all over again, which can make things tense.

Rehearsal Time

The question of rehearsal time is a controversial and important issue (see Chapter 6, "Rehearsing the Cast"). Actors need to rehearse, but some directors claim that too much rehearsal dulls spontaneity. I have to refute that argument. I agree instead with actors like Paul Newman who insist that lack of rehearsal is often the result of studio executives looking to save money or of directors who don't understand their value. I suspect that some directors wouldn't really know how to rehearse a cast even if they had all the time in the world.

The value of rehearsals is incalculable. To begin with, they save a great deal of money because actors will know what is expected of them. Rehearsing also establishes a rapport, a sense of trust and teamwork, among the actors and their director. At the rehearsal, directors also learn how each individual actor works and what kind of support that individual needs. Directors develop avenues of communication with their cast that create trust. If that doesn't save time and money, I don't know what does. A productive director-actor relationship is best-established in rehearsals.

See to it that time is set aside for rehearsal before shooting begins, no matter how much pressure you're under in the pre-production phase.

The Imposition of Strict Concepts

As a director, it is vital that you free the actor to create, rather than imposing your concepts on them. The different styles of two directors central to the development of the Stanislavski System in this country demonstrate the importance of freeing the actor. Harold Clurman was a brilliant theorist and critic, a noted director, and one of the founders of the Group Theater in the 1930s. Several actors I know told me that they felt stifled when working with him. At the first day's rehearsal, Clurman would read the entire play to the cast and then impose his concept on them by giving them line readings and telling them the results he wanted and how he wanted each part played.

On the other hand, we have Elia Kazan, who was an actor and also a member of the Group Theater who went on to establish the Actors' Studio. He inspires his actors to use themselves in the most creative ways possible. In the documentary *The Outsider,* directed by Michel Ciment, Kazan talks about how beautifully "the Method" works. He talks about how he trusts his actors and allows them the freedom to follow their impulses.

Kazan also discusses the scene in his film *On the Waterfront* in which actors Marlon Brando and Eva Marie Saint take a walk during the winter. It's early in their characters' courtship. They haven't declared their love for each other yet, though the chemistry between them is definitely there. Eva Marie Saint accidentally dropped her glove during the shot. Brando leaned down and picked it up. Saint reached for the glove but Brando kept it and then put his own hand in the glove. None of this was staged and Kazan commented, "That said it all." That moment is a beautiful example of a director knowing when to leave actors alone.

Most directors would have called "cut" because the action was not planned. But the imperfections and the accidents are the exciting things in a performance. Prescribed bits of business tend to produce mechanical behavior. Don't obligate your actors to certain choices. This can stifle their impulses and their freedom to create a sense of truth and immediacy in a performance. I try to make the directors I teach understand that if they set up a relaxed climate in which actors feel respected and confident, "happy accidents" will occur.

I consider Elia Kazan the most brilliant actor's director of our lifetime. His work in that area in both theater and film is unequalled. I regret never having the privilege of being directed by him, but I have many friends who did and their stories are very inspiring.

The Actor's Trust

Often, directors are unclear about what they want. As a result, actors become confused and communication breaks down. This is a detriment to both parties and it puts the director at a great disadvantage. If one of your vehicles of expression is the actor and the actor is confused, that individual is not going to express what you want him to. Confused actors will be, in effect, paralyzed. They may wear the mantle of their role on the outside, but they will not be able to convey a complex character with all the wants and contradictions of a real human being.

It's important to remember that actors are very vulnerable and, at the same time, courageous. They have to perform exceedingly private functions in public. By this I'm not necessarily referring to physical activity that may be embarrassing, though this is sometimes the case, but to psychological activity — behavioral or emotional intimacies. Even if the moment isn't particularly private, actors are constantly putting themselves on the line. They have to use the full range of their instrument, meaning that they are exposing their feelings as well as using their vocal, physical, and intellectual skills. Under such circumstances it's important to gain their trust, for the circumstances under which actors work don't exactly foster confidence. They may have had little or no rehearsal (time is short), and they are surrounded by the bustle of equipment and technicians, which makes concentrating difficult.

There are things you can do to gain the trust of your actors. Get to know them socially, as people rather than cogs in the machine. Rehearse if you can, and welcome their opinions and input. Even if circumstances force you into the no-rehearsal mode, you can still find quiet moments to talk with your actors while the crew is doing its work. Above all, when you give your actors a note, take the trouble to talk with them privately rather than shout it across the set for all to hear. It preserves the actor's dignity and you will be well rewarded for it.

None of this means that you have to pander to the over-developed sensitivities of an actor. You must be assertive because you have to get what you want. You have to break through their walls, bad habits, and personal obstacles. You have to penetrate each actor's defensive barrier. You must be a strong but benevolent leader if your actors are going to have confidence in you. Otherwise, like children, they'll rebel because they feel endangered following someone who doesn't communicate clearly or even understand the acting process.

If you want to be a director, you have to make statements. You have to be hungry and you have to take risks. To do this, you must engage your actors. You have to stick your neck out, and that means being able to communicate. Sometimes the indirect approach is best; you will encounter actors who resist your direction, and in some such cases, you may have to back off rather than coming on too strong. This resistance can be a very short-lived problem because actors aren't blind. Once they are convinced of the quality of the work you're doing with other members of the cast, they'll come around to your way of thinking.

Being strong does not mean being a bully, however. Insulting, undermining, or blaming are methods for tyrants, not directors. Regard your actors as partners who bring original insights to their roles. Respect their ideas, but always be clear about *your* goals and motives. Remember that ultimately, the decisions are yours.

CRAFT-PROBLEMS ACTORS BRING

No one is perfect, and thus, while you may cast the best actors for your project, each one will bring a unique craft-problem to the set. If you understand some of these potential problems and the language actors use (as discussed in Chapter 3, "The Actor's Language"), you'll be able to offer constructive suggestions to overcome these issues.

The Solo Actor

Be aware of actors playing by themselves. By this I mean that they are not relating or responding to what others in the scene are doing or even to their environment. Acting is a give-and-take process that depends on very real contact between actors. They must play their "action" towards their partner to achieve their "objective," and must be open to the "action" their partner plays to them.

The unfortunate result of self-immersed acting (or bad acting, if you will) is a discordant scene, one that has negative effects on other actors in that scene. Self-involved acting gives the other actors nothing to react to. This lack of chemistry makes for a very dull exchange. To circumvent this, relax your actors and recommend a strong action for them to play — one that is sure to arouse a reaction from the "solo" actor. This should suffice to put the scene back on track.

Generalizing

Sometimes you will work with actors who are not fully in the moment but, rather, playing generalized emotions. This could be caused by several possible factors, but is most likely because they haven't found anything in the scene to motivate them to pursue a specific goal. Characters are always trying to achieve *something,* and directors should encourage active behavior to help actors discover what it takes to do so.

Sometimes actors aren't entirely engaged in achieving something. Instead they act a general emotional state, such as being happy, sad, angry, petulant, or aggressive. They may do this because they haven't prepared or they haven't made the character's needs and goals meaningful to themselves. Perhaps the whole process has moved so quickly that they have had no time to prepare, perhaps they just don't know any better, or perhaps they are simply lazy.

Whatever the reason, generalized performances are not engaging because they lack individuality and spontaneity. Be on the alert to spot such performances. Once you have, you can do something about them. In Chapter 6, "Rehearsing the Cast," and Chapter 7, "Resolving Problems on the Set," I address several quick, non-intrusive methods you can implement without turning your rehearsal or filming into an acting class.

Indicating or Pushing

When we say that actors are indicating, we mean that they are resorting to external, physical ways of showing what their character is experiencing. Affected facial and vocal expressions, gestures, and body language are the tools actors use when they are indicating. They may furrow their brows to show concentration, roll their eyes to show exasperation, bite their lip to show contrition, drum their fingers on the table to show irritation, and so on. They will display physical expressions commonly associated with a particular emotion, but the realism of that emotion does not seem to come from within. An actor who indicates informs an audience but does not involve them. This mode reveals that the actor doesn't know how to make a personal identification with the character or the circumstances of the scene.

Pushing occurs when actors experience a germ of emotional reality within themselves but don't trust it to grow, when they feel obligated to produce a stronger and more intense feeling. They will tighten their muscles to "push" it into being. They are also afraid that what they are feeling won't come across, so they over-express themselves or indicate what they *should* feel, not what they *truly* feel. In other words, they are focused on how they are performing. This strained effort not only distorts the actor's face and body, but also destroys the very thing they want to produce: depth of feeling. In acting, relaxation, trusting your instrument, and the willingness to let things be as they are are the only answers to escaping such contrived moments. In real life, people tighten their muscles in order to suppress their feelings, not to free them. This is the paradox and the difficulty of acting. If we allow muscular tension to take over, we destroy the very feelings we work so hard to arouse.

Pushing is easy to recognize on a set because the distorted expressions are obvious. Indicating is more difficult to catch.

Under some early theatrical conventions, "indicating" performances was the norm. One such example is Francoise Delsarte's codification of performance gestures in the late nineteenth century, when it was standard practice to use set gestures to reveal specific emotions. Actors learned the gestures and were judged by how well they applied them. Similarly, in silent films, set gestures suited a performance style that had to "show" rather than suggest, given the absence of language.

However, when we turn to contemporary drama, whether on stage or screen, such conventions are not only inappropriate but also embarrassing. Actors need to convince the audience that their characters are real people experiencing real feelings. Actors must internalize what their character is going through and let body language, vocal timbre, and empathy spontaneously reflect that inner state.

There is a noticeable difference between "indicating," "pushing," and a genuine, powerful expression of feelings. In a tight close-up, Al Pacino's reaction to his daughter's murder in *Godfather III* is a strong case in point. He looks toward the camera with an expression of anguish, his eyes and mouth wide open in a silent scream. Pacino's incredibly intimate close-up did not embarrass the viewer or come across as forced because his face did not just "indicate" grief; the emotion was deeply felt and therefore convincing.

There is an old adage in films that says "less is more." True sometimes, but not always. Sometimes "less is less," particularly in film because of the intimacy of the camera and how much it reveals. The camera picks up subtleties; being too powerful and over-the-top can therefore be unwise.

If, to the naked eye, it seems that an actor is doing nothing, that does not mean that he is empty. On the contrary, that actor may be alive within, and the lens will pick that up. If the actor *is* empty of thought or feeling, the lens will pick that up as well. Think of the many close-ups of characters you've seen that revealed nothing. But also consider the many close-ups that were so gripping you'll never forget them. Conveying genuine emotion without indicating or pushing — or without giving too much or too little — is not easy, especially when working with a camera.

Playing Actions, Not Results

Actors are psychologically geared to action. It is counterproductive to talk to actors about the emotional results you want from them. Instead, talk with them in terms of the specific tactics they can use to deliver results: to get that wallet from that man, to make that person love you, to get that cigarette, to break up that relationship without causing too much pain. Don't talk with your actors in terms of results, such as "be angry here," or "you are happy there." Realize that emotions are a result of actions, interaction, and conflict. If we pursue a goal and achieve it, we will have a strong emotional response. If we fail, we will have a different response. Later chapters of this book will go into more detail about this issue.

On the other hand, and despite all you've read so far, there are actors who want to play results and want to know exactly which emotion you want them to express, and where. They want all the results ahead of time. Blame it on their inexperience, poor training, or tension, but whatever the cause, you're stuck with the challenge. The situation does not, however, have to be a disaster. It's unlikely you will have much time to have your actors adapt to your approach, so give them a good reason for every emotional result you want.

For example, let's say the action for a character in a scene is to cross to the window and open it. The emotional root or motivation for that action, what I refer to as the "why," could be, "Because you feel sick to your stomach." Another action is, let's say, for the actor to cross to the bookcase and pull out a book; the "why" for that action is "Because you want the other person in the room to leave." The notion of motivation is sometimes used to ridicule any method-based approaches, and the need for an actor to know a character's motivation before being able to act is often questioned. However, in actuality, such an approach transcends many theories because it is logical and true to the way humans behave. Everyone does something for a reason and, often, that reason is unconscious.

One of your responsibilities is to perceive whether this result-oriented style of directing produces the effects you want in an organic and believable fashion. Be on the lookout for physical tension, pushing, indicating, or the actors watching themselves. By isolating the symptom, you can find the solution.

Playing On One Level

Actors who lack a range of emotion and stay on one level are usually not connected to the inner life of their characters. Such actors often go through the motions, mouthing the dialogue in a natural way and simply following the blocking (the physical moves set up by the director). This kind of acting is often referred to as "mailing it in" or "walking through it." Sometimes it is caused by actors either being unprepared, not knowing any better, or thinking that "less is more." A more likely cause is that the actors have not fully lived through what their characters are experiencing. They have not made the character's needs important to themselves and, therefore, they lack energy.

Usually, actors whose performances lack emotion or who perform on one level have, at one time or another, been put down by their directors. As a result, they give up trying and play it safe. They are afraid of being told "no, no," that they are doing too much. A director may say, "Just say the lines," or, "Remember, less is more." True as that is, it will only work if there's something going on below the surface. Otherwise, less is less.

One of my goals is to provide you with techniques you can use to make sure that your actors' performances are full of moment-to-moment colors. The solution isn't to ask the actors for more variety, but to encourage them to have a strong need, stay connected to the other actors, follow their instincts, and respond in the moment. The answer is in the details of performing.

Actors Who Play Quality

Oftentimes, actors are recognized for having created a particularly memorable character. The performance seems to be the result of a perfect confluence of the actor's personality and that of the character. Thereafter, they may be offered the same type of role over and over again, and if they continue to play it, all but the most gifted actors can be in danger of becoming living clichés.

There are actors who have a talent for playing a particular character trait or quality or range of qualities, such as intensity, naïvete, vulnerability, or the traits of a menace, a bumbler, etc. Woody Allen and the late Jack Lemmon are examples of brilliant actors who can play quality: both were adept at portraying bumblers. Lemmon, particularly in his comedic roles, stuttered and stammered his way through entire films. However, he was equally successful at playing other roles in which such mannerisms would have been inappropriate. Woody Allen, in contrast, only writes about that one type of character, but he is able to play it and make it compelling in all kinds of different circumstances and storylines. An actor who can play "quality" makes it permeate every moment of the performance; acting such roles is not easy. While a "one-note" portrayal offers nothing, a "quality" role, although limited, contains truth.

Actors Who Watch Themselves

Beware of actors who "third-eye" themselves. These actors sit in judgment on and direct and program themselves, rather than being in the moment by truly looking and listening to their partners and responding spontaneously. How do you recognize this tendency? First, be aware of the vocal patterns with which actors speak each line. Do they sound the same each time, regardless of what fellow actors are feeding them? This is a dead giveaway. Second, be aware of feeling bored by a performance and thinking of what you'll eat for dinner. In other words, you're not emotionally engaged because the actor isn't either. Remember, acting in film or theater is meant to create an empathetic experience for the audience, and if the acting is empty, the audience loses interest. Finally, look for the actor doing a "star turn." I once saw George Bernard Shaw's *Pygmalion* on Broadway with Peter O'Toole and Amanda Plummer. No two actors could be more different in approach and quality. O'Toole was amusing, but he gave a "solo" performance, being overtly clever in the way he used his body and voice. She, on the other hand, was in the moment, emotionally involved, simple, and related to him in a very direct way. The audience's reaction was interesting. They were thrilled to see a movie star like O'Toole onstage, but they were not fooled. As the audience left the theater, all I could hear were comments about how good Plummer was and about how they could not believe O'Toole, even if he was fun to watch.

My purpose in this section is to make you aware of the various ways actors can, unwittingly, sabotage themselves and their performance. I believe, as I have said, that being forewarned is being forearmed. If you can identify a problem and understand its cause, you are better equipped to tackle it instead of being at the mercy of your lack of knowledge. How do you, as a director, solve some of the dilemmas I've outlined? Each situation varies, but an excellent start is to identify the problem first, then work out a solution.

THE DIFFERENCE BETWEEN STAGE AND SCREEN ACTING

To end this chapter, we'll take a brief look at the differences between stage and screen acting and attempt to clear up the misinformation and myths that surround the issue.

One popular myth is that stage and screen acting require two different styles, but the difference between them is not a matter of style but of size and artificiality. When a performance on screen seems to be unreal, it is because the camera doesn't allow for fakery. If it is unreal on the screen, it is just as unreal on stage. But theater audiences, unfortunately, have come to accept this myth as valid. Conversely, a performance first created for a film and then brought to the theater may seem too subdued for a theater audience even though the performance is honest. Making the adjustment to a larger space is a rather simple matter, unlike trying to make a false performance truthful.

There are, of course, technical differences between stage and screen acting. The most important difference is in the intensity of the performance. In theater, an actor has to reach the whole audience, even those members sitting in the back row of the balcony. Sometime, somewhere, these actors were taught to be seen and heard above all else. Little if any attention was paid to their believability and spontaneity. Much discussion may have taken place in rehearsal about style and characters, but what happened to the reality of the characters onstage? Apart from the technical aspects of vocal projection and physical expansiveness, if there is no reality behind the words an actor speaks, the rest of the performance appears false and theatrical. This is why so many theater productions are an empty experience for audiences.

Too many theater directors seem to spend their time staging the production of a play that has already been produced many, many times before. Wanting to bring a new approach to the play encourages directors to focus on style rather than content. In these productions, the actor is just another prop to be physically manipulated in order to create the stage picture, which can be detrimental to any sense of truth. This problem can occur before a camera as well. Directors focus on positioning and moving actors around to create a particular composition within the frame while ignoring what is going on within and between the characters. Actors refer to these directors as "traffic cops."

Theater does have advantages for actors, which is perhaps why it is often referred to as the actor's medium. For instance, there are day-long rehearsals for four to six weeks, and during this period, actors have the time to create solid relationships with each other and with their director. Scenes are generally rehearsed in sequence, and actors can build their characters slowly, with a well-developed feeling for the arc of the characters' development. By opening night, they are well immersed in the play and their characters, and, finally, have an audience to connect with. Every night can be a different experience, depending on the emotional makeup of that audience.

That mystical connection between players and audience is an extraordinary exchange that cannot be found in film. It can, however, occur in television programs taped in front of a live audience where the rapport between cast and audience is like the rapport in theater.

A lot of the comedy in a television show can be spontaneous because of the interplay between the cast and the audience. Though sitcom casts may rehearse the general shape of the show, the final ingredient in the equation is the audience. The audience pretty much teaches the cast where the comic takes should be and how long each one can be. This interplay between the actor and audience puts the final polish on the production.

Theater has its own particular problems for actors that they won't find in film or television. On stage they have the responsibility and pressure of keeping their performances alive night after night, month after month, and even for years during some Broadway runs. This is a draining obligation. Film's major advantage is that once a moment is achieved, it never has to be reproduced. In film and television, actors have the advantage of being able to do the scene over and over until it is right. In theater, once you are in front of that audience, you can't say "cut" and repeat the scene if it isn't working.

Another important advantage of film is the absence of pressure to "show" an audience that there are real thoughts and feelings going on within the actors. The camera, because of its intimacy, will pick things up without the actors having to *do* anything. Many times I've heard actors say they felt they were doing nothing during a take, only to discover during the dailies that the performance was full to the brim.

In the theater, once the curtain goes up, the actors are in charge. Film, in contrast, is the director's medium, leaving actors at the mercy of the director and editor, as these are the two people who can help make or break the performance. Whatever the medium, true creativity demands taking risks, and what can be more rewarding than setting your sights high and relishing the journey?

DIRECTOR: KNOW THYSELF

"Working with actors is the single most important thing a director does. Drama is about people, and you'd better know a lot about people, actors, and acting or you won't get a layered performance."

— *Martha Coolidge*

It's a sad fact that all too often, directors and actors are not always cognizant of the difficulties the other faces. Directors, for instance, often seem totally unaware that at any one time most actors are unemployed and desperate for work. Actors recognize all too well that, as soon as their role is finished, they'll be searching for work all over again. It's not surprising, then, that during casting sessions and throughout the production period they see directors as gods who have unlimited power over their lives. At the same time, actors are often woefully unaware of the difficulties of the director's life.

The power actors believe a director has may not, in reality, exist. Too often, directors don't have that much clout. Casting for a television series is usually done by casting directors and producers. Directors are merely handed preordained leads and guest stars. The artistic and production team is put together not by the director, but by the producers.

In features, a director has more input regarding casting but often the real job is reduced to "shooting a schedule." As soon as that's accomplished and the director's edit is done, the footage goes to someone else to finish.

Seasoned directors, however, will usually make the final casting decision — with producer approval, of course. Star directors usually cast whomever they want. Independent film directors are generally in full control because they initiated the project in the first place. For everyone else, it's a matter of learning to work with what they are given, while at the same time working to gradually increase their say.

There are, of course, fewer jobs for directors than there are for actors. Any film or television project has scores of actors but only one director. Even in stage plays, however small the cast, directors are out-numbered by the actors. How do directors compete for these scarce opportunities? Ingenuity! The drive and imagination that young directors employ is awesome. They audition, so to speak, with their films — short or long — which have put them into debt of five or six figures. They have maxed their credit cards, borrowed bundles from relatives and friends, and, if lucky, they have completed the film that will have taken at the very least a year out of their lives.

Once it's made, there are no guarantees that it will open any doors, be accepted at any festivals, or find distribution. This is the last hurdle independent directors face. Chances are, it will be as long and frustrating a business as making the movie in the first place. Faced with such daunting odds, many would-be directors turn to other ways of establishing a career.

THE DIRECTOR'S OPTIONS

Directors have a number of career options available to them. Many turn to writing screenplays as a way of creating a directing job for themselves. Unfortunately, when taking on this artistic discipline, which may not necessarily be their strongest suit, they end up confronting the same obstacles: closed doors, lack of connections, no financing, rejection, and agents or producers who insist on rewrite after rewrite. By the time these writers — who are really directors in the first place — are finished, they don't really know who they are, what they are supposed to be doing, or what their original story was about. Despite the successes that occasionally make the news and sometimes win awards, writing can be a tortuous and frustrating business that often results in being no help at all to the would-be director.

Another way to get a job is through broadcast television. There are a number of director slots, but the same problems exist so it's not necessarily any easier. Since television directors are usually hired project by project — like hired guns — they have little or no meaningful input into the show. They are not members of the original team that conceived the idea, established the tone of the show, and cast it. By the time the new director appears on the set, the cast and crew have been together anywhere from six months to five years. Direction from a newcomer is often met with resistance and the director finds himself reduced to being little more than a traffic cop. This resistance may be warranted or it may be shortsighted. Either way, the producer and writer will have the final word. Although the assignment will pay well, the creative experience may not match the financial rewards.

In the theater, the director's life is usually not quite as overwhelming. Depending upon which part of the country they are working in, and their status within the business, they may be engaged by the producer of a theater or by actors who want to showcase themselves because, like directors, they worry about where their next job is coming from.

Directors may also initiate a project themselves. If so, like an independent filmmaker, they will have to find the funds, rent the space, act as producer, and carry on their work as director — right through opening night and beyond. Even so, the stress of mounting a production does not equal that of an independent filmmaker, and the theater director, at the very least, has the satisfaction of bringing a project to a close in a reasonable amount of time.

For theater directors, salary is never part of the appeal unless it's playing on Broadway or major theaters throughout the country. In local theater, directors — like actors — are paid a stipend: enough for gas money, basically. So, for one and all, it is truly a labor of love and not a career-building endeavor.

One avenue film directors can pursue to make a career for themselves is to become a writer/producer/director. This gives them the advantage of full creative control. Some directors make it, and Gary Ross' busy career is evidence of that fact. Ross has regularly mixed producing, writing, acting, and directing. For the film *Pleasantville,* he was writer, producer, and director. He wrote *Lassie, The Flintstones, Dave* (in which he also played a role), co-produced *Big,* and produced *Trial and Error.*

Such careers point out the importance of flexibility. If up-and-coming directors have their heart set on only directing, they might not break through. They may have long periods without work or they may remain stuck at a certain level if they are unable to get a foot in the door. In contrast, someone who alternates different roles in the film or television industry might find that the experience they gain, the reputation they earn for themselves, and the contacts they develop open doors that might otherwise remain closed.

It is not easy to develop such career paths, and new directors should keep three things in mind. First: writing and producing are not as simple as you might think. Second: it is important to understand how much hard work, rejection, disappointment, and false starts such a career will contain. For every success there will always be many more failed projects. It takes a resolute personality and a lot of stamina to productively live such a life. Finally: it is also worth keeping in mind that it is not possible for everyone to achieve successful careers of this type. Young directors should not live with false hopes.

PROBLEMS DIRECTORS BRING

Performance artists, particularly actors, know that their development requires the exploration and training of their physical instrument and inner selves. This is not expected of directors and writers. Consequently, this lack of self-awareness can create quite a few problems. In the following pages, I will point out some personal specifics that, when understood, shed light on your work.

Ego

There are certain types of personality problems that show up over and over again. One of the most common is that of the overwhelming ego. This isn't meant to be a complaint about directors with strong personalities or about ego per se — far from it. Certainly you need a strong ego to make it in this business. I'm referring to how a director's ego can limit them to only one possible interpretation of the material; directors who want every line to be said as they would say it and for the characters to behave as they would. The problem with such an approach is that it allows no room for the actor's input and finally encourages empty behavior because they are not playing from an impulse, but from an obligation.

A closely related problem is when directors fixate on their own mental image of what should happen and fail to realize that their vision can only be achieved through the actor. This is not to say that directors should not have a vision. They must. That being said, they need to recognize that actors strive to give a director what they want, but inevitably bring in other colors, nuances, and feelings, as well. If you are wise, you will incorporate these new colors into your idea. That can only occur if you are open and relaxed enough about your work and are not locked into a previous image.

Direction by Tyranny

Usually, everybody respects organized and firm directors who know what they want and how to get it, yet remain open to actors' ideas. Directors who bully and humiliate to get what they want do exist but only succeed in shutting off the actor, who is rightfully fearful. Such behaviors can only stem from a profound insecurity on the director's part. Fear of not being able to fulfill their vision through the actors plays a major role. It's easier to blame an actor than it is to appear ignorant.

It's far better to work in a spirit of encouragement and cooperation that will creatively involve your actors and show them that their professional input matters. Make them feel part of the team. Being polite and welcoming doesn't hurt either. Rather than diminishing your status, it actually increases it.

Insecurity

Directors at the other end of the ego spectrum create problems for themselves, too. If directors are too insecure, actors lose respect and can eat them alive. Insecurity reveals itself by how you treat your material and actors. If you are insecure, you'll most likely hedge your bets about what the material means and how to handle it. Insecure directors vacillate, use language full of expressions, such as "sort of," "kind of," or "what do you think," slide around issues, fail to commit, and change their mind frequently. They may be overly deferential with actors and accept whatever is thrown their way.

You must realize that actors are invariably focused on one thing — their role. They rarely have an overview of how their role fits into the mosaic. This can very easily affect the balance of your entire project.

Remember that being a director means giving direction, and though there may well be several routes to get there, someone needs to know the destination. It's your job to lead your cast.

Fear of Actors

Closely related to the problem of insecure directors are those who are afraid of their actors. This comes as a surprise to many actors, given the general image of directors. But I've found that one of the reasons directors don't talk to actors — besides not knowing what to say — is because they are afraid of them. They are afraid because they know that they are dealing with human beings, not machines. They are dealing with people's feelings and may be reluctant to say the wrong thing. These directors feel safe with machinery because machinery doesn't talk back; they feel safe with the technical people because their discussions are about objective issues. With actors, however, subjectivity is ever present. Ask yourself if you are afraid to hurt your actors' feelings, sound stupid, be too judgmental, ask for more or less emotion, push them to the edge, or of your ability to communicate in a productive way.

Please understand actors are desperate to work with someone who understands their medium. They reach out by asking questions, but because the director is inhibited, afraid of the actor, or insecure, he or she often says something like, "Let me see it. Just do it." Do what? Actors will do something but it may not be the best option. In short order they will ignore you, turn to each other, turn off, or take over because nobody's there as a trustworthy leader.

My teaching and directing in Europe and America underscores the fact that all actors long for real and meaningful communication with their director. Unfortunately, they are rarely in a position to demand it — only stars can do that (recall the conflict mentioned earlier between Marlon Brando and director Frank Oz).

Narcissism

Also noteworthy are the problems caused by directors who are on narcissistic trips. Young directors often sentimentalize and romanticize themselves when, in fact, they don't really know what they are doing. They are in love with the idea of themselves as *directors,* rather than with the *art of directing.* We may all start out with narcissistic needs and hunger — the need to be admired, to be loved, to stand above the crowd, and to be validated. All of these are probably the reasons we were drawn to this business in the first place but, at some point, we have to grow up and take responsibility for the art.

Directors have to learn the craft of their art. It isn't enough to do finger painting all your life and say, "Aren't I wonderful?" It's not enough to love the art form. You have to respect it and want to fulfill its intent. As directors we are not really creators but interpreters of someone else's material. If you respect the material, you'll master all the elements used to bring the vision to life. If you are true to art, you will speak to the human condition through whatever medium or style you choose. Love the art in yourself and not yourself in the art.

> A Hollywood director, entering the Gates of Heaven, sees God and goes over to him to thank him profusely. "Oh, never mind that," God says, "I need to talk with you. Do me a favor... What I've really wanted to do is direct..."
> — *Delia Salvi and Joseph Sargent*

The Manipulative or Exploitative Director

The problem of manipulation extends much further than the sexual exploits on the casting couch. Exploitation comes in many forms. It is certainly true that the casting couch used to be rife with sexual innuendo in Hollywood, and, to a degree, still is. This form of exploitation is not confined to directors or even within the film and television industries. Wherever there's a man or woman with power, there is the potential for exploitation. The casting couch is one of the worst forms of sexual exploitation and has no place in this or any other business.

Manipulation goes much further than sexual harassment, however. Directors should have ethical limits as to what they'll do to get good work from the cast. Brutality and intimidation are not only reprehensible but are counterproductive. Actors will tighten up, become frightened, and inhibited. It's not just a matter of morality but of practicality.

Directing is a form of manipulation — there's no question about that. But a line must be drawn between brutality and the rather painful road that often has to be traveled to reach achievement. Remember, there's pain that produces good results and there's pain that does not. An ethical person knows the difference between being cruel in order to feel powerful and being cruel in order to get a good outcome: an outcome that will please the actor, as well. Most will say, "That was so tough but it was worth it." Sometimes, creation isn't easy.

Recognizing the necessity for manipulation doesn't mean that you run the risk of losing touch with your own creativity; it's all part of the normal process. It's taking the material in front of you and molding it. That's creative. That's what you do when you are sculpting or painting: taking the material and molding it to fulfill the image you have in mind.

Being Emotionally Detached

Directors must have an emotional connection to the world around them. If you remain detached, you can theorize and politicize all you want but you will never touch the human core. I don't care what language we speak, we all respond to the same things. We respond to the sound or touch of something, its color or tone, and to the relationships of objects together. It's not enough to be analytically astute or imaginative for its own sake.

Directors who are cut off from their feelings bring problems to their work. This type of director may well be hard working, assiduous, and organized but these academic virtues don't go very far. Excelling in the analytical part of the process is easy, but when it comes to really dealing with the human condition and feelings, perception and shaping that piece of material (the actor), can be much more difficult. You have to be willing to experience other people's feelings and be willing to share your own. That's when magic can happen but, with an emotionally distant director, that's when things fall apart. As a teacher, my most important job with detached directors has been to awaken them both to their feelings and those of others.

Grasping the Subtext

Keep in mind that invariably, there is much more going on in a story than there appears to be on the surface. There is a subtext that's usually quite emotionally complex and, sometimes, involves sexual matters. Your character, personality, and life experiences can either help or work against you. For example, a director in my class couldn't see the implications of a piece of business — the physical activities — employed by the woman in Chekhov's *The Seagull,* who fears losing her young lover. By using some subtle pieces of business she reveals her true intent: to hold on to him through sexual means. The young director couldn't see why the older woman had her hand on the character's thigh. I asked him, "What do you think she's doing with her hand on his thigh?" "I don't know." "Well, think about it. Is she mending his pants?" "No." "Well, what could it be then? And how do you think he feels about it? And what do they do when they are alone and who is usually the aggressor?" These are the kinds of questions you need to ask. There are many layers to a scene and you must dig to unearth them.

Fear of Working With People's Feelings

It is apparent that directing involves dealing with feelings. Since some directors may have difficulty with this, it's appropriate at this point to elaborate on exactly what's involved when we talk about the issue.

Often, people, including directors, are not open to their feelings or the feelings of others due to their conditioning. We are taught to hide our feelings and reactions — to put on a polite mask. But you can't empathize with your characters until you can identify the various feelings within yourself. Human drama is all about a clash of feelings and needs, how people deal with these issues, and how they try to solve them. Isn't that what the Greeks were writing about all the time? Sleeping with your mother, killing your father, loving your brother, ripping your eyes out — very strong stuff and it still works today.

It is precisely in defining various feelings that your actors can help you. Physical action is relatively straightforward and we are at the stage when computer-generated effects can replicate physical action. But computers are no substitute for feelings: that is what actors do. Don't be afraid to encourage them. Actors are a golden resource that can put your work into a different league altogether.

Actors aren't afraid of their feelings and feel rewarded when they can use them to imbue their character with the depths of true life. And, believe me, if it's too much for them, they'll let you know.

The Character's Feelings

Directors have to work with feelings on two levels: the feeling of the characters and the feelings of the actors. Directors can sometimes have a reticence or fear about fully engaging in the human material that comprises their work. The events of a story are straightforward: action and special effects are mechanically choreographed; and blocking, marks, and business may be complex but are without any emotional requirements. In contrast, the internal life of their characters involve feelings that are not so straightforward. They are often messy and don't involve simple "Yes" or "No" responses. Some examples may even cut close to the bone, touching on our own internal emotional life that we might find disturbing.

Simply suggesting that directors get over their problems is of no help because our psychological makeup rarely responds to being told what to do. Indeed, the fear would probably be exacerbated. Instead, the most useful solution to this problem is twofold. First, it certainly helps for directors to realize that it is the actors' feelings that provide richness and depth to the work. If you can find a way to handle these feelings, you will have a wonderful tool for turning run-of-the-mill material into quality work — be it drama, comedy, or action.

The second aspect of the solution doesn't involve an attitude change at all, and so, is probably a lot easier to accomplish. All it involves is realizing that there are tools for analyzing the characters' feelings, processes for actors to create them, and a common language with which to communicate. In other words, the very process of directing which this book espouses, provides the tools to bring you closer to the characters' feelings *and* your own.

The Actor's Feelings

With regards to the feelings of actors, directors may have problems because their actors are not inanimate objects that can be turned on and off. Instead, they are people with all the emotional complexities that being human implies. They have hopes and ambitions, fears and phobias, likes and dislikes, dignity, and a sense of self-worth. They will react to what is going on but try to hide any setbacks, disappointments, or slights that they may experience. You might think this means there is no real problem or that directors need not worry about their actors' feelings if the actors usually hide them. In fact, it's a much more serious problem than if actors came out and directly let you know what is affecting them.

Often, directors avoid actors' feelings because they fear tampering with the actors' psyche by pushing them too far or saying the wrong thing. Some directors fear any emotional display at all, while others fear the actor may go out of control. All in all, actors can seem like dangerous territory.

I had a directing student who was afraid to work with people. Eventually he explained that he felt as if he had no right to intrude on other people's feelings and that he felt insecure and stupid when doing so. He shared that in front of the entire class. It was so personal and honest. I am still touched by the power of his courage. He had originally said, "I am just a cinematographer. I don't know how to deal with people." Yet that is exactly what a director must do. Not only is this human material the subject of a director's work, but it is also the means by which they work because they have to engage directly with the emotions of their actors in order to move the audience.

TRUSTING YOURSELF

Being a good director starts with trusting your instincts and abilities. Focus on your core talents before beginning your work with your actors. Without this crucial step, you won't know where to begin and you'll doubt your ability to direct the cast.

Use Your Instincts

Beyond creativity and knowledge of one's medium, imagination, self-awareness, sensitivity, perception, and trusting one's instincts play a major role in becoming a fine director.

Most people haven't been encouraged to trust their instincts. Although we are naturally observant and inquisitive, and indeed our very survival once depended on it, our upbringing tends to encourage the opposite. We are socialized to not look too closely and are repeatedly told to mind our own business.

Though your conditioning may inhibit you in your social life, trust your instincts in your work. When you realize that you have this inner barometer to *sense* what is going on, you'll trust yourself to observe details and will be better able to recognize what's going on within the actor. Quite often, the difference between a good director and a mediocre one is that the good director sees what's going on within the actor and is in a position to know if further direction is necessary. Meanwhile, the unreceptive director doesn't notice that anything is amiss, allowing for a nondescript performance to slide through.

Inner Awareness

The most important tool against an exercise in futility is inner awareness: really being able to see with your inner eye and hear with your inner ear. That's where being in touch with your own sensitivities as a human being comes into play. You may hear the words but you also need to deduce the subtext. Know the difference between your engaged thoughts and feelings during a scene and a wandering mind. This is crucial. Your inner self will tell you that the scene is empty and boring — that the actors in front of you are just reciting empty lines. It's what stirs you as a human being that really counts, so be aware of your gut feelings. Therein lies the real "magic."

Your Body

Pay attention to your own body's response as you watch a scene. If you feel a knot in your throat or tension in your neck, pay close attention to your actors for signs of trouble. Most likely, that lump in your throat is telling you one of your actors also has a lump in his or her throat because they are unconsciously holding back feelings. Again, remember that you are involved in an emotional, rather than a mental experience. That's what acting and directing are all about: creating an empathetic experience between the actors and the audience. If an actor is blocked, you will experience that block as well. And if you experience it, imagine what the audience is going to feel, particularly in a theatrical production.

Using Yourself Fully

If you want to make the best use of your actors, recognize that it's a complex situation that requires employing a multilevel process: observing, diagnosing, and problem solving.

The three levels at which you will need to simultaneously function are:

- the human level
- the diagnostic level
- the prescriptive level

The human level involves perception, empathy, and trusting your instincts. You must be able to discern what your actors are doing, both in terms of human behavior and the quality of their acting.

The diagnostic level: you've noticed a problem by trusting your perceptions; diagnose the nature and the cause.

The prescriptive level: now you need to come up with a solution. This is when knowledge of the actor's language and processes are especially helpful.

On paper, these points can be set out in a linear fashion but when you are working, you need to do all of these things simultaneously. No easy task, but it can and should be done.

Interpersonal Skills and Communication

Directors aren't beset with any more personal problems than any other occupational group. Nevertheless, as a director you need to be aware that any personal problems you bring to the set will have consequences. I think it is fair to say that the director-actor relationship is one that depends on personal qualities more than many other professional relationships.

Directors are dealing with human material. To start with, the subject matter is about people, what makes them tick, their needs, their fears, their relationships, their inner and outer conflicts. Sometimes these subjects are messy, especially when dealing with physical and emotional areas that many prefer to keep private. You will have to take a stand on these issues and talk about them, sometimes in great detail, with your actors.

At times, you may even find this as embarrassing as your actors might.

In directing, all the complex ins and outs of relationships are at play. Given that your actors are in a vulnerable position, that you are all under pressure, and that you have to get your actors to deliver what you need, a premium is placed on interpersonal skills.

Put this aspect of your work together with the humanness of the material and it is easy to see that your personal qualities do matter. Being warm and encouraging does matter. A considerate director is more likely to get results than a rude one, as would a director who persuades rather than browbeats, who encourages rather than forces, who helps rather than demands, who earns the respect rather than the fear of his or her actors.

You need to understand that if you bring negative attitudes and personal problems to the project, the entire company is affected. Directors must set the atmosphere and serve as a guide while still being open to new ideas.

Most directors go into production with the best of intentions, but sometimes these good intentions fade over time. The director is then hard put to understand how or why harmony between him and his cast has disappeared and distrust and frustration has taken over. The usual, self-consoling answer is that actors, in general, are very, very difficult to work with. Little do directors realize how they have helped create this discord.

A lack of knowledge about the nature of actors is a major contributor, but a lack of self-knowledge about one's communication skills can be equally undermining.

From my experience as a director and actor, the best performances come from an interdependent, give-and-take relationship between the director and the actors. Your actor's challenge is to fulfill your concept of the scene, even if their interpretation differs from yours. Your challenge as director is to clearly communicate your concept in playable terms. Objectives, action verbs, and needs are "in." Long-winded, intellectual pontification is definitely "out." Your actors have already read the script several times, so a lengthy reiteration of the plot accomplishes nothing. It simply numbs their imagination. Look into their eyes while addressing them. Are they bright or glazed over? Are you talking them to death? This is why your script and character analysis is so critical. Your homework should prepare you to be concise.

Another consequence of a director's failure to clearly and simply communicate with his or her cast is confusion. Initially, actors try hard to understand and to create your concept. But if communication keeps breaking down and their frustration grows, they'll try to direct themselves. By becoming detached, they can lose their impulses and act in a prescribed manner. They might even resort to indicating or mailing it in. Either way, the result will not be satisfying.

Lack of Acting Experience

Directors with some acting experience are relatively common in theater but rare in film and television. Most film directors have come up from film school or through the medium itself. That invariably means the technical end. They started out as production assistants, assistant directors, writers, or editors. Not only does this mean they have no experience in directing actors, but they have bare knowledge of the actor's instrument. While acting experience is not a necessity for being a good director, a complete lack prevents directors from looking past the actor's façade. They are blinded by the look, the quality, and the superficial skills of the actor. For them, looking the part is enough. This has fostered a widespread acceptance of mediocrity in performances. You must understand the instrument you'll be working with if your work is going to be something more than just pedestrian.

People assume that any director would inevitably want good acting in their productions but recognizing the difference between good, mediocre, and bad can be difficult. That's why directors who have experienced stage fright, the difficulty of bringing themselves to the character, problems of concentration, and the rewards or frustrations of working with other directors have an advantage.

COMMON DIRECTORIAL MISTAKES AND TRAPS

Directors whose background and training has been grounded in technical areas are usually at a disadvantage. I've no doubt that their strongest suit is the camera with the screenplay a runner-up. Lagging far behind is the business of acting. The goal here is to make directors aware of how they themselves can create problems on the set. We all have traps we fall into and, hopefully, by putting a spotlight on some of them, I can diminish their power over you. Since recognition is the first step toward growth, the next few pages will point out the various ways in which directors inadvertently create problems with their actors.

Directing for Results

Both experienced directors and actors often tend to assume that directing for results is the appropriate way to work. Directing for results means telling actors what you want to see and hear: that they should cry, laugh, shout, or be excited. However, this is without giving them any clues as to why or how they'll get there. The problem lies in not realizing that these emotions are the result of needs and wants. Emotional responses come as a *consequence* of people actively trying to fulfill a need. Essentially, directing for results means telling actors the end product you want to see. When you address them in this manner, they immediately decide you don't know how to direct and lose all faith in you.

On the other hand, you'll encounter some actors who want to be given result-based direction. There are actors who can't work from actions or personalization but can instead only smile when told, cry when asked, or show anger when instructed. They have no technique, but in their childlike desperate need to please the world, will give you exactly what you are looking for. "If you want anger, sure, I can shout. I'll give you anger." And they will, but you'll soon discover it's not likely to be the most original or subtle acting that you'll ever see.

In contrast to actors who can only follow superficial instructions are actors who work the other way, that is, from analysis, personal identification, impulse, and action. This leads to the emotional result. They are well-trained actors who know how their instrument works and have the skills to employ when interpreting your material. These are the actors you want to work with, for they are like gold. But if you keep asking for results, they will feel you don't trust them, feel stifled, and then shut down. When that happens, not only will you sacrifice trust and communication but antagonism may develop and that is the last thing you need.

The Tyranny of Line Readings

Although there can be justification for a director to give a line reading, some actors may take it as a personal affront. They feel the director thinks they can't act. This results from poor communication on the director's part. It needs to be made clear that you're only trying to point out the sense of the line and not "how" it should be said. By making it understood that your intention is to clarify the meaning of the line, you won't encounter any resistance or resentment.

You can also trap yourself by expecting to hear a line read a particular way and rejecting a more truthful, and consequently, more original way. Does, "I love you," always have to be said softly and romantically? Of course not. Shouting, "I love you," can be much more effective sometimes. When receiving bad news, do people always react with tears, horror, or shock? No! For some, the response might be anger or even laughter.

Another innocent error directors often make is in pointing out a moment or line when the actor was particularly effective. "I loved the way you said that line," or "The way you touched her..." or "The way you picked up that cup was terrific." Actors are hungry for this kind of affirmation, and no doubt deserve it, but it can also backfire. Drawing too much attention to a detail could encourage the actor to repeat that precise moment in exactly the same way. In so doing it stifles an in-the-moment impulse that had produced it in the first place.

Rather than risk actors imitating themselves, it is safer to compliment the basic reality they had created and their courage in following through on their impulses. Positive feedback is very nurturing, but avoid making actors self-conscious.

This brings up an important point: don't expect nor encourage your actors to come to the first rehearsal knowing their lines. Once the actors connect with their character's needs, identify with the relationships between characters, and understand the events of the scenes, the lines usually come as a natural consequence.

Of course, there are some actors who feel paralyzed if they haven't learned their lines right away. If an actor has established this habit early in life, there is no point in trying to change them overnight. However, you will have to make sure that they don't get stuck in line readings without emotionally connecting to them. The most telling symptom of this is a vocal pattern in which the lines have exactly the same tone and rhythm each and every time. If this happens, give specific adjustments such as, "You're late for an appointment," or, "Joke with your partner." In other words, give them anything that will encourage their spontaneity and take them out of their rut.

To those of you who direct your own scripts, be aware that your writer-self is much stronger than your director-self. I've never seen it otherwise. Realize that no actor is ever going to say a line the way you heard it in your head as you were writing. You may have labored painfully over each line but it's doubtful that the lines are poetry and that you're the second coming of Shakespeare. When you hire an actor, it's because they come close to your concept of the character and you feel they can bring that to the role. Let them! Don't expect your actor to be a carbon copy of what you had in your head. This will only lead to trouble.

Being Too Literal

Another directorial pitfall is being too literal. Plays and screenplays always have descriptions attached to the dialogue such as *lightly, angrily, lights a cigarette, frightened,* etc. This is the writer's way of communicating the overall emotional content of a scene to enhance your understanding. However, many directors and actors take these comments literally and fall into the trap of "obligations" — playing the moment as described rather than allowing for a fresh reaction.

Find your own truth in a scene. There's no danger of it becoming something other than what was intended. The actor may never cry or laugh on the same line but it doesn't matter as long as the overall emotional content of the scene is there.

Not Merging Actor and Character

Avoid maintaining a distance between the actor and the character. This encourages a schizophrenic state. The actor is the character now, so when the actor enters or leaves a scene, it is the character doing so. Speak to your actors as the character. This helps them step into the reality of the role more easily. To help close this identity gap, address them personally, such as, "What do you want?" or "How do you feel about what he just did?" instead of asking them, "How does your character feel?" or "What does your character want?" The sooner your actors and characters begin to merge, the faster you achieve your goals.

Traps in Terminology

When directors are familiar with the right terminology but don't know how to put it into action, we have a problem. Terminology is not a guarantee. Directors may learn these useful terms but may think of them as magic tools without somehow validating them by their own experience. They tend to believe that all they have to do is use the right jargon, apply the right formula, and they are guaranteed results. Unfortunately that's not the case because there are too many factors that may undermine your efforts.

Actors may know the terms too, but may never have behaviorally experienced them in their bodies. There have been many instances when I've told an actor to "make that person laugh" and their initial response was to laugh themselves rather than doing something to the other person to arouse *their* laughter. In such instances, if you truly understand the term, you'll be able to paraphrase until the actor commits to what you're saying.

Blocking Camera or Actors

It is important to work from the material and the characters, regardless of the medium. As you will discover in Chapter 9, "Conversations with Directors and Actors," these directors all share a similar approach to directing — be it situation comedy, television drama, or feature film. They avoid a "formula" style of shooting by concentrating on the story. They feed off the actors; then they block the camera. The angles and interesting camera moves are not solely dictated by a visual aesthetic but by the story and the meaningful behavior of the cast. In this way, not only are predictable camera moves avoided, an organic whole has been created.

Style Over Truth

Instead of fixating on how actors look and sound, directors need to focus on how they can help actors create a life that is believable. Sometimes a script seems to demand a certain style, but the style should not obliterate the reality needed behind it. The style is in the writing and is enhanced by the visuals, not the other way around. Your actors may be required to underplay or overplay their roles, but behind that must be a foundation of truth. Putting your cast into an interpretive and stylistic straightjacket works against the truth of the material and produces empty shells.

Emphasizing Special Effects

Special effects films are extremely popular these days, and even though there may well be an intrinsic value in the visual aesthetics of special effects, they can swamp the story and the characters the audience wants to relate to. If you're really trying to do justice to your material, to make the viewer sit up, take notice, and feel something, the characters need to be recognizable. Don't assume you can avoid the need to work creatively with actors by concentrating on special effects. It doesn't work. While the audience's senses may be assaulted, the heart is not.

Why Imitate?

It is an irony of this business that the success of a film initiates imitations, copycat movies, and sequels. Though the sequels may well make money, it is a bittersweet success because the films will rarely have the positive qualities of the original. It's almost axiomatic that, sequel by sequel, the quality of the original is gradually watered down — if for no other reason than the behavior becomes predictable rather than original. Even successful films such as *Star Trek, Lethal Weapon,* and *Die Hard,* though occasionally throwing in a surprise in their ever-expanding episodes, generally prove the rule of diminishing quality.

The problems of imitation are every bit as severe in television, as a personal example will illustrate. A few years ago, a friend of mine read for the lead role in a new series produced by the same team that had produced an earlier, successful series. She noticed enormous similarities between this role and the one in the original series because the character's attitude, rhythm, and style were the same. She never dreamed they'd want a carbon copy of their original series. She was wrong. She decided not to play her role like the woman in the first series but to play it as her original instincts had suggested. Needless to say, she didn't get the part. The actress they finally chose was a carbon copy of the original series' character. Success breeds imitation, but not success. In this case, it was deadly. The show never sold.

THE ACTOR'S LANGUAGE

> "Very few [directors] know three-quarters of what they're doing. To have a clear picture of what you want and to be able to convey that in a way that an actor can understand, that's a real gift."
>
> — *Paul Newman*

There is a language actors use to talk about acting — whether it is for stage, film, or television. Directors who are fluent in it are more productive because they are able to employ terms that trigger appropriate and instant responses in their actors without the need for long-winded and potentially confusing conversations.

Directors ignore the language of actors at their peril because, like it or not, it's there. There are words that refer to certain aspects of the script and to the characters and their relationships; there are terms to describe the work that actors do; and those that can trigger certain responses to get the results directors need. If you only know how to give your actors basic direction along the lines of, "A little slower; A little faster; You know what to do; Give me more; Give me less," you will find yourself in trouble. So will your actors. Under such circumstances there is a real likelihood of actors losing respect for you. It will be clear to them that you don't know what you are doing. Alternatively, they may feel that they are failing. Either way, you'll all have a problem, resulting in tension and blocked actors.

Keep in mind that not all actors have the skill to surprise you — to bring a layered reality to their character — and may need your feedback and assistance. Knowledge of their vocabulary allows you to communicate with them in a concise and imaginative way that stimulates the response you need.

There is no great mystery about the actor's language, so there's no need for directors to feel that it's impenetrable jargon. The opposite is true because as the language evolved during the course of the twentieth century, it came to dominate mainstream American stage and film acting and, consequently, the way most people speak about acting. Originating with the

Stanislavski System, it was strengthened through the work of Lee Strasberg, Stella Adler, Sanford Meisner, and Robert Lewis. Today, it is an actor's natural language. It's the automatic way they talk about interpreting their characters and what they do to bring this interpretation to life.

This vocabulary not only provides tools for analyzing script, character, and performances, it stimulates actors into delivering performances needed to make your interpretation of the script a reality.

The language helps at all stages of the process. At the beginning, it is the language of preparation because you use it for script analysis. It helps define the given circumstances and theme. It helps analyze character and understand what is meant by a character's objectives and needs: the *why* of what they do, and what is meant by characters playing actions in pursuit of their objectives. The actor's language also helps break the script down in ways that enhance the emotional and behavioral texture of a scene through the use of *beats* and *actions*. The language gives you tools to name what you observe in rehearsals and on the set. If you see a problem and have the vocabulary to talk about it, you can save the scene by suggesting the use of an appropriate process. These techniques aren't complex, let alone esoteric, and can be easily learned.

Before I get into detailed definitions, be aware that you may encounter other terms that might be confusing. They are essentially synonymous and I will include the common ones where appropriate.

ACTING TERMINOLOGY

The vocabulary is a shortcut to communication and its specificity disallows confusion and generalization. For example, rather than asking your actor, "What does the character want in the scene?" one instead asks, "What is your objective? What do you want?" It discourages a separation between actor and character and brings the questions closer to home.

Given Circumstances/Place

The information supplied by the author — period, time, and place; the characters, their backgrounds, and relationships; the society and its culture; events that preceded the first act and those that occur during the play; the climate and time of day — are all factual details forming the foundation upon which we build our interpretation.

Place (environment/setting). It's not enough to simply note the place in which a scene occurs. You must consider how factors such as weather and time of day can impact the behavior of your character and how you can utilize the "place" to tell your story. Despite the existence of certain universal truths, people behave differently in different places.

The environment/place can also suggest daily activities, not directly related to the story, which enhance the reality of the scene. These activities allow actors to express or redirect their feelings into the surrounding objects and how they use them.

Theme

The theme of a script is the unifying idea that makes it different from other manuscripts. It is the main concept that makes the story hang together and make sense. It's not necessarily a moral or ethical statement (a "message"), though it may be. It is certainly a creative concept. All good screenplays and plays reveal an attitude about their subject matter and that becomes the theme. It can be as simple as "crime doesn't pay," or it can be more complex.

The theme provides unity, purpose, and credibility. It causes all the other elements in the production to come together to create a whole. It is the foundation for your vision of the design, staging, music, camera work, and, most importantly, the acting. Theme is the reason for the film's existence.

Working out the theme is the first thing directors need to do as part of their preparation, because once you have done so you'll know how each scene, character, and event serves that theme and the point you are trying to make. This will make it easier to direct each scene. Your decisions about events, scenes, and characters are determined by your theme.

Determining what the theme is and how to use that knowledge in your work is explored in Chapter 4, "The Director's Preparation."

Character

Character needs definition because when I refer to it, I don't mean external characterization that has to do with the physical traits of a character. I mean the internal or inner qualities. By asking the right questions about each character's background, drives, relationships, objectives, and conflicts, you'll be able to define their emotional, psychological, and behavioral characteristics; their strengths and weaknesses; and their inner contradictions. In so doing, you and your actor will create identifiable characters with depth and individuality.

Physical Characterization

You need to understand what actors mean when they refer to "inner" and "external" work. The inner work of an actor is a character's emotional and psychological inner life and their state of mind.

External work, on the other hand, focuses on the physical characteristics of the character: how they move, speak, dress, and relate to other people. These specifics are determined not only by where they were raised, but also by their socioeconomic background and their education. Tense, shy, or aggressive characters will have traits that are an outward manifestation of that inner life.

Different professions and occupations result in differing physical traits. For example, an accountant's physical makeup is different from that of a professional athlete. Similarly, certain periods in history, certain societies, and geographical locations have their own lifestyles and cultures that affect the physical traits of the people who live in those communities. As a director, you need to research these backgrounds to determine what physical traits your characters should have. Again, asking the right questions will guide you to truthful characterizations as opposed to stereotypes.

Super-Objective

You discover a character's super-objective by asking questions such as, "Who is this person? What do they consciously want out of life? What is the unknown driving force of the character? What drives them in life?" This drive is always unconscious and usually has its origins in the character's childhood. Characters are not aware of why they make certain choices in life but we must know. This is what Stanislavski meant by a character's super-objective (which some people also call the character's spine). Whatever name you use, it's this inner force that impels the character toward certain goals in life and influences their choices. This drive will always be there. It's our job to ask the questions that force us to dig deeper for the answers. That is why we must always be students of human nature, observing the world around us and asking ourselves why anything is the way it is.

Overall Objective

The overall objective of the character is the conscious drive toward a particular goal that is unconsciously influenced and determined by the super-objective. This, in turn, determines each scene's objective. As the given circumstances change from scene to scene, the objectives differ and there are new obstacles to surmount, which affect how the scene is played.

Scene-Objective

The scene-objective, unlike the super- and overall objectives, is confined only to that particular scene and is something the character consciously desires and wants to achieve. It serves the character's overall objective in that it's what the character does in the pursuit of this goal, which, in turn, ultimately fulfills their super-objective.

In a story, characters rarely get what they want without difficulty. How they go about trying to fulfill their objectives is what makes for interesting drama. There would be no drama if the characters got what they wanted right away. It is these specific, scene-by-scene objectives that draw us in as we watch our heroes overcome obstacle after obstacle in the pursuit of their dreams.

Let's take the example of the character whose super-objective is to outdo his father in life. This drives him to seek power. A scene-objective might be to cast doubt within the company president's mind regarding a competitor. If he succeeds in this objective, he will come closer to rising up the corporate ladder and achieving a position of power. He will behave in certain active ways to influence the other person in his attempt to fulfill his objective. These specific behaviors are known as "actions" that we will discuss soon (also see the Appendix).

As a model, let's use a very attractive, intelligent, and successful woman who, for some inexplicable reason, always falls in love with men who are physically or emotionally abusive. Her overall objective — which is conscious — is to marry, have a family, and a career. We meet her at the beginning of a relationship. It soon becomes clear to her friends — and to us — that he is a poor choice. Yet, she perseveres in trying to be everything he wants and supporting him in every possible way.

We would have to question if she truly wants what she professes because she is nourishing a no-win situation that is destructive to her. We might conclude then, that she feels unworthy of "the big prize" so she unconsciously seeks relationships that are guaranteed to fail. In so doing she gets what she really wants: proof she's a failure at love. From that we can conclude that her super-objective is to prove her unworthiness. Since she doesn't feel worthy of a fulfilling relationship and is afraid of being abandoned, she selects men who are unable to commit emotionally, which guarantees the fulfillment of her super-objective. The answers we are led to by the circular path of our questions give us a new, profound interpretation of our characters.

Needs, or the "Why"

There is an important clarification about objectives that must be made. Take care not to confuse objectives with *needs*. They aren't the same thing. The objective, say, is to "make you love me." The need is the why. "*Why* do I *need* you to love me?" "Because you have been unfaithful to me and I need reassurance," or "Because I have never felt loved." Or it could be, "I need to feel someone loves me because I've been betrayed." Whatever the specific is, the actors have to find that need and create it within themselves. Then they have a reason for their behavior. In other words, the actions won't really ensue naturally if the actor isn't in touch with the need, the *why*. The why affects *how* the objective is played and gives subtext to the lines. The actions played to fulfill the objectives might be to charm or to seduce, but they won't have any subtext or be organic to the actor unless he or she is in touch with the needs *behind* the objective.

Conflict

Conflict, which is the essence of drama, is the result of two objectives in opposition to each other (the hero versus the villain). It is not about shouting at someone. These overall objectives are what drive the entire play or film forward and create a state of suspense that generates audience involvement. What will the outcome be? Who wins in the end?

Each scene must also contain a conflict that derives from the characters' opposing objectives. An example could be a husband whose objective is to go to the ballgame but his wife's objective is to get him to a movie. Therein lies the conflict. A conflict shouldn't be any more complex than that. A scene without a conflict would be a bore because it would lack dramatic tension.

Inner Conflict

Inner conflict is another important element. It is formed by finding the opposite of a character's objective or need. It is important because it creates more dramatic tension, as well as a richer subtext. Inner conflict results when what we want (our objective) clashes with an opposite feeling or need within us.

Inner conflict is not in the lines and it is not easy to spot. It lies just below the surface, adding an indefinable texture to a scene. For instance, imagine the role of an actor auditioning for a part who is suddenly attacked by stomach cramps that he has to overcome. He wants to succeed in the audition but also needs to ease his stomach pain. In another instance, another actor — also auditioning — sees a mouse behind the casting director but has to continue the audition. In this case, the objective is still to win the role while at the same time wanting to flee from the mouse. The inner conflict makes the playing of the objective much more complex and dynamic.

Subtext

Whether we realize it or not, we always have an interior monologue going on. We are articulating our thoughts and feelings to ourselves, while at the same time deciding if we wish to outwardly express any of them.

When this "subtext," the meaning or story beneath the surface, is strong, it comes through and colors how the dialogue is delivered. How often have you received a compliment from someone and felt that it was very insincere, that you sensed anger, resentment, or indifference? Often enough, I'm sure. You were responding to the subtext and not the words.

This subtext communicates that more is going on within that person than they are sharing, that an inner conflict is present, that the person is thinking or feeling something other than what they are saying or doing. Having subtext behind an author's lines reveals the truth behind the event. A way of creating this subtext, besides just discussing it, is through the use of the "inner monologue," which is addressed in more detail later in this chapter.

Obstacles

Obstacles are what stand in the way of a character achieving his or her objective. This obstacle intensifies the conflict because it's harder to achieve the objective. Obstacles can be of an inner or external nature and this is when terms and tasks begin to overlap.

The inner conflict of a character can be an obstacle, in and of itself, when feelings toward another present a problem. An external obstacle, on the other hand, might involve someone eavesdropping or trying to make oneself understood in a noisy place. In other words, it is something that must be overcome to achieve the objective.

Titanic is an example of a film with strong external obstacles — money and social class keep the lovers apart. Once they consummate their relationship, there's a certain irony in the external obstacle: the ship. It brought them together in the first place and then separates them forever. The internal obstacle they would have to overcome, however, has its roots in their social backgrounds. Her fear might be that he is using her to assure his entry into the United States and his fear may be that her family would never accept him.

Actions

Action is probably the most confusing word in the language of the actor. Historically, it has had different meanings for directors and actors, as well as in film and theater. When using the term with actors, you need to clarify that you aren't referring to "action" as a filmmaker's command to start the scene. In the actor's language, it is an active verb. Action is something one character does to manipulate another character in order to achieve his or her objective.

If, for example, we are talking about a man with the objective of undermining his competitor because he craves power, we need to look at how he goes about it without relying on the author's words. We are talking about behavior. If the line is, "Where did you get that new suit? It looks great on you." It can be done in several ways: to charm, to amuse, to tease, or to build up. So, if the character's objective is to influence the CEO, then any of these methods would be appropriate. An action is an active verb: something one person does to another person to influence a change. Keep in mind that behind every action there has to be a why, which is the need/why behind the objective.

The specific defining of an action is crucial because it needs to propel the first actor into a behavior, which, in turn, stimulates a reaction from the second actor. Defining an action also enables the director to suggest playing new actions when a scene becomes one note (predictable). Change of actions (behavior) also helps define the beats in a scene.

Beats

Beats are the sections we find within a scene that are defined by changes in circumstances or transitions in behavior. Though they can sometimes be determined by a change in the circumstances, such as another character entering or exiting the scene, they are more likely to be determined by a change of action (behavior).

A beat can be one sentence or half a page. Whenever something changes in the scene or whenever new behavior occurs, that's the start of a new beat. Suppose a third character comes in to introduce good or bad news; that creates a whole new beat. When that character leaves, a new beat begins because the people in the scene will do something else as a consequence of his leaving.

Don't be too rigid in your approach to beats. However, it is important to know where they are or could be. If your actors are in trouble, you can recommend new actions that, in turn, could change where a beat occurs. To sharpen your insight into the scene, I suggest you list where the possible beats are and possible actions to be played within each beat.

THE ACTOR'S PROCESS

Even if you have learned the language of script analysis and characterization, and as a result have done a good job with your preparation and casting, you may still find that your actors are not delivering. In such cases, relax because there is plenty that you can do.

Rather than resorting to telling your actors what emotional result you want to see, guide them — through your pointed comments — into discovering what is missing. If the actors are too general, remind them of their character's needs or objectives. If they seem unsure of what should be going on in a particular scene, ask them where the character has come from, about the relationship, or the consequences of not achieving the objective. If the problems are more focused on individual moments, suggest different actions to play or change the obstacles being faced.

If none of these suggestions work, don't resort to directing for results because there are other procedures and exercises you can call upon. These processes are explained below and full details of how you can use them appear in Chapter 6, "Rehearsing the Cast."

A word about directing for results: most actors look down on this form of direction because they find it demeaning. If a director directs for results, actors generally consider him a traffic cop. But, because their obligation is to give the director what he wants, less experienced actors will end up pushing, indicating, or faking whereas well-trained actors may produce the result as realistically as possible knowing full well it will not work as well as when the result is spontaneous and organic. They may also feel the direction they are asked to follow is merely to create an effect rather than a logical response to a particular moment in the scene. All of these doubts can block an actor, making the director's goals even more difficult to achieve.

Many times, we hear an actor described as "dangerous," meaning that the actor's performances are unpredictable. You never know how they will behave in certain obvious situations. They will surprise and delight you each and every time by behaving in ways one would not anticipate but their behavior strikes a chord of truth within people. This is the kind of performance I would like all directors to recognize and strive for.

Sense Memory

We've seen that actors often have difficulty making relationships, events, or issues involving their characters real. There's one well-established exercise that can help here. It's called sense memory and it is one of the important Stanislavski processes. Lee Strasberg further developed the process into the popular tool we know and use today. In essence, sense memory is the re-creation of objects on a sensory level by using the five senses of sight, taste, smell, touch, and hearing to stimulate the imagination. It is the means to an end, not an end in itself, and can also be used to create physical sensations such as pain and temperature.

The value of sense memory is that it restores the impressions, feelings, and relationships of anything we have experienced. The way to bring back that event, that object, that physical or emotional reality is by re-creating the sensory objects that are associated with that person, place, or thing. You don't aim for the emotions. Instead you re-create the objects that were associated with that event without anticipating the results. The actor must accept what feelings emerge, because reaching for a specific emotion will make it disappear.

Upon first hearing about this process, some directors may think it sounds strange or that it is some half-baked actor thing. But there's nothing mysterious about it. It is a proven scientific fact that all memory is stored in the senses. Memories are revived within us accidentally, every day. We hear a particular song, smell a type of cologne, see a person or object, experience a specific texture and are transported back to a time and place and experience the feelings associated with that event.

Dr. Ivan Petrovich Pavlov, a noted Russian scientist in the early twentieth century, conducted experiments with a hungry dog. Each time the dog was brought food, a bell rang. The dog salivated at the sight and smell of the food. Eventually, the hungry dog would salivate at the sound of the bell, even though no food had been produced. The dog had a strong physiological response to the bell as a result of its association with food. We, in turn, do the same. Think of biting into a lemon and notice what happens to your salivary glands — they actively respond.

Sense memory occurs when we are dreaming. We dream pleasant or unpleasant things and our whole organism responds, emotionally and physically. Our heart pounds, we wake up sweating, crying, screaming, laughing, or smiling. We have physiological and psychological reactions to what is, essentially, a fantasy. That monster is not chasing you. You are not literally flying off the building. But you can smell it, taste it, see it, and respond to it accordingly. However, that's on an involuntary basis. Sense memory, on the other hand, allows us to re-create these responses by design.

Sense memory is the foundation upon which other important processes are built. It is used for affective memory (for very specific and very emotional realities), for substitutions and personalizations (which enable actors to re-create various meaningful objects which, in turn, affects them emotionally), and for overall physical conditions. Sense memory helps open up the unconscious. In addition, a wonderful byproduct of this process is relaxation. The actor is so focused on the sensory process that there's no room to worry about themselves.

An actor's craft involves voluntarily reaching for certain emotional realities called for by the text. Re-creating past events and objects through the use of the senses is all that sense memory is. How it is done and when it should be applied is outlined in Chapter 6, "Rehearsing the Cast."

Affective Memory

An affective memory is created through the use of sense memory and is called for when actors need to deal with one of their most common challenges: the creation of very profound and specific emotions. Also known as emotional memory, it is the process most often associated with the Method. Over the years, though, a great many misconceptions and half-truths have clouded what is, in essence, a very straightforward technique.

Affective memory has received a great deal of bad press, usually from those who know little or nothing about it, who have never used it themselves, or who have seen it applied incorrectly. Some actors are fearful of experiencing intense emotions, while others believe it can cause nervous breakdowns. In fact, just the opposite is true. It can be quite cathartic. Of course, we are not concerned with therapy here but how emotions can bring truth to an actor's work.

Let's define it. Affective memory is the re-creation of a very intense and specific event through the use of the senses in order to arouse a specific emotional response required by the scene. It is a very powerful tool and not something you would frequently use. Many times, it isn't necessary at all and it would be counterproductive for you to encourage it. Most of the time, it will only be needed if the actor is having difficulty identifying with a very powerful event through his imagination. But remember that a director must be pragmatic. Use a process only when it is absolutely necessary.

Personalization and Substitution

Another opportunity to call upon sensory work is when creating specific places or people is needed. This is known as personalization or substitution. These interchangeable terms refer to actors substituting something personal from their lives that parallel the character's life in order to arouse within themselves the same emotional connection that the character has to the subject. This process provides a more reliable way of working and brings real meaning to an actor's work.

Let's see how substitution/personalization can work. A scene calls for a sense of physical and emotional abandon but the actors aren't quite able to convince you of their complete freedom. Their behavior is more acted than experienced. Now would be the appropriate time to suggest re-creating a place or object that would stimulate this overall response. The beach might do it for one actor or a piece of music for another.

Once the actors have chosen their specific objects (a place or thing), the next step is to re-create all the specifics using the senses: the play of sunlight on the water (sight), the scent of the ocean (smell), the warmth and texture of sand under their feet (touch), the sound of the ocean (hearing), and the sea salt on their lips (taste), until they have arrived at a very specific state of being. We, the viewers, don't know what the actors are using, but we do know that what we see are people with a great sense of abandonment and joy. By substituting their sensory memories of a beach, they have created the required state of being for the scene. When using a piece of music, the actors re-create the specific sounds of the instruments and experience the rhythms in their body which, in turn, stimulate the actors' bodies to move to the sounds and beats they are experiencing through their sensory imagination. The result, for the audience, will be a free and thoroughly expressive character.

Personalization can also be used to create specific types of relationships. Perhaps two actors have to play a love scene and either they have only just met and are quite uncomfortable or they dislike each other. Though they should start by trying to find elements in each other that they can use to create the relationship, sometimes that doesn't work. In such cases, they can substitute a parallel: someone they feel more intensely about. This is not encouraging schizophrenic behavior but simply a starting point to create a specific relationship with the other actor. By re-creating specific physical characteristics of their personalization and projecting that onto their partner, he or she will take on the qualities of the personal object.

Remember, Pavlov's dog? Bell, food, salivating. Here we have personalization, partner, and arousal of specific feelings.

Let's use a more concrete example. Two actors who have never met before are playing the parts of a husband and wife in the middle of a quarrel. (Let me remind you to be specific and consider what it is that starts the quarrel. Perhaps the husband is perennially unfaithful and the wife has had enough. Her objective is to force an admission from him.) If imagination alone doesn't fire up the actor/wife, then she can create someone in her life who has betrayed her trust: a family member, a teacher, a friend, a former lover. She doesn't have to find a direct parallel. Eventually, by projecting these sensory specifics onto the other actor, he starts to take on the properties of the personal object that has been created via the senses.

Like many of these processes, personalization and substitution may sound mystical but is really quite straightforward.

The Inner Monologue and Speaking Out

This process is employed to deepen the actor's identification with the inner life of the character that then creates subtext. Its purpose is to generate "here and now" feelings within the actor which would be logical to the character. The need to employ an inner monologue is a result of recognizing there is nothing behind the words the actor is speaking. There is no subtext.

This process may not always produce the desired results because, unknowingly, the actor intellectualizes these inner thoughts by *writing* what they *think* the character would be thinking, rather than experiencing feelings in the moment. This misapplication of what can be a very productive procedure leaves the director and actor frustrated.

A much safer approach to creating the "here-and-now inner life" is by having your actors *speak out*. This exercise is much more effective in the long run. Have your actors get in touch with their inner and outer selves by articulating, either silently or out loud, every physical and emotional moment they are aware of. For example, "I feel my heart beating. I just moved my hand. I feel like taking a deep breath. I feel like crying," etc. In the event you hear the actor verbalize a feeling without expression, encourage them to express and release that "here-and-now" feeling.

As you proceed, you will begin to notice the actor relaxing and then discovering that certain feelings are emerging. With encouragement from you to relax and express themselves, you will find the actors becoming centered, free, and in touch with their moment-to-moment inner realities. Once the actor reconnects to himself, he'll be able to breathe new life into the author's lines imbuing them with a rich subtext. This process is usually used during rehearsals. But once understood and experienced, your actors can keep this going during the performance to keep their performance fresh. This exercise is also helpful to actors who have become emotionally blocked and are consequently performing mechanically.

Actors' Preparation

Actors need to pay attention to their preparation to begin a scene. They need to know where the scene fits in the through-line of the story. At which point in the evolution (arc) of the character's life does this event take place? At which point in the script does the scene occur? This is particularly important in film since scenes are invariably shot out of sequence.

Actors need to know where their characters have just come from and what they have just experienced. The actual scene may not even exist in the script but it needs to be created so the actors know what emotional state they should be in when the scene starts. They need to know why they are there and what they are expecting to find in the room, what their relationship with others is at this juncture in the story, and so on. Remember, many scenes — especially in film and television — begin in the middle of an event with the action well under way when we cut to it. They need to know what has gone on just before the action begins, not just the events of the story but the psychological and emotional ramifications of what has occurred up to that point.

It is incumbent upon you to notice whether the actors begin a scene in a full and specific emotional state. Sometimes, actors need help with this sort of preparation and though, in theory, they should have done their own work, you may still have to offer a few reminders or suggestions.

A brief discussion on what the previous scene has meant to their character may be all that is needed. Or you may need to suggest something such as a substitution. Whatever it is, you won't be able to do it unless you know the through-line of your film — not just what happens but the emotional evolution, the arc, of the characters.

Actors can also use an affective memory as preparation. For example, if a character is in a state of fear as he enters, the fear has to be created before the scene starts. The actor needs to come in with the life of the character already established within so that whatever is said or done is affected by this state of mind. This will color how the actor deals with what the other person in the scene gives him. The emotional state may change in the scene but that's the way life is. Isn't it? Moment-to-moment changes occur in life and the development of your scenes should reflect that.

Improvisation

Improvisation as an exploration tool was developed by Stanislavski and is now commonly used by directors and actors. However, as with sensory work and affective memory, there's a great deal of misunderstanding associated with it.

It is important to stress that improvisation should not be an end in itself, even though it may be used that way in areas such as comedy-improvisation groups. For our purpose, improvisation is a problem-solving device. It is a way of freeing the actor from the lines and any other obligations inherent in the text. By setting up a parallel situation, the actor is about to discover something personally meaningful that triggers strong identification with the role's situation.

As an example, let's use a scene between Biff and Happy in *Death of a Salesman.* Biff is disillusioned with his life. He would like to go out West to work on a ranch but needs financial and moral support. His brother, Happy, loves Biff and would like to see Biff fulfill his dreams. But selfishly he needs Biff to stay in town so he can help take care of their aging parents.

Parallel example: Actor #1 (Biff) has not done well with his career in Hollywood and would like to go to New York City to find acting work. However, he can't afford to live there alone and needs his best friend to go with him to share costs, as well as for moral support.

Actor #2 (Happy) doesn't believe his friend is talented enough to make it in New York but would never say so directly. Besides, he wants to stay in Hollywood because he has been getting some roles and feels optimistic about his future career. However, he does not want to alienate his friend.

Actors can easily identify with this parallel situation. The emotional needs, circumstances, and relationship are all clear. Consequently, in the playing of the improvisation, the actors find the link between themselves and the characters that make them identify with the needs and problems of Biff and Happy.

Finding an equivalent experience within themselves frees actors from hiding behind the author's words or chained to predetermined emotional obligations. It allows them the freedom to tap into their own experiences and imagination.

All we're ever really doing — whether through sensory work, improvisation, or the use of objectives — is trying to open the actor's imagination so that he or she can believe deeply in whatever the character believes in by finding the deep connections between themselves and their characters.

Creating Unique Characteristics

Although a great deal of emphasis needs to be placed on interior work, sometimes you also need to pay attention to the external, physical work: the body language, gestures, and mannerisms of a character. Of course, you will cast someone who bears the physical likeness of the character. But at times the actor, in his or her rendition of the role, is not specific enough. In some situations the actor hasn't done research or explored how the character's background determines how to speak and move. In other situations, the actor's body language may not reflect the inner state the scene requires.

Physical tasks can help solve such problems. This is not result based but through the use of physical tasks, one can arouse a character's inner life. It is achieved by giving the actor simple activities that create certain physical modes of behavior. These behaviors have logically grown out of the character's psychological makeup. For a hyperactive character, you might suggest he or she has a rash all over and they aren't allowed to scratch, or perhaps ask him or her to make sure their clothes are always in perfect order. The actors may exaggerate at first but don't worry, they will become more comfortable as they rehearse and the revealing character behavior will have been created.

Another phrase you will hear bandied about is "using an animal." This is another acting process from Stanislavski that was further developed at the Actors' Studio. Beyond benefits for actor training, it is extremely useful in creating unique characterizations. The actor studies and emulates the physical behavior of an animal or insect: how it walks, sits, sleeps, eats; observes and/or interacts with other animals or people; how it behaves when it is content, tired, angry, or bored, etc. By imitating these specific physical characteristics and doing them properly, the actor begins to experience an altered state of mind: a psychological mindset different from his or her own. This metamorphosis is extremely important because it puts the actor directly in touch with the character's inner essence that will alter the actor's perceptions and reactions to the world around them.

Additionally, the physical behavior, once humanized, becomes the outward manifestation of a specific type of person. It is said that Marlon Brando used an ape to create Stanley Kowalski in *A Streetcar Named Desire* and, upon closer observation we see this in how he listens to others, how he hangs on to door jambs, and how he handles physical objects.

Naturally, working on an animal takes time. It's something an actor would do to prepare for a role before production actually begins. But even last-minute suggestions from the director can still create interesting behavioral results.

Tasks

A task, in and of itself, is unrelated to the text and is only used as a means to an end. It is a simple, physical and mental activity that can be used to achieve a particular result in the here and now. This is not substitution and personalization, affective memory, or a heavy psychological process. For example, if a character is supposed to be worried and the actor either doesn't come across that way or is faking it, propose a little task to accomplish. It is as simple as asking the actor to multiply 632 by 59 in their head without writing it down or writing in the air. This will preoccupy the mind and give you exactly what you need — a person whose thoughts are really elsewhere and not fully focused on what is actually taking place around them. Or you might suggest he or she recall what time they awakened on Monday four weeks ago. What did he or she do upon waking? What was the first conversation of the day? What was served for breakfast? How did he or she dress? Where did he or she go in the morning? Having your actors try to recall every incident of that particular day gives them something to actively think about in the present. What you are doing is getting your actor to do exactly what the character is doing at that moment — solving a problem. In addition, such tasks also create a rich subtext.

Knowing what you specifically need helps you create tasks to get what you want in a simple and expedient way — particularly on a set. Tasks help relax your actors and produce very interesting behavior. Besides, you and your cast can have a great deal of fun using tasks.

Don't worry that this might violate the integrity of the script because it doesn't. As a director, you should use whatever works to make the acting organic. Having the actor fully engaged in a simple task helps make the work more truthful at that moment, which guarantees the integrity of the script.

Adjustments

"Adjustments" is another word you will hear a great deal and is very important to understand because it is a very valuable tool. Adjustments are not complex exercises but relatively simple suggestions made in the moment. They can be used in rehearsal and are even more valuable when used in the case of little or no rehearsal time. They can even freshen things up or help focus your actor when they become general.

Adjustments are often the natural consequence of an obstacle. It is the term used to identify what has to be done to underscore the event of the scene.

Let's use the common scenario of espionage as an example. The scene requires the passing of information or money between two people in a European café. The danger lies in their being observed and overheard.

The logical concern would be how to camouflage the transaction and still behave in a natural manner. An adjustment the director might suggest would be to have one character "turn this into a party." Or, suggest one of the two is grieving and seeks consolation from the other. Please note that the adjustment taken is to play an objective that has nothing to do with the actual transaction but is used as a camouflage.

Fact and Fantasy

Not every personal object an actor uses has to be literal or have actually occurred in his or her life in order to draw upon it. By recognizing how much we all build fantasies in real life and respond to these fantasies as if they have actually happened, I put together the two most important elements in our lives: fact and fantasy. They form a new yet familiar act we practice daily without even realizing it and it works beautifully.

We start with a meaningful object and then add the fantasy, the "what if." For example, there is a scene in which a woman is preparing a surprise birthday party for her husband. Many guests are present while she's busy with finishing touches. There's a knock on the door and when she opens it a policeman is standing there. After checking that he has the right house and person, he tells her that he has come to report that, unfortunately, her husband was killed on the freeway. Now that is a difficult transition for any actor. They can't make it work by indicating, pushing, or even by doing nothing. But it's guaranteed to work very well if the actor uses a personalization of someone they love and imagines them mangled on the freeway. That will work. I call this process "fact and fantasy" — starting out with a personal object and fantasizing on it, something we do spontaneously every day of our lives. How many of us have fantasized about an actual person or event and experienced strong feelings as a result?

Applied to a script, the process also works well for actors who can't fully believe in the given circumstances or can't relate to a character or situation. At times, even when circumstances are clearly defined, the actors are unable to identify with the situation or behave in a specific way, let alone work with intensity or urgency. This is where the "what if" concept can also be a very useful tool. In such cases, you might suggest something that is not in the script at all such as,

"What if you have just discovered that your apartment has been ransacked" to an actor whose character has just discovered that a colleague has been spreading lies about them.

Using a "what if" is especially useful when you need to come up with something on the spot. It is also helpful when the actor needs a fresh stimulus for repeated takes or close-ups. Focusing on a new stimulus reawakens the imagination and allows for new and fresh impulses.

Another variation is the "as if." By telling an actor to treat the other characters "as if" they were royalty or treat them "as if" they might snap at any moment, generates a very specific and active behavior and, at the same time, tells us a great deal about the relationship at that moment.

Though tasks, adjustments, fact and fantasy, what ifs, and as ifs are unrelated to the script, they all help the actor achieve a desired state of mind and behavior. Such specific suggestions do not go against the truth of the script: They merely pump life into what has become stale and empty. If the suggestion works, the actor will soon segue into the actual circumstances of the scene but this time with renewed energy that freshens the event and reveals a subtext that enriches the performance.

THE DIRECTOR'S PREPARATION

> "Art is the retelling of certain themes in a new light, making them accessible to the public of the moment."
>
> — *George Lucas*

Detailed preparation is a vital part of the director's work. It will help you to understand the script, to make clear how best to bring it to life, and ultimately it will assist you in your work with the many and varied collaborators who will be part of your creative team — including the actors.

Every director's preparation begins with the script. For the absolute beginner and the seasoned professional alike, the process starts by asking questions about the script. What is the author's point of view about life? What is your interpretation of the author's view? What is a possible theme? How do the characters embody this point of view? Does the script suggest a realistic style or a more theatrical approach? The more you analyze the script, the more questions arise.

APPROACHING THE SCRIPT FOR THE FIRST TIME

Begin by writing down your reactions to the material. You probably won't hit on a theme right away nor on all the other points I'll ask you to address in the "Director's Notes" section of this chapter. In fact, you will have many ideas before you hit on one that feels right. Unless you write them down as you go, however, you are likely to forget some of your ideas and you won't be able to compare them to each other. More importantly, the discipline of writing down a theme and your impressions encourages you to come to grips with the script's issues. You can't direct a script well if you haven't analyzed its elements carefully. Answering detailed questions about the script forces you to figure out what you think it means and helps you to dig deeper, to go beneath the surface.

Furthermore, a director must ask specific, probing questions about the characters. What makes the characters tick? What kind of people are they, really? In what way do the characters differ from each other? How do they feel about each other? What do they want from life? What do they want from each other? How do the relationships between the characters change?

Once you've recorded your original impressions, systematically focus your vision by considering the points outlined in the "Script Analysis" section of this chapter. These questions are the heart of your director's notes.

Preparing the director's notes incorporates both an intuitive response based on your first reading of the script and a deeper analysis based on your subsequent multiple readings. Establishing your particular interpretation of the script and its theme will help you decide on more specific choices for a scene. The primary function of preparing these notes is to help you shape your vision of the script.

Instead of querying oneself in a general way about a script and settling for obvious, superficial answers, a deep analysis helps you bring the screenplay and its characters to life. Good characterization goes beyond cliché. Not every detective is tough. Not every hooker has a heart of gold. Yet these are the stereotypes we see over and over again. Not every housewife is tired and not every gangster is mean. Some of them have families that they love. Even if a script is written in a clichéd manner, it does not have to be played that way. This is when true creativity enters the scenario. You need to know how to ask and answer the right questions. When this happens, you and your actors can work together to bring dimensions to a role that aren't there on paper.

In my classes, I ask my students to take the notes even further. They are required to write out the problems that arose with the actors in rehearsal and the solutions they applied to remedy those problems. As you work with actors, this creative problem-solving method will become vital to your success because you'll be able to guide the actor into identifying with the character's philosophy, goals, relationships, likes and dislikes, needs, despairs, and joys. You will be in a position to help your actors find specific, urgent feelings and needs in themselves that are comparable to those of the characters.

An analysis of the text improves your ability to communicate with your actors because your direction will be more specific. Generalizations never inspire strong work from your cast. Clarity and depth of understanding allow you to be a better leader.

You may get lucky if one of your actors makes an unconscious connection with the text. Sometimes an actor has an instant identification with the role and delivers an amazing performance. These moments are golden and inspiring and, if you are very lucky, sometimes they will stick. However, all too often these precious moments fade away after the first flash. When this happens, it's your job as the director to help your actors again find the connection between themselves and the text. While doing that is never easy, it is possible if you have a deep understanding of the theme, the characters, and the actor's instrument.

With the solid foundation of your director's notes, you'll be in a better position to reinforce work that fits your vision of the story, and you'll find ways to bring your actors closer to your ideas. For an example of this process in action, read Chapter 8, "Director's Notes: *On the Waterfront*."

One last note: I strongly advise directors not to share their written notes with the cast because rather than stimulating instinctive responses, doing so can often lead to over-intellectualizing.

DIRECTOR'S NOTES

The first reading of a script is an exciting and emotional time. As the director, you see glimpses of the script's potential as a performed piece. Some characters may speak to you, and a couple of lines of dialogue may stick in your brain. This emotional response is vitally important to your later conception of the film. Immediately write down all of your feelings, thoughts, impressions, and ideas — even if there seems to be no connection between them. First impressions can be the most valuable reference you have because they have come from an inexplicable but strong response to something in the text. As you work the material over and over, these initial insights will provide the fire to keep you going.

Further read-throughs will offer more insights. At this point, continue to trust your unconscious to feed you ideas. In this way, you continue to keep the door to your feelings open so that you can confront questions you'll need to answer later without being inhibited. Be aware of what feelings the script provokes in you and which characters you identify with most. The more you define the subject's affect on you, the easier it is to understand the material. The effort of all this personal identification with and exploration of the script results in a clear vision that will, in turn, influence your choices as a director.

Script Analysis

Now that you've noted your intuitive impressions, it's time to work through a specific list of questions that make up the heart of the director's notes. The topics these questions address are succinct — they are those that are absolutely necessary to your investigation. When you actually apply these questions to a text, don't settle for the first answer that comes to you. Keep exploring by always asking what and why.

The list of questions and the detailed explanations of them that follow are intended to give you focus, to heighten your awareness of what is inherent in the script, and to stimulate your imagination and your unconscious to pick up clues that can lead to enlightenment.

* What is the *story* about?
* What is the *backstory?*
* What are the story's *given circumstances* (place, time, characters, and events) and why are they significant?
* What is the script's *theme* (the author's point of view about the subject)?
* What is the purpose of each scene and how does each *further the theme?*
* How does each character *embody the theme?*
* What is each character's *super-objective?*

* What are the *characters' relationships* to each other?
* What is the story's overall *conflict* and what is its *climax?*
* The *director's goal*: What is your goal as the director of this story?

What is the story about?

Look beyond the obvious elements of the plot and answer the following queries: With what issues does the plot deal? What happens from beginning to end? What do we learn about life by examining the characters' relationships to the world? Is the story about trying to escape from the past? Is it about people learning how to make a difference in the world? Of what issues does the writer make us aware?

What is the backstory?

Characters' lives and the events that occur in them do not begin on the first page of a script. A script continues a story of lives, experiences, and past events into the present; it builds on the assumption that the characters' have had experiences outside the boundaries of the script's scenes and time frame that have led them to their present condition and circumstances. This is what we mean by "backstory" — backstory is the history of each character. A well-written script offers clues to who the characters are and what elements have led them to this point. What is not immediately obvious can be easily filled in by your imagination. Exploring the backstory creates a solid foundation for all your interpretive choices. If you don't delve into their history, your characters will seem one-dimensional.

What are the story's given circumstances and why are they significant?

A script's given circumstances such as who, what, when, where, and why establish the facts and conditions from which your entire interpretation will come. You cannot identify a theme unless you are aware of the significance of such given factors as: place, time, and events. These facts help us understand what brought the characters to the point in their lives the script addresses.

These details are not open to interpretation, even though so much of what you and your actors do *is*. For example, in the play *Hamlet,* you can't ignore the fact that Hamlet's father, the King, has just died, that his mother Gertrude quickly married her brother-in-law, or that the ghost of the King has appeared before Hamlet. Nor can you disregard the fact that this is a royal family in a certain period of history. If you ignored these facts, your work would lack justification, logic, consistency, and credibility.

But don't approach these as just cut-and-dried facts, either. They provide the stimulus from which everything else springs — whether that means considering the theme, developing your director's goal, or working with your actors.

Given circumstances have an importance that goes beyond their mere surface characteristics. What do they mean in terms of the theme, plot, the characters, and their behavior? Think about it. A story set in the 1950s will not have the same values and behavior as a story set in present times. Different scenes will take place at different times of day and will also affect human behavior. Some characters are morning people, while others don't come to life until the sun sets. And, while it is true that characterization is based on individual personalities, you can't ignore the characters' backgrounds either: a group of uneducated, rural folks will behave differently than a group of city sophisticates.

Don't generalize. For example, *place* is broad in terms of the big picture but it needs to be examined in detail in relation to each scene. You then need to do the same thing for the other given circumstance, *time:* What occurred before each scene and how does each scene affect the ones that follow?

It may seem that some aspects of the given circumstances have no bearing on the work of the actors, but that is not true. They all do. Good actors will have done their own research. However, if you're working with actors who haven't done their homework, your knowledge and awareness of the implications of the givens will be critical.

What is the script's theme?

Identifying the theme of a script is the foundation upon which all your other preparatory work as a director rests. When you identify a script's theme, you are communicating what you consider central to its meaning; you are coming up with an interpretation of the message the author intended to convey in the work. Don't worry about coming up with an objective, definitive interpretation of what the author intended the script to mean because that is impossible. All scripts contain ambiguities, unresolved questions, and therefore, possibilities. Understanding theme, then, is not a matter of understanding *exactly* what the author meant. It's about arriving at your interpretation of the author's work. That's why we have so many different productions of *Hamlet* and so many interpretations of *A Streetcar Named Desire.* Your choice tells us something about you and makes your production unique, rather than a carbon copy of all the others.

The theme of the script is a central, unifying idea that ties all the scenes and characters together. It is the concept that makes the story hang together and make sense. Theme gives the story purpose — it is the reason the story is being told and the reason for the production's existence. By adhering to the same central theme, the different elements of your work will combine and create a whole, a gestalt.

To come up with a theme, ask yourself what the moral of the story is. For instance, a story's moral could be, "We are doomed to live unfulfilled lives if we deny certain truths." A theme relevant to our time could be, "If we live only for the sake of profit and progress, we dehumanize mankind and ourselves." Any story concerned with such a theme will reflect a society's moral values. Another interesting theme could be, "We are destined to destroy ourselves if we live too much by either our passions or our intellects. We must achieve a balance." Greek drama often dealt with this theme, which is essentially the struggle between our Dionysian selves (ruled by passion) and our Apollonian selves (ruled by intellect). A script's biggest thematic clues come from the behavior of its characters.

It may take some time to discover a theme. You may change your mind several times before finding the idea that feels right. Once you do state a theme, even tentatively, you will have a jumping-off point. Knowing your foundation will allow you to undertake the rest of the analysis and make some decisions. Don't be afraid to change your mind. At this early stage, nothing should be set in stone.

What is the purpose of each scene and how does each further the theme?

The questions to ask yourself about individual scenes are as follows: What is the purpose of each scene as it relates to the theme? Does it establish atmosphere? Does it introduce a new character? Does it reveal character development? Does it provide the climax of the story? Does it advance the theme? Does it reveal any consequences of our leading character's struggle?

Once you have determined each scene's purpose, you'll know what has to be emphasized in it. For example, the first scenes in a script are expository. They expose information about time and place, and they introduce characters and establish the atmosphere.

Using the theme "we cannot live for progress alone or we will lose ourselves" implies that a company concerned only with profit would be efficient, tense, and impersonal. Let's say a film opens with a shot of a Fifth Avenue skyscraper in Manhattan. We see people going into the office building. Then we cut to the lobby and see our leading character entering an elevator. He is quite preoccupied with something important. We might also see many others in the lobby who appear concerned about being late, or who are looking over some notes, etc. If this were a story about the relaxed nature of corporations, you, as director, might choose to have our hero enter the lobby and elevator casually and greet a cheerful, relaxed staff. However, given that our opening is supposed to establish a tense atmosphere, we should see our leading character enter preoccupied, barely greeting anyone. Others characters in this scene are also under pressure to complete a task. From these first few scenes, we know where we are, we meet our hero, and we experience a specific atmosphere that sets the tone for the film because you have been specific about your interpretation and therefore know exactly what to emphasize.

As the director, you must not depend on the dialogue to convey such information; the script isn't going to have a character always come out and say, "Gee, I'm really nervous about today's meeting." Good exposition is achieved through an actor's behavior and emotional energy, not by spelling out the facts.

How does each character embody the theme?

Each character represents an aspect of the story's theme. The hero, the villain, and the other characters support one element of the story or another and reflect some facet of its environment. The dramatization of a character's life choices, values, relationships, and behavior are the means by which the author manifests his point. Also, be aware that the antagonist and protagonist could actually shift positions during the course of the story, thereby teaching us a different kind of lesson about life. If such complex shifts occur in the script, you must keep track of when and how they reveal themselves.

What is each character's super-objective?
Once a theme has been determined and you understand who your characters are, it's time to move on to the characters as individuals.

The super-objective is the character's driving force; it determines the psychological and emotional makeup of the characters and is the key to their inner lives. What do they want out of life? What drives them? The answer lies in their unconscious.

Whatever name you give it, this drive was there before we met them and will probably be there after we leave them. In Chapter 3, "The Actor's Language," I cited a person who needs to feel powerful and in control of every situation, be it personal or professional. That inner force motivates all his actions. Unconsciously, he may be trying to replace his father in his mother's life, kill the father's power, protect his own extreme vulnerability, or gain parental approval. Of course, he may be trying to accomplish all of the above objectives because they could be interconnected.

Precisely examining the characters' personalities, their behavior, and what they say about themselves and others will give you clues about what is really driving each of them. Is he shy? Is she a do-gooder? Does he need to please all the time? These questions lead us to the characters' super-objective — their spine — because people's inner drives often determine their choices and behavior. Conversely, their behavior provides clues about the deeper needs they are trying to fulfill. These drives are not conscious ones of which the characters themselves are aware, but we need to know about them. No matter what answers we come up with, it is important to keep asking why until we feel we have found the core of each character.

This isn't as complicated as it sounds. You don't, for example, need to be trained in psychoanalysis to be able to figure out a character's super-objective. There are only so many basic motives. Make a decision and go for it. Once you come to a decision about a character, other things will make themselves known. Remember that you can always change your mind and that you probably will. Making a decision doesn't mean you are committed to it forever. The more you examine the characters' behavior and relationships, the more insight you will gain.

What are the characters' relationships to each other?
Too often, directors focus on the obvious aspects of characters' relationships. They define them simply as being married couples, best friends, enemies, or colleagues. While these obvious details of relationships are important, focusing solely on such basic, external facts yields a lack of depth in the relationships between characters.

Relationships can be very complex and are based on the mixed feelings characters have for each other. External facts tell us nothing about the true nature of a relationship. Take a brother and sister, for example: They could be best friends, enemies, or even lovers. Remember, things are not always what they seem to be on the surface. When relationships turn out to be different than what they initially seemed, the characters involved in them become even more interesting and engaging.

When considering the connections between characters, look beneath the surface and discover how each character really feels about the others. How are the characters different from each other? What do they want from one another? How do different relationships change during the course of the story? What does each character like and dislike about the others?

What is the story's overall conflict and what is its climax?

Conflict is the essence of all literary genres, whether drama, comedy, tragedy, romance, or action. There is no dramatic tension without it. Conflict draws the audience in and keeps them engaged. Conflict occurs when the intensity between two opposing forces grows until it finally climaxes in a showdown. These opposing forces, such as good versus evil, profiteering versus humanitarianism, or blind ambition versus social conscience are embodied by particular characters. The conflict between such forces and the resolution of that conflict dramatizes the issues the author has chosen to present.

For those who are more familiar with plays, be advised that although screenplays do not designate the end or beginning of an act, their basic structure is exactly the same as that of a play.

With that in mind, let's look at the structure of a typical script that has been designed to deliver maximum dramatic conflict. If we look at the arc of a script, we are first introduced to the time, place, and atmosphere of the drama — the exposition. Then, the characters are introduced: Who they are, and whether they are the protagonist (the hero) or the antagonist (the enemy) are established. By the end of the first act, we get a sense of the story's conflict. By the end of the second act, that conflict comes to a head in the story's climax. In the third act, the conflict is resolved somehow, and the consequences of the conflict for the characters and their world are revealed. This is a simplified description of a screenplay or play's structure, but it is sufficient for our purposes.

The director's goal: What is your goal as the director of this story?

It is important to clearly define what you want to say through this story and what you wish to arouse within the audience. Do you want them to feel more positive about life? Should they be angry so that they will take action on certain social issues? Should they laugh at themselves? Be grateful for what they have? Are they inspired to put their faith in love or a spiritual entity? What philosophical, romantic, or absurd elements will you need to emphasize to accomplish your goal?

Having a clear goal helps distill directorial choices so that character and production values both serve one purpose. This helps you determine the characters with whom you want the audience to identify, despise, ally themselves, or to feel emotionally conflicted about. An excellent example of a character who provokes emotional conflict in the audience is Matthew Poncelet in the film *Dead Man Walking*. Without the director's clear goal of allowing the audience to see both sides of Matthew Poncelet, played by Sean Penn, the audience could have dismissed his character as just a cold-blooded murderer. What makes the character and the film interesting is that director Tim Robbins arouses the audience's compassion *and* repulsion for Poncelet. Directorial choices become easier and are more successful when your vision is clear.

Scene Analysis

Many of the following questions may seem repetitive, but upon closer examination you'll discover that they relate to the dynamics of each individual scene within a script. Keep in mind, however, that the script's theme and the characters' super-objectives are the foundations upon which all the answers to these questions rest.

* How does this scene further the script's *theme?*
* Where does each scene take *place* and what is that location's effect on the characters?
* What is the *"scene before the scene"*?
* What is each *character's scene-objective?*
* What is the *why* behind the objective?
* What is the *conflict* in the scene?
* What is each character's *inner conflict?*
* What are the *obstacles* faced by the characters?
* What are the *"beats"* in the scene and what are the *"actions"*?
* The director's goal: What is your *goal* for the scene?

How does the scene further the script's theme?

Having decided on the theme, you can now begin to judge how each scene supports it. Asking yourself what elements in each scene relate to that theme helps clarify the way that scene needs to be played and what should be emphasized in it. If the script's theme, for example, is that "money corrupts," and one of the scenes finds the protagonist severely tempted to "sell out," we would want to emphasize the process by which our hero weighs all the benefits he would garner from succumbing to the temptation, even though that process may not be presented in the actual dialogue. This scene introduces a crisis in his life, and leaves the audience wondering which choice he will make. Previous scenes have revealed the character's lack of satisfaction with his life, which makes him vulnerable to temptation. This scene also addresses the issue of character development by revealing an aspect of the protagonist we have never before witnessed. Look at the actions and details in each scene; develop the elements that could manifest some aspect of your theme. Look for subtle ways to draw out, suggest, imply, or symbolize the overarching idea you want the script to dramatize.

Where does each scene take place and what is that location's effect on the characters?
In a broad sense, the environment from which the characters come (or in which they find themselves) helps define their personalities more specifically. If the characters come from the slums, for example, their environment has influenced their behavior and attitude about life. We can see that when they are in their own environment, they behave significantly differently than they do when they are in a chic hotel lobby.

Defining and using a place requires selecting appropriate, logical daily activities that the characters perform in each scene that are often referred to as "business." These daily activities are determined by the actual physical environment of the scene. For example, if the scene takes place in a kitchen, the possibilities for activities are endless: the characters could be preparing a meal, putting away groceries, making a shopping list, cleaning up after a meal, eating, or looking for a recipe.

There are many reasons for directing such activity. It adds credibility, realism, and logic to the scene and, most interestingly, allows actors to express their inner feelings in the way they perform these activities. This gives the audience insight into the kind of person each character is and what they are really feeling in each situation.

How you direct your actors to use the setting and its objects in a particular scene gives the audience a great deal of information without having to spell it out for them. Here's an example: We have no previous information regarding a married couple when we first encounter them. We see a table set for a dinner party for four. We see the husband reacting to their best china and silver adorning the table, as well as the flowers and candles. He observes his wife silently as she enters and exits the room, busy with last-minute details. She adjusts and readjusts the table-setting and seems nervous about the arrival of their guests. How the couple has been relating to and using these objects has already told us that a problem exists between them. The tone of the scene has been set and finally confirmed when he speaks his first line:

> He: Is that what you're wearing?
> She: Yes.
> He: If we're cooking out, why are you so dressed up?
> She: She'll be dressing up.
> He: Are you competing?
> She: For what?
> He: What women always compete for, I guess. Do you think he's attractive?
> She: Who?
> He: Her husband.

What we see in this scene, before anyone has spoken, is worth a thousand words. Behavior is all!

What is the scene before the scene?

Most often, events that precede particular scenes are not part of the script. However, when a character enters a scene, knowing where they have just come from or what state they are in when we first see them has significant influence on the way we experience that scene. Examining these specifics helps determine what thoughts and feelings the characters are having as the scene begins. Having your actors create such background details for their scenes makes their work more effective.

What is the character's scene-objective?

Every character has an objective in a scene. This scene-objective always serves the character's super-objective, which, as you will recall, is unconscious. The scene-objective is quite conscious, as is the reason for it.

Using the example we considered earlier of a man's need to outshine his father's accomplishments, we know that is his super-objective. When directing specific scenes, you must be specific about how and in what ways you show that character's need. What happens in that scene that hints at or reveals the character's super-objective? Asking this, in turn, helps the director choose what the character does to achieve it and how the character relates to others. The "why" behind this scene-objective is a conscious one, but ultimately serves to gratify a deeper need.

What is the "why" behind the objective?

Objectives aren't the same as needs, but are there to help fulfill a deeper yearning. The objective may be to win the boss over, but the character's need is not necessarily just to "make herself indispensable." *Why* does our character need to influence her employer? Does she eventually want to take his place or is she competing with another colleague? Perhaps she needs to prove to herself that she can win at anything she tries? The why behind a need fires a character's engine and colors how the scene is played. This character's subtext (the implicit or metaphorical meaning) affects the way the scene-objective is played, and what the real feelings behind the characters' behavior and words are. The "why," or motivation, for a character's drives and behavior is something she does not want to reveal to the other characters or, often, even to herself.

I emphasize the why behind the objective because too many actors play the objective but forget to create the why. The why makes all the difference. Let's use an example of a physical task: cleaning the car. There's only one person involved, but how the actor cleans the car tells a story. Suppose the character is cleaning the car because last night he killed someone in a hit-and-run accident and there's evidence on the car. The objective is to clean the car and the why is to get rid of the evidence. The way he cleans the car and his reason for doing so is quite a bit different than the way he would clean it for a big date that night. The outcome is exactly the same, a clean car, but the why tells us a totally different story and determines how the objective is played.

The relationship between characters also affects how an objective is played. A character asks for a raise: This request can be colored either by his fear of his employer or his lack of self-confidence.

Other factors affecting the way a director may choose to dramatize an objective include the presence of another person, and how the character feels about the other person, himself, or his physical condition. The character's behavior will be influenced by the fact that he has an enemy in the room, a headache, a pounding heart, or a hangover.

What is the conflict in the scene?
Remember, every character in a scene has an objective and the clash of these objectives creates the conflict. Sometimes, the conflict is very much out in the open, other times it is the subtext — keenly felt but not expressed.

What is each character's inner conflict?
Inner conflict is the war characters fight internally as they struggle to achieve their objectives. What they are saying or doing externally is often different from what's going on inside them.

Take a person visiting a friend who is dying. Her objective is to comfort her beloved friend because she doesn't want to feel guilty later (the why of her objective). Her inner conflict comes from revulsion over the patient's condition, which makes her afraid of being in the same room. Thus, inside she is struggling with revulsion and fear, but externally, she is comforting someone she cares about. Let's ponder another situation. Man's objective: to get his girlfriend back by proposing marriage. Inner conflict: terror of being emotionally trapped. Woman's objective: to get him out of her life. Inner conflict: she's still madly in love with him. The dramatic tension within such a scene comes from the conflict between the two objectives, while the inner conflicts create an intense subtext for each character and make the pursuit of their objectives more difficult and dynamic. Inner conflicts arouse our curiosity — they create a sense of mystery because they are sensed but not known.

What are the obstacles each character faces?
Obstacles are elements that interfere with the characters' pursuit of their objectives and that complicate the characters' ability to fulfill their goals. Obstacles may be created by other characters (usually in the form of clashing objectives, which is what give us the protagonist/ antagonist conflict of classical drama), plot developments, external factors, or a character's internal conflict. Obstacles can be physical, such as a headache or a broken leg, or external, such as cold weather or a crowded street. They can be internal, such as a fear of being overheard, a fear of noise, or a chronic fear of rejection. Usually, you will find that the obstacles are already suggested in the script, but you can also create them to add more levels to the scene or energize the actors. If a performance is flat, create an obstacle by telling the actor — whose objective is to break up with her boyfriend — that she can be overheard by strangers. Creating obstacles

encourages more interesting behavior. It gives the actor concrete obstacles to deal with, which focuses their concentration on the problem within the scene.

Where are the *beats* in the scene and what are the *actions?*

In your preparatory work, look at how a scene breaks down into beats (changes of circumstances or behavior). This is part of the common language between directors and actors.

You can determine when a beat starts and ends by finding the transitions in a scene. Every time a character changes from one action to another, the old beat ends and a new one begins. A beat can be as short as one line or as long as a page, although beats are rarely that long or short. It is important to realize that there is no set space for a beat. If your actors instinctively create the beats and develop a multi-layered scene, then you are in luck. If your actors do not create them spontaneously, the scene is in grave danger of being played on one level. In this case, you can achieve variety and different levels by scoring the scene, beat by beat. If you very specifically say, "On this line I would like you to charm her, then at this point, mock her," one beat has been completed and a new one begun when the new action is played.

Be flexible in your approach to beats. Use beats as guidelines to grant your actors the freedom to be spontaneous. If actors are truly connected to the needs of the character, they will pursue their objective actively and the beats and actions will differ each time. That's because in reality, we never pursue something in exactly the same way twice. When directing, only suggest various actions to be played if the behavior is too general or you want more colors.

The result of clashing objectives between characters creates conflict within individual scenes. In order to fulfill the objective, the character will perform different *actions.* The goal of those actions is to influence another character in some way. Since each character pursues a different objective, their actions in certain scenes are bound to clash. For example: Susan wants to stay at home and have a cozy evening in front of the fire because she needs to feel that John still loves her. But John wants to go bowling because he feels suffocated. Her actions may be to seduce him, coax, plead, or attack to get him to stay home, while he might try to convince, humor, ignore, demand, and, finally, reject her in order to get what he wants. You now have a dynamic scene, one with objectives and actions resulting in conflict. These are the elements used to achieve, on a moment-to-moment basis, the greater goal: action creating reaction. Unless we're arch manipulators, in everyday life we spontaneously employ many actions in order to achieve our goals. What we do unconsciously in our personal lives, actors must do consciously when they dramatize a character's actions.

It is unwise for directors to speak to an actor in terms of results such as, "Here I want you to cry," or "Here I want you to smile." Although actors who are worth their salt can do it, the result will be predictable, empty behavior. Or, even worse, it can lead actors into strained and uncomfortable forms of expression. Instead, give them actions to play using active verbs such as demand, defy, wheedle, etc. The ensuing interaction between the actors will create the desired emotional result. If it doesn't, try changing both characters' actions and run the scene again. Once an actor desires something badly enough, you will get the results and emotions that you are looking for. Better yet, you may achieve emotional responses and behavior you hadn't even considered.

By concentrating on playing actions, the actors avoid generalized emotions. By truly being engaged in wanting something from the other character (the objective and the why) the actor will engage in specific behavior (the action) that will encourage counter-reaction from others in the scene. This interplay between action and reaction encourages actors to live in the moment, in a give-and-take situation — each action affecting the other. This, in turn, stimulates and encourages strong responses from the audience.

Giving actors specific actions to play also helps get their minds off themselves. When actors feel insecure or obliged to play a scene in a certain way, they tend to watch themselves. This results in playing the scene "by themselves" or reaching for predetermined emotions. If this problem develops, suggest a very active verb to get them to focus on the other person in the scene.

A word of caution however: If you suggest a certain action and the actors don't play it as you anticipated, don't worry. It simply means that words evoke different responses from different people. Keep in mind that actors' instincts may be more in tune with the truth of the action and their way of playing it may add more to the scene than your initial concept. The bottom line is to use whatever actions spur involvement.

If one action doesn't work, suggest another — use a synonym for your previous suggestion or choose a more active verb. If the action is to "make the other character laugh," the action "tickle her" (not literally) or "make her smile" may do the trick and spring them into active behavior. As an experiment, say to yourself, "I'm going to make you smile," then, "I'm going to tickle you," and see if the different wording makes you react differently. By experiencing the effect different actions can have, you realize how actions can be one of your most productive tools as a director.

Some examples of effective actions include: demand, deny, threaten, console, charm, reject, and degrade. Simple active verbs are best because they are easier to play. These active verbs should always be kept in your back pocket to use as a resource when you see a performance lagging. Again, actions are not the dialogue or stage directions in the scene but the active behavior characters employ to achieve their goal.

The director's goal: What is your goal for the scene?
First of all, don't lose sight of your theme or your character's relationship to that theme. Then ask, is this the scene:

* in which the characters reveal their true intent?
* where the characters reveal their insecurities?
* where the protagonist is struggling between principles and revenge?
* where other characters choose one side or the other or switch allegiance?

* where you want the audience to change its mind about a character?
* where you want to create some humor by underscoring a character's faults?

Being this specific about each scene's function in the overall scenario gives you a very clear path toward your vision of the entire piece. Knowing what to emphasize in each scene supports your interpretation of the material.

CHARACTER ANALYSIS

The stories that seem to touch us the most and that are, in my opinion, the most fun to direct, are character driven. People are so multidimensional and their relationships so complex that trying to fit all these pieces together is a demanding but exciting challenge. The next step for directors and actors is to bring the characters to life so people can recognize themselves or people they know in them. Avoid stereotypes at all costs. Clichés are boring. We must instead flesh out each character by including their flaws as well as their virtues. Remember, one-dimensional characters can lead to melodrama.

Sometimes, audiences can learn from the characters' attempts to straighten out their lives. At other times, their experience is cathartic because the audience can laugh at themselves or shed the tears they've been bottling up.

As a director, you should pay attention to the physical characteristics of your characters such as posture, weight, dress, and mannerisms. These externals relate to internals in two principal ways. First, they are an expression of the inner life of a character. Body language alone can reveal a great deal about a character's inner life and background. It also works the other way. Externals can influence the inner life. If you are doing a period piece, for instance, the manner of dress is a key to a character's social status. At the same time, it influences how that character moves, feels, and uses his or her body. When you are dressed formally, you sit differently than when you are wearing jeans. Something happens to the body, something happens to the spirit, and that is when we see the marriage of external and internal qualities.

Such a marriage is difficult to achieve if you don't have a map that helps you know what to look for in a character and where to look for it. The following pages will guide you toward a clear understanding of your characters and keep you from going around in circles. Think carefully about the following details regarding the characters and create your own questions. If some of the questions that follow are difficult for you to answer, keep in mind that they are not supposed to be easy; on the contrary, they are designed to stimulate your imagination and curiosity.

* What is the character's biography?
* What is the character's backstory?
* Describe the character's values and principles.
* Describe the inner conflict of the characters.

* Describe the arc of the characters' development through the script.
* Describe the relationships between the characters.
* What are the physical attributes of the characters?
* How do the characters embody the script's theme?

What is the character's biography?

Biography is the character's background from childhood to the present. The whole purpose of a biography that a director and actor build is to understand why the character does what he does and feels what he feels. In other words, a biography provides the roots of the character's being and the elements that helped create the person we meet. This kind of exploration allows actors to identify with the character's problems and encourages them to dig into their own similar needs and experiences in order to bring the character to life.

For me, the word "why" is essential in character analysis. If I don't understand why the characters are who they are or what made them arrive at this point, how can I justify what they do? The more aware I am of their roots, the more specific my choices will be. For example, consider the role of Beatrice, the mother in *The Effect of Gamma Rays on Man-in-The-Moon Marigolds*. Beatrice lives with her two teenage daughters in the back of her vegetable store. One daughter is unpredictable, highly emotional, and given to epileptic seizures. The other is quiet, introspective, studious, and loving. Beatrice was raised by a protective father who was the buffer between herself, the world, and her ridiculing classmates. Seeking that same protection, she instead found a husband who deserted her. As both breadwinner and mother, she is now overwhelmed by fear, resentment, and rage, all of which are taken out on her daughters.

While it would be easy to play Beatrice as a wicked mother, it would be clichéd to do so unless we understand the source of her anger and frustration. If our goal as a director is to present full human beings driven by unresolved issues, then it is our responsibility to help our actors develop, in this case, the undertones of fear, loneliness, and frustration.

By understanding the "why" of it all, you'll find the virtues in villains and the flaws in heroes. In this way, you will create memorable performances.

Asking questions opens our imagination and provides answers that will resonate within us. Exploring a character's background helps us get in touch with their roots and understand why they need to do what they do. It also determines what major elements influenced the choices they have made that have brought them to this point in life. These answers help actors find parallels within their own lives and encourage a deeper empathy for and identification with the character.

Take notes on everything the author says to describe the characters, including:

* What were their roots?
* Where did they grow up?
* What was their childhood like?
* How much education did they have?

* What was their economic and social situation?
* How did their social background influence their character?
* How would you describe their personality?
* What kind of relationships did they have with their parents, siblings, friends, and teachers?
* Were they bright, outgoing, or introverted?
* Did they feel free to express and assert themselves?
* Were they a dreamer or a doer?
* What are they like when alone?

What is the character's backstory?

Answering this question involves examining all the events in the character's background that brought them to the point when we meet them. The writer offers some details, but as a director, you can fill in the gaps with your understanding of human nature. The biography and backstory help us understand what forces led the characters to make certain choices in their lives.

Questions to ask in creating this backstory:

* What circumstances led to this current problem?
* As a result of previous circumstances, has the character arrived at some determination about themselves or their relationships?
* What problem does the character need to solve?
* Have any of the characters met before?
* How did they feel about each other?
* Did something change this relationship?

Once you have determined each character's history, you are better prepared to answer more comprehensive questions about the whole story.

Describe the characters' values and principles.

Believable characters are born when the actor — and audience — understand where this person is coming from. Delve into the underlying values and principles that make your characters whole by asking these questions.

* What are the characters' private thoughts?
* How do they feel about themselves?
* How does this affect their relationships and behavior?
* How do the characters feel about their lives?
* Describe their ideal life for themselves and for man in general. (A moral ideal, as opposed to goals.)

* What are their moral values?
* What are their greatest dreams and hopes for the future?
* What are their greatest fears regarding their future?

Describe the inner conflict of the characters.
An actor can only make a character interesting if he brings that character's inner conflict to light. This conflict will make them wrestle with themselves, the environment, and other characters. Such struggles make the performed script interesting and true to life. Think about the following issues.

* What unresolved emotional issues do the characters harbor?
* What lies within the characters that they could never reveal?
* Of what inner conflicts are they unaware?

Describe the arc of the character's development throughout the script.
An arc is the development of a character over time. Where does the character start? What happens next? How does the character change and when? Understanding and developing this arc allows the entire story to take shape.

* Do the characters change in the story?
* Who is each character in the beginning and who do they become?
* What causes the change?
* What issues and flaws are resolved?

Describe the relationships between the characters.
No two people are exactly the same and no one reacts to a situation in quite the same way. Understanding how characters perceive each other and relate to each other is very important. Define your characters' relationships by asking these questions.

* How do they relate to others? Are they open or defensive?
* What attitudes and feelings (conscious or unconscious) do they have towards the other characters?
* What specific things do they like and dislike about each other?
* Whom are they the most sympathetic towards?
* Whom are they most indifferent to?
* With which person do they disagree most?
* What is the specific nature of their relationships with each character?
* Whom do they love, fear, resent, envy, trust, distrust, and why?

What are the physical attributes of the characters?
Creating a rich subtext for your characters includes a dose of physical reality. Make sure each character stands out as an individual and relates to the real world via everyday mannerisms.

* Do they have an accent?
* Do they take good care of their body?
* Is their posture athletic or do they slouch?
* How do they enter or leave a room?
* What aspect of themselves do they like and dislike?
* What are their physical mannerisms?
* Do they have stiff shoulders?
* Do they resist being touched?
* Are they always smiling no matter what they feel?
* Are they very meticulous?
* Are they always touching people and objects?
* Are they aggressive or passive?
* Do they remind you of some animal?

How do the characters embody the script's theme?
In order to concoct believable, moving films and plays, the director must determine how each character participates in, or adds to, the overall theme. Strip down the layers until you get to the core by asking these questions.

* Which side do they represent?
* What are their super objectives?
* What drives them in life and what determines the choices they make?
* What is their overall objective in the script?
* What are the obstacles (inner and outer) that are in opposition to the character's objectives?
* Do we learn anything from this character?

The author will probably have supplied you with a great deal of information about your characters, but the more you probe their past, present, and future on your own, the better your work as a director will be.

Putting It All Together: Atmosphere, Mood, and Pacing
We've spent a great deal of time discussing the meaning of the script and understanding characters and actors, but you may wonder about pacing, timing, atmosphere, and mood. Well, wonder no longer. These things are a consequence of what is taking place in each scene and not separate elements to be tagged on at some point.

Atmosphere and Mood

Atmosphere, and the related element of pacing, has a great deal to do with how a scene is played. When directors think of atmosphere, they often try to first determine the scene's mood. (Try to remember that "mood" spelled backwards is "doom.") Often, directors rely heavily on production values to create mood — lighting, camera, editing, and music, and the actor is reduced to a mere prop. Production values are meant to support a director's vision, but they can also assault our senses and ultimately leave an audience with an empty experience because the person we are trying to identify with is overwhelmed by special effects. Realize that atmosphere is a result of what is literally taking place between people. If a woman is preparing for an exciting date, she will create an atmosphere filled with anticipation and excitement. If she is getting dressed for a funeral, the atmosphere will be totally different. The given circumstances suggest what the character is thinking, which suggests how he or she feels, which dictates how he or she moves about the room. This is body language. Thus, the actor, being in the reality of the given circumstance, creates the atmosphere.

Trust that when you work from the specifics, the atmosphere will come as a natural consequence of the given circumstances, the relationships, the objectives, and their actions. If two people are dining at a gourmet restaurant to celebrate their engagement, the atmosphere will be quite different than if they were going to be late for the theater or having just come from a wake. People create atmosphere and mood by just going about their business.

Pacing

As a director, you need to recognize the relationship between pacing, the given circumstances, and the actions. If a couple is getting ready to go to a banquet in honor of the husband's employer and the wife can't decide what to wear, there would be a sense of urgency in the scene. If there isn't, however, many directors will attempt to create it by telling the actors to "pick it up." Well, any actor can do that! By speaking to actors in mechanical terms, you encourage mechanical behavior. If you want the pace to quicken, give the actors an adjustment that will naturally create a sense of urgency and thereby spontaneously create a faster pace. Try raising the stakes for the wife by suggesting they will be seated at the CEO's table or that the CEO is a stickler for promptness.

Conversely, actors can often race through a scene. If you decide you need a more languid pace, suggest the couple is in a sauna or sunbathing — anything that will relax them. Any adjustment should trigger an organic, natural reaction that results in your desired pace. Deal with actors as vital flesh-and-blood human beings who can slow down or speed up a performance spontaneously and naturally when given a human reason for doing so.

A note on the director's impulse to say, "Pick it up." That impulse is not necessarily unreasonable because, in fact, it may be an instinctive response to the symptom of a problem. When the exchange between two actors seems to drag, it is usually the result of the actors not being fully involved in the situation. Perhaps their needs aren't strong enough to pursue the objective.

Maybe they are thinking too much about what they are doing rather than just doing it. If you are correct in your assumptions, then saying "pick it up" won't be so dangerous because they won't have the time to watch themselves. What you are doing, in essence, is helping them get out of their own way so that their impulses are freed.

EXERCISES

Select a published script you would like to use for the exercises in this chapter. Find one that has something to say about the human condition or society in general, with characters that have strong emotional desires. Working on such scripts is interesting because of all the levels of meaning you can explore; it's also actually easier than working on scripts that lack substance — making something flimsy seem interesting is quite difficult.

Do not, however, choose material you've already seen and admired. By selecting such a piece, your natural inclination is to duplicate it. Where, then, would your vision be? Give yourself a chance to be original.

I don't recommend using something you've written yourself either. "Why not?" you may ask, "I intend to direct my own pieces." Of course, but my years of experience have proven that the writer part of you becomes much stronger than the director part of you, and it's a no-win situation for the director. When working with screenwriters in my classes, I like to kid them by saying, "I don't care what the Bible says. The word did *not* come first. The impulse came first, then the grunt, then came the second grunt, and that made a word." That little joke brings any screenwriter back to reality.

Since you are learning a new process here, you'll be much better served by using material that intrigues you and leaves room for your own vision to emerge.

Director's Notes

1. **Describe the theme.** List one or two possible themes in one or two sentences.

2. **Describe the given circumstances.** How do the elements of time, place, and background support the writer's theme?

3. **Describe your goal as director.** Write one or more brief sentences about what point you are trying to make with this script. What would you like to arouse within your audience? Again, do not write an essay because you could clutter your thinking. Write succinct sentences and come to grips with what you are trying to accomplish.

4. **Describe how each scene furthers the theme.** Select a two-character scene you wish to work on in detail and, in one sentence, tell the story of the scene (describe what happens). Then describe how the scene relates to the theme and, finally, how the characters serve the theme.

5. Describe each character's super-objective. Decide who the protagonists and antagonists are. In one or two sentences, state their super-objectives.

6. Describe the scene-objectives. Describe each character's objective in the scene and be very clear about *why* they need to fulfill that objective. Be aware that one character will drive the scene more than the other, making one more active and the other more reactive, and that the power can shift from one character to the other.

7. Describe the conflict in the scene. Keep in mind that conflict is caused by two clashing objectives.

8. Describe each character's inner conflict. This inner life is often the opposite of what the character reveals on the surface.

9. Find the beats. Before you choose actions played by the characters in a scene, it is helpful to first break the scene down into beats. Read your selected scene several times, and when you feel you can clearly understand its beat structure, mark the beats with a pencil line. Remember that beats will vary in length and will even change.

10. Describe each character's possible actions. Write down the actions each character could play in each beat. Be sure to use active verbs and do not elaborate. Example: "Fend off, seduce, amuse, charm" are all you need for each beat.

11. Describe the character relationships. Examine how each character feels specifically about the other's appearance, personality, behavior, intelligence, values, and habits. Do the characters resent, envy, admire, appreciate, or love the others? Careful exploration of the text, as well as your imagination, will supply you with many clues and answers. Make a separate list for each character.

An example of Director's Notes can be found in Chapter 8, "Director's Notes: *On the Waterfront*."

Practical Exercise for Objectives, the Why, Actions, and Personalization

The next exercise is practical rather than analytical. Try it with the actors with whom you have chosen to work. It will help you recognize the impact these specifics have on playing the scene.

The only dialogue to be used in this exercise is the following:

Character #1: Give me a cigarette.
Character #2: No.

Under no conditions should dialogue be altered or added to.

1st run-through. The objectives:

Character #1: To get a cigarette.
Character #2: To refuse.

2nd run-through. Now add a specific "why" for the objective such as:

Character #1: Stopped smoking two weeks ago and has an unending craving.
Character #2: Wants to break Character #1's addiction.

3rd run-through. Add specific actions to play such as: beg, plead, demand, tease, warn, soothe, etc.

4th run-through. Add a personalization and substitution. Be sure to free your actors from the previous actions they played and encourage them to be completely spontaneous.

Character #1: Substitute something they crave in lieu of a cigarette, such as a beer or chocolate cake.
Character #2: Substitute someone they love or hate for the character relationship.

This exercise not only trains you to be very simple and specific when building a scene organically, but also develops and heightens your awareness of the difference between just good acting and acting that is truly alive.

When watched closely, the exercise also demonstrates how genuine identification with the characters' objectives and needs leads to playing specific actions organically. These actions and reactions spontaneously result in beat changes and subtext.

CASTING THE PRODUCTION

"Not everybody can star in a movie. The rest of the people are the characters supporting the stars. They are the people who make the movie work."

— *Mike Fenton, casting director*

Casting is a crucial aspect of the director's work. Many say that casting is 90 percent of a director's job, and there is some truth to that statement. By casting actors with characteristics similar to their roles, it wouldn't be necessary for a director to work that hard to help his actors identify with their characters. Intelligent and sensitive casting has often led to noteworthy productions because of outstanding performances. However, even good casting isn't foolproof, as evidenced by many talented actors appearing in failed productions.

Unfortunately, casting is influenced by less than idealistic considerations. Often, directors aren't the ones calling the shots and such decisions are left to producers and distributors. If you are lucky enough to take part in the process, there are many factors that can affect your choice for a part besides an actor's absolute perfection for the role. One factor is the overwhelming influence of economics. Producers, studios, and distributors are very concerned with the marketability of leading actors. Will the actor's name help raise money needed for the production? Will this name draw audiences to the theater or will it be box office poison? As a consequence, economics can have a major impact on the script. Each time a "name" agrees to come on board, his or her demands require that the script be rewritten to suit his or her particular quality or ability. This can happen more than once on any project. Inevitably, the integrity of the script is violated and the project becomes the weaker for it.

The other, and more prevalent, factor is finding the right look, which can lead to clichés and stereotypes. It may be an easy way out for directors, but it is of no value to a production. Unless directors become more aware of talent, skills, and what true actors can bring to a production, their work will remain shallow.

To cast well, there are several factors to keep in mind. If your training and background has emphasized the more technical aspects of film direction, these truths will be especially helpful. In many cases, directors with a theater background have had the advantage of casting and directing already and have been exposed to great, dramatic literature. Whatever your background, there is much to become aware of, more to learn, and many bad habits to overcome.

FINDING YOUR CASTING DIRECTOR

Having the right casting director will make your life much easier. Casting directors are the liaison between you, actors, and their agents or managers. They are up to date on the pool of talent and the availability of the more seasoned players. They are able to keep tabs on every actor who has impressed them in a performance, audition, or an interview. Time permitting, they will hold general auditions to meet new actors and view their tapes — a compilation of excerpts from their television and film work — to get a better sense of their capabilities. Their after-hours job is to attend many theater performances and view as many films and television shows as possible in order to find new talent.

Once hired for a new production, the casting director's primary function is to contact the actors' representatives to set up preliminary auditions. During this phase they will narrow down all the actors they feel come close to your vision of the role.

They will also set up the audition appointments for you and negotiate salaries and billing with the actors' representatives. In other words, they save you an enormous amount of time and energy that is better spent on other matters. In a different, but just as meaningful way, they can also open your eyes to other possibilities of interpretation and introduce you to unknown but very impressive talent.

Finding the right casting director is not as daunting a task as it may seem. However, you must have a clear vision of what you want to do with your script, your characters, and the emotional energy of your production. Your vision will help during initial meetings with different casting directors.

What should you specifically look for in a casting person besides their professional credentials? Compatibility and compassion! How do they connect and emotionally respond to the story? Do they have the insight and sense of the script that supports yours? What is their perception of the characters? Do they see traits in the characters you never thought of? Do they have original ideas about casting or are their suggestions conventional? Do their casting ideas reveal courage and imagination or do they have a stable of reliable but not necessarily inspiring actors that they use all the time? And, finally, do they really understand, respect, and love actors?

Now that you know what qualities to look for in a casting director, the next step is to know where to look. Ask your director friends for referrals. They will most likely be more than willing to share their experiences about every good and bad casting director they've met. When you see a film with strong acting and interesting casting, be sure to note the casting director's name. Before making a final decision on the person for this position, view other projects they have helped cast.

Once you have found a compatible casting director, breathe a sigh of relief. You now have someone who thinks the way you do and will support you.

If, on the other hand, you can't afford an experienced casting director, ask your director and actor friends to recommend some actors for the roles. If you must, advertise in film and television periodicals such as *Ross Reports, Backstage West, Backstage East,* or online (www.castingsociety.com and www.LA411.com). You might even consider taking on the daunting task of attending many theater productions in search of actors who might be right for you.

Other valuable resources for finding actors are theater groups. These groups are more than happy to post your casting notice to help their fellow actors find a good role. If you are looking for seasoned professionals, many theater groups count older actors in their ranks. Due to the nature of the business, these elder statesmen may not be getting much film and television work. (Youth is gold. Old is out.) There are also social clubs, activity groups, and senior citizen theater groups that promote activities and may yield talent for you. For young actors, check various college and university theater departments in your area. And, last but not least, review the Academy Players Directory published by the Academy of Motion Picture Arts and Sciences.

If you begin casting without benefit of professional assistance: a word of caution. While reviewing actors' photographs and résumés, keep in mind that some hungry and ambitious individuals may embellish their credits and training. Only the audition will truly reflect their capabilities.

PREPARING FOR THE AUDITION

Once you have the right casting director by your side, you're almost ready to see actors. The casting director will have first submitted a script to a breakdown service such as Breakdown Co. or Castnet whose readers provide — for your approval — a description of each character, incorporating whatever unique specifics you deem necessary. A synopsis of the script is also provided. These character breakdowns are sent to agents and managers who will submit headshots and résumés of the actors they feel might fit your roles.

For your auditions, select each character's key scenes. Since film scenes are usually quite short, try using scenes with no more than two people. This gives actors a bit more to work with. If the role requires strong emotions of any kind, be sure to use scenes that test their emotional range.

You must also determine who will read opposite the actor you are auditioning. Casting directors or their assistants usually assume these roles. However, unless they have acting backgrounds, they're often not exceptionally helpful. Casting directors or assistants tend to bury their noses in the script, giving the auditioning actor only their foreheads to react to. They may read their lines without expression or simply rush their dialogue. There is nothing worse than reading with someone who gives you nothing to react to. How anyone can expect an actor to give a good audition under such circumstances is mystifying. This approach is to nobody's advantage, least of all the director who may ultimately be the loser. Insist on having an actor assist with the readings. By supplying a giving partner, you give your auditioners every chance to show what they can do.

Actors for major roles will receive the complete script in advance and be advised of which scenes to prepare for the audition. For minor roles, scenes are always available at the production office for actors to study before reading for the casting director.

With certain exceptions, your casting person will conduct preliminary auditions and narrow the choices for each role. Occasionally, they may even videotape an actor or two for your consideration.

Once you have analyzed the script, developed character profiles in your director's notes, and all the organizational work has been done, you are now prepared for the audition.

The Perils of Typecasting

The easiest and most seductive trap during auditions is typecasting. If you only think of roles as large or small and use this as the standard, you'll be doing yourself a great disservice. Typecasting limits the depth of characterization that can be achieved.

There is some mistaken belief that casting the right character type is enough. It's enough — if your view of people is shallow. Typecasting leads to stereotypes that are boring and, at times, downright insulting. Since nothing more is expected from actors other than that they look the part, typecasting becomes a waste of talent and directorial imagination.

Naturally, the basic psychological aspects of characters have tremendous importance in casting. Certain physical characteristics, such as ethnicity, age, height, weight, and body language matter if they reflect a certain lifestyle or inner quality of the character. In fact, certain physical qualities will indicate where the characters were raised, their education, their profession, and how they have lived their lives. The obvious logic of the story's milieu dictates the physical nature of the characters. For example, a film about boxing will demand certain physical types, as would a film about a starving nation. Pay attention to these details but don't let them be the sole criteria upon which to base your judgment. More important is whether the actor can act and identify with the character's needs and problems. Resist the obvious!

A romantic lead, for example, doesn't have to be clean-cut and handsome. He could be rough around the edges but so charismatic and personable that women would find him difficult to resist.

A similar but slightly different trap is the danger of casting to an ideal. The ideal person that you envisioned walks into your office. They've got the look and quality you dreamed of when you worked on the script — and here they are! Keep your feelings in check. I've seen more independent films hurt because directors were blinded by the embodiment of their fantasy, only to discover that these people could not act. All the actor had was what he walked in with and nothing more. The dream turns into a nightmare and the director is left to make do with what he got.

A classic example of not casting to type is Marlon Brando as an Italian-American mafioso in *The Godfather*. Instead of playing a stereotypical killer, he was a loving, warm, affectionate family man. Who can forget the scene when Brando discusses murderous business in his office while stroking his cat?

Gifted actors will bring unpredictable behavior that makes people sit up and take notice. But directors can initiate unforgettable moments if they think of their characters as multi-faceted human beings rather than types. Look for the unexpected in characters — the opposite colors. A friend can be impatient, a killer can be tender, a brute can be childlike, and a loving wife can also be a bitch. Don't play it safe. Use your imagination.

CASTING SMALL ROLES AND NON-ACTORS

Since so much emphasis is generally placed on casting the major roles, creative attention is rarely given to small roles or "bit parts" as they are referred to in the film industry. In theater, they are referred to as "walk-ons."

Not all roles have enough scenes to allow for character development. A character that appears in one short scene makes a statement and will be who they are, nothing more and nothing less. Naturally, you'd cast actors whose personal characteristics would make the statement. But how nice it would be to have one more dimension at the same time.

"Bit parts" populate a large portion of a production and can add greatly to its texture and tone. They can even provide comic relief. Again, not every courtroom judge need be austere, not every salesman need be slick, or every waitress tough and saucy. Why can't the judge be a Santa Claus type, or the salesman a bit paranoid, and the waitress motherly or shy? Wouldn't that be refreshing for a change? Be inventive when casting these roles and have fun. You won't regret it.

Some directors may even be tempted to use non-actors for bit parts. My advice? Use them at your own peril. The justification we often hear from directors is that they "want to use real people." Why? Aren't actors real people? While directors who think this way have a valid point, they are unaware of what is influencing their thinking. To put it simply, they have seen too many actors "acting" or are put off by the perfectly manicured, safe, and predictable Hollywood types. They now prefer people who have uniqueness about them: men and women with all their imperfections readily perceivable.

In motion pictures and especially on television, leading men and women are so perfect, they become dull. The system encourages beauty and stereotypes but rarely individual personalities. Yet most of these actors are skilled and eager to take direction. They are able to give more than is expected of them. Non-actors may look more interesting but they may not know how to be natural. They don't know how not to "act," how to reflect on a moment, or how to sustain emotion. It is rare, indeed, to find a non-actor who can really bring himself to the role or a director skilled enough to make it happen.

The supposed glory of using non-actors is a misleading myth and, therefore, dangerous. The rationale is usually based on Vittorio de Sica's *Bicycle Thief,* where a non-actor was chosen as his lead. After all, if de Sica could comb the streets of Rome to find the perfect cast, so can you.

The fact is, de Sica didn't just go out into the streets. He interviewed about 500 people and followed dozens of them around on the street until he saw somebody that appealed to him. The man he ultimately chose looked the part, had the right quality, had imagination, and didn't try to "act."

Keep in mind that de Sica started out as an actor and continued to act when not directing. Elia Kazan, also started out as an actor and cast the lead role in *America, America* with a young Greek man who had never acted in his life. However, he had similar life experiences to those of the character. Although this individual was very effective in the film, he never worked as an actor again.

CONDUCTING THE AUDITION

The audition is a multi-layered process. It encompasses a basic interview to get a sense of the individual and an actual reading of key scenes from the script. This preliminary process leads to callbacks. During these callbacks you may work with the auditioning actors more carefully, checking their interaction with other actors, and even taping them to review later. During these steps, particularly the first reading, you must do your best to create a relaxed atmosphere.

The object of the audition is to learn as much as you can about the physical, psychological, and emotional makeup of each potential cast member. But, keep in mind that the actors will be nervous. Therefore, be sensitive to each actor's mood as they enter the room. They may have gone through an internal preparation for the scene and to engage in small talk can shatter their concentration. Allow them to read first and chat later. Some actors may want to chat first and then start the reading. Be attuned to each actor because the more relaxed they feel, the better the reading.

The Interview and What to Look For

The interview portion of the audition is when you discover what sort of people the actors are and their suitability for a specific role. Put the actors at ease because if they are tense, you will never know what they are really like and whether or not the two of you can really work together.

It is during the interview and reading process that you discover the actor's "take" on the script and the role, how close they come to fulfilling your concept, or what new ideas they might bring to the role. Your casting director may have recommended someone whose uniqueness is compelling and against type. This type of casting is both adventurous and exciting.

Directors learn everything they need to know by asking questions. Begin with questions of a social nature. Once the ice is broken, review the actor's credentials as listed on their résumé. It is often useful to talk about the most interesting and unusual aspects of the actor's work. There may be a play they were involved in that interests you, a director they may have worked with, or some such "hook" on which you can build your conversation.

Although you are looking for actors who possess the physical traits of the characters in your script, keep in mind that these aspects are some of the most flexible elements of your search. Details such as hair color, height, and build only matter if they have had a specific effect on the character's sense of self and background.

More important is the actor's personality: innate qualities such as energy, presence, outlook on life, psychological makeup, emotional qualities, intelligence, and sociability. These factors are important because they fulfill, without effort, the inner life of the character. In the Michel Ciment documentary *The Outsider,* Elia Kazan describes his first meeting with James Dean. He was casting *East of Eden* and found a sullen young man whom, out of his discomfort, invited Kazan for a ride on his motorcycle. A terrified Kazan felt it was worth the risk to get to know him better. In subsequent meetings he discovered Dean had problems with his father — similar to those of the character — and there was more. Dean also had a profound need to please, yet get away from his parents. This actor could identify with the character and bring the necessary emotional range and depth to the role without too much effort. Kazan had found his leading man.

Some actors are very good at auditioning and present a polished and finished product during auditions. This sort of actor may be a good choice, if capable of growth and development during the rehearsal and shooting. But, it may also turn out that what the actor demonstrated in the audition is all that they can do. Their glibness may merely indicate inflexibility, not accomplishment.

Again, don't dismiss actors because they don't fit the obvious mold. The necessity of finding actors with obvious characteristics of the role may blind you to other considerations. Actors who are well prepared for their audition will fundamentally bring you a particular emotional reality but it may not be the one you had in mind. Don't be hasty in your judgment. Instead, be impressed by the fact that they bring that much to the audition. The advantage for you is that these actors are willing to tap into their own feelings, have worked on the role, and bring fresh ideas. Besides, at this point of vulnerability, they are also easily malleable and will be more responsive to suggestions.

Although props are not expected, some actors will bring their own. Don't let that surprise you. Similarly, many will come in full costume but don't be seduced by this. Look beyond the surface. A costume may illustrate the type but is there something behind the façade?

Most importantly, don't lose sight of your characters. Keep in mind who they are, what drives them, and what their objectives and relationships are. This knowledge makes it infinitely easier to cast correctly because you can match actors who are effortlessly in tune with the character. Such awareness makes for fine storytelling and direction.

Here are a few specifics to cover during the interview and audition:

* The actor's innate character: psychological traits, confidence, outlook, energy, and sociability.
* Information regarding the nature of the actor's social and family relationships.
* Is the actor sensitive to others and capable of self-exploration?
* What is their concept of how the role fits into the script?
* Are they expressive and energized?

The First Audition and What to Look For

During the actor's first reading there are many specifics to watch for. In fact, there are so many that they might blend into one general goal: to find the perfect actors. Don't panic. Don't rush to judgment and avoid being seduced by a good reading and an overall "rightness" for the role. You may later discover there is an inflexibility or an inability to relate to other actors. Instead, assess the first and second readings with the following questions in mind.

* Do the actors have a clear-cut idea about the role? Are they connected to it or are they just playing the surface and what is obvious?
* Do they bring something different to the role?
* Do you believe what they are doing?
* Do they listen well and respond in the moment?
* Does the actor offer insights into the character that you never thought of?
* In what way do they believe they connect to the character?
* What similarities and differences do you find between the actor and the character?

Once the actors have read the scene, you have the opportunity to test their flexibility by giving them various suggestions to see how responsive they are to direction.

Asking actors to cry, laugh, or be angry is a result direction. I am opposed to such direction since it encourages indicating. Yet, such direction could reveal how adept they are at applying their craft. It may show that — despite your poor direction — they can produce a result in an organic way. However, the responsibility of recognizing the difference between faked or genuine emotions lies on your shoulders.

It is far better to suggest different adjustments, change the circumstances, have them play a different objective, or give an "as if" adjustment as described in Chapter 3, "The Actor's Language." Also, don't be reluctant to ask actors to totally reverse their concept of the role. Obviously, you have found something compelling about them but need to know if they can come closer to what you have in mind. Be aware that if actors are emotionally open, they will be able to make the switch.

As you can imagine, the interview and audition are wildly important. A poor selection on your part might make you feel like the butt of this joke:

Actor overheard during an audition: *"Who do I have to 'do' to get on this picture?"*

One week later on the set after getting the part: *"Who do I have to 'do' to get off this picture?"*

Casting the right actor for each role is a difficult task. But, when done correctly, your selections can make your film stand above the others.

Taping the Audition

Taped auditions have replaced the old Hollywood screen test. Although they are not often used by older, seasoned directors, younger directors may find taping helpful. It's an expedient way to refresh your memory and it helps foresee how the actors come across onscreen and how they will interact with others.

Since just about everyone has a camcorder these days, expense is not an issue. In fact, it's a handy tool to help make your final decision. I highly recommend taping auditions.

Callbacks

The first audition will produce some possible candidates for each role. Callbacks will now offer you the opportunity to decide which actor is best for each role and to discover whether the actors are open to further character developments. A callback also gives a good sense of what works best for each actor. Never forget that, regardless of similar training, each actor will require different directorial approaches. Observe whether they are able to process ideas on their own or whether they have to be spoon-fed. Note whether they took your suggestions from the previous audition and incorporated them.

In addition, callbacks give you the ability to test whether the actors are too set in their line readings, responses, and behaviors by pairing them with different partners. Some actors develop such a set attitude about the behavior of their character that they play it the same way no matter whom they are reading with or what their partner does. Because of its intimate nature, one of the most important aspects of film acting is the ability to listen and respond to what the other actor gives in the moment. Callbacks will also reveal chemistry between actors: how well the actors communicate; how interested, responsive, and free they can be with each other; the possibility of sexual tension between them, and the degree to which this creates onscreen interest and excitement.

Some directors like to employ improvisations during callbacks. This is a sound idea because it can give you clues as to how well the actor's imagination works, how spontaneous they can be, and what their emotional range is. However, this freedom can also be misleading. They must also be able to bring the same freshness back to the script. Many a young director has been seduced by the results of an improv only to learn later, on the set, that the actor has been overtaken by the lines and concepts and is no longer the "live" person the director thought he or she had cast.

EXERCISES

The beauty of doing exercises is that you are not bound to a concept, but are free to let your instincts and imagination serve you. The following exercises are intended to encourage awareness of the world around you, in particular, your internal world. Allow yourself to soar. You don't have to be "right."

Developing Trust in Yourself

This exercise is intended to sharpen your awareness of what you see and to trust your intuition beyond surface qualities. Focus on the actors who are going through these exercises with you. List as many of their personal qualities as you can.

* List the physical characteristics of each actor: age, height, weight, hair color, eye color, and any unique characteristics.
* List your thoughts about the psychological and emotional qualities of each actor.
* Are they sentimental or hard-nosed?
* Are they prone to angry outbursts or are they more placid?
* Do they think quickly or slowly?
* Are they generous or not?
* How do they feel about themselves?
* How do they relate to people?

Creating more questions of your own will help develop your ability to go beyond the surface of a person and enable you to make more subtle and profound casting choices.

Writing Character Breakdowns

Using the script that you are working on for the exercises in Chapter 4, "The Director's Preparation," take the time to practice writing character breakdowns for your major roles. Limit each breakdown to a short outline.

* List the basic facts of age, education, occupation, relationship to the other characters in the script, and their joint history.
* Then list, for each character, their psychological and emotional makeup, their life needs, and the major conflicts they face.

Playing with Casting

Actors bring their own personality and qualities to a role and the following exercise demonstrates how this impacts the character.

* Using your actors, cast a scene from your script in the obvious ways and then read the scene. Now switch roles, going against type.
* Have your actors read the scene again and list the different qualities they bring to each role. With each actor, give them specific actions and/or adjustments to play and note how well they incorporate the suggestions.
* With the consequences of both castings in mind, go back to your original casting, read again, and note the differences. Which casting do you find more interesting?

This exercise should illustrate that the most obvious choices are not necessarily the best ones.

REHEARSING THE CAST

" . . . that relationship between actors and directors. It is really misunderstood by the public [and] misunderstood by lots of directors . . . The great director [makes] an environment comfortable enough for you to create within."

— *Helen Mirren*

One of the most controversial aspects of filmmaking is the rehearsal. For those with a theater background, preparing a production without rehearsals is inconceivable. Yet, with extremely few exceptions, that is the modus operandi in films. For the average filmmaker, such an issue is of little consequence since their backgrounds have focused on the artistry and technology of filmmaking to tell a story, rather than the people that inhabit the film.

Producers and studios reinforce this thinking because they see no reason for the additional expense of rehearsal salaries. Supporting the argument is the nature of the film media itself. The ability to shoot take after take and edit later enables directors to juxtapose one shot against another to achieve the best possible result. It also permits directors to eliminate a bad performance by piecing together snippets of multiple takes to create one acceptable performance. This dependence on the camera's flexibility and the editing process has put directors at a disadvantage by undermining the importance of rehearsing actors to get the best possible performances.

In actuality, the absence of pre-production rehearsals can actually be more costly because the medium itself places a burden on actors' shoulders. The absence of emotional continuity, having to keep track of who and what they are supposed to be at any given time in the script, and having no time to develop character relationships can have a major impact on the quality of an actor's performance. In addition, an actor's most important scene is often scheduled for the first day of production. Yet, if they have never worked with the director before, don't know what will be expected of them, and don't know anyone on the set, they can feel very isolated and worry about doing a bad job. These concerns create an inner tension that can interfere with an actor's concentration, lines, and spontaneity. This results in additional takes that can affect the shooting schedule and send cast and crew into overtime. In short, saving money on pre-production can cost more money on the set.

The value of rehearsals can't be denied. It is the one and only time that a director, free of the pressures of the set, can give individual attention to the cast. It is the one time that the entire company is together and has the opportunity to exchange ideas with the director in a relaxed atmosphere. Questions and answers can be aired without pressure. Rehearsals allow directors to discover how their actors play off each other and provides the opportunity to find the best approach for each actor. It is also the time when actors begin to get comfortable with one another and start to learn about the director's vision. This period establishes a common bond between both the director and actors, and actors to actors. As a consequence, the time spent on rehearsals may limit problems on the set.

In the film world, actors are valued as a moneymaking commodity. Whereas in the theater, the actor is king. These different perceptions greatly influence how actors are dealt with.

Usually, theater-based directors come from a tradition that understands acting and knows full well that it is the human component that has a lasting effect upon an audience. It is not surprising then that such award-winning directors such as Martin Scorcese, Elia Kazan, Francis Ford Coppola, Sidney Lumet, Lawrence Kasden, and Barry Levinson clearly demonstrate this in their films.

Theater directors have generally developed an approach to rehearsals. For the filmmaker, the medium itself can cause actor-related problems not encountered on a stage. Therefore, what is covered in the ensuing pages is relevant for all directors for, after all, actor problems are just that — problems — no matter where they are performing.

CREATING A RELAXED ATMOSPHERE IN REHEARSALS

The chief ingredient in making a story soar and creating a vicarious experience for the audience is the actor. In order to use their inherent brilliance, actors need to unlock their fertile imagination. A vivid imagination fosters the actor's belief that what is said, done, and felt is appropriate. Imagination helps the actor believe the stimuli and awakens sensory, emotional, and motor responses. These responses propel the actor's first leap or impulse. As a result, the director's primary goal throughout the rehearsal process is to use various methods to excite and stimulate the actor's imagination so that their instrument becomes open and responsive to direction. None of this is possible, however, without relaxation.

If the actor's worst enemy is tension, this enemy is yours as well. Tension blocks impulses and leaves actors unresponsive to both their colleagues and their environment. It causes them to act in a vacuum, it blocks the release of necessary emotions, and it can distort the expression of these emotions, making the actors appear false, strained, and empty.

Actors become tense for many reasons. The more they work, the less apprehensive they are about their effectiveness. However, since only five percent of Screen Actors Guild members are working at any given moment, each time actors go to work they often feel as though they are staring all over again. As a director, put your actors at ease by treating them with respect and by making them feel valuable to the production. If you can create an atmosphere that says, "We're all in this together," you will help alleviate a significant amount of your actor's tension.

Of course, whether you are working with well-established stars or with relative beginners, you are working with individuals who walk into rehearsals with all sorts of stress from their personal lives. Before actors can inhabit the skins of their characters, they need to shed the tense baggage they've brought to rehearsal or onto the set. The amount of time it takes for an actor to relax will vary based on their training and the intensity of their personal feelings. After they are relaxed, the true creative work can begin.

The simplest and most effective approach to release tension is to be empathetic. As your cast settles in for the day's work, interact with them while simultaneously checking out their mood. Are they preoccupied, anxious, or putting up a façade? Your sensitivity to their emotional energy will suggest what they need from you that day: more clarity, reassurance, guidance, etc.

Being a Strong Leader in Rehearsal

When you're wrong, be the first to admit your mistakes. Don't blame your actors. Actors are sensitive and they want to please their directors, so don't panic if you give a piece of direction and it doesn't really work. Instead, view your choice as an interesting experiment. Never be afraid to admit that you are wrong or that your idea is leading the group in the wrong direction. You may discover that the problem is not your ideas but rather the phrasing of your direction. Words have a different impact on different people. Try to find the word or phrase that will ignite your actors. By taking responsibility for what doesn't work and by giving praise when it does, you will make your actors feel supported. In this way you foster a creative partnership.

CREATING A COLLABORATION BETWEEN DIRECTOR AND ACTOR

We've already established the need for directors to communicate at a meaningful level with their cast. Directors need to have analyzed the script, know what they want from their actors, have the language to communicate, give clear and articulate direction in executable terms, and avoid generalizations and directing for results. If your actors are having problems, you need to be perceptive enough to see it and have the language to give quick and useful direction.

Why Communication Matters

Communication is the key aspect of the director-actor relationship. Directing actors is a complex business and though it certainly includes careful preparation done in the calm of your office, most of your work is done face to face where you're dealing with reality. You are now reflecting back to them how well they've created the characters, the relationships, and the dynamics of the scene. If what you see needs work, it's essential you give directions that will lead them to the appropriate behavior. Yet, all too often, constructive and specific feedback is lacking because the director's ability to communicate isn't what it should be. Either you — as director — aren't clear about what you want, you don't know the language to use, or neither you nor the actor is very articulate. Sometimes, the issue is nuances of feeling that require even more precise description.

If directors can't provide proper feedback to their actors, then both are in trouble. Most actors will think they are failing, become tense and unfocused, or resentful and frustrated.

Clearly, lack of communication is a problem shared by many and it takes time to develop sophisticated skills in this area. In the following pages, I explore a few fundamental skills that all directors can develop.

The Director's Attitude

Your attitude is very important. Harshly spoken commands called out across a set aren't going to help an actor live the precise nuance of a delicate moment. Not only do they have to go through a series of imaginative processes — as they have been trained to do — but they also need to relax enough to do them. Creating a positive and relaxed atmosphere is your responsibility and works to your advantage.

This doesn't mean you should be patronizing. Instead, assume until proven otherwise that your actors have done their homework. Talk with them as collaborators with an equal level of understanding while possessing different, specialized abilities. This way, you create a positive and productive relationship.

Actors also need to feel that someone is in charge: a benevolent captain of the ship who knows in which direction to head. Only then can actors safely put themselves in the captain's hands. Actors sense when a director is insecure which leads them to lose respect and trust or simply take over. Why should they put themselves at risk?

Empathy

A person with empathy has the capacity for participating in another's feelings or ideas and this is crucial. Without empathy, how can any director or actor create characters that touch the audience? This sensitivity that encourages you to comment on the human condition is the same tool that guides your actors. Empathizing with your actors means not only being in tune with them but checking out all of the things that could possibly interfere with the work you are trying to achieve. True, a poor performance might be due to lack of preparation, a problem with interpretation, a certain lack of technique on the actor's part, or an inability to find the right actions to play. But equally, it could be due to outside matters: production pressures, finding it difficult to connect with another actor, or the issue might be entirely personal. If you can empathize, you can zero in on what the problem is and come up with a solution.

The Value of Precise Language

If an actor says, "Yes, I understand, I understand. Let me try it," you probably made your point. But if you talk and talk and the actor starts the scene again and nothing's changed, there's obviously something wrong with your communication. You have not been clear. Get to the point as quickly as possible.

The more specific you are, the better. If you are not specific, you may create confusion. Actors can be easily confused, not because they are idiots but because they are working with their instruments. They are not playing the violin or a piano, nor painting a picture. The only instrument an actor has is the body, voice, mind, and heart. It's impossible for actors to watch themselves and still be involved in the scene. You should not expect them to split their focus.

Be precise and avoid telling the actors what to do through result-based direction. ("Cry when he slams the door.") When I was in the pilot episode of a television series called *They Came from Outer Space,* my partner and I created a flirtatious relationship that was not indicated by the script. The exchange became very strong and the director simply said, "I think it's become too intimate." So the two of us pulled back physically and flirted at a greater distance. He didn't tell us how to pull back but gave us a short description of the problem that we then solved ourselves.

That director was concise but others will digress into a long explanation of the entire story. The scene was there to establish who these characters were and how each of them related to the other (which, in essence, was about outrageous characters chasing each other). That did not invalidate what I brought to the scene: a love-hungry, tough waitress who put the make on all the men who came into the diner because she was hoping to find a mate. Playing this objective is what got me the role, but on the set the flirtation became too intimate on both our parts. Overall, my objective added an element to the scene that was interesting and funny, while at the same time my action "to pursue" contributed to the overall notion of everybody being on the chase.

A director can, if necessary, discuss larger issues of theme and story with the actors. By "if necessary" I mean that the actor may say, "I don't understand why you want me to play it that way." The director might answer, "I see this script as a microcosm of how people chase each other for different reasons. The two boys, aliens from another planet, are chasing a dream because they want to meet Malibu Lisa. They've seen ads about all these sun-tanned, gorgeous girls surfing in Malibu and they are chasing that dream. The two hoods are chasing the boys because the aliens are driving a hot car the hoods want. The two Navy officers are chasing the two kids because they are aliens. The waitress chases all the men because she's hungry for love, and the sheriff is chasing everyone because he wants to do the best job he can. Everyone has a stake in the plot. If you approach the actor with that kind of logic, there's no way that actor is going to argue with you because it all makes sense. It all fits. It's all the facets of the diamond. They are all connected and they all make a point. Many people call this the spine of a script.

The words you use to communicate with your actors matter. Sometimes that's because you are dealing with complex nuances of human feelings. This whole vocabulary of acting terms provides a useful shorthand for you to use when directing your cast. The value of this vocabulary is largely in the way the right word can trigger an instant and appropriate response from your actor, saving you both a great deal of time and angst.

Suppose a director says to me, "I love what you're doing but I'd like to see a tough, hard edge to it." This is result-based direction and could lead to playing an attitude, causing meaningless behavior. But if the director asked me to challenge the other character in the scene, the hard edge would come from a driving force within me, rather than the overall cliché of a tough woman. This would help me focus more intently upon my opponent.

The need to know this actor's language is well illustrated by an experience a director from Australia, Richard Franklin, had. He had been directing for fifteen years and amassed a long list of features and television programs to his credit. Franklin was directing a feature in New York with a cast of well-trained, theater-based actors. At one point, he was telling the actors, as usual, to move from here to there. Finally one of the actors said to him, "Yes, but what's my objective in the scene?" Franklin didn't know what she was talking about. "Objective? What's that?" And not having a major ego problem, he thought, "You know, there's something here that I am missing."

He realized that by not knowing the actor's language, he had no way of helping them and he realized he was at a disadvantage. A friend brought him to meet me and we spent the entire afternoon talking about acting terms and their meanings, what he should be looking for in a performance, how to analyze the script from a character's point of view, what books to read, etc. He then went back to Canada to start shooting the film, *FX2,* the sequel to *FX.* I sent him a tape of my lecture with a note saying, "Just in case you want me sitting on your shoulder at midnight, here's my lecture. Good luck." He responded with a beautiful note saying that for the first time in his career, he demanded rehearsal time before shooting started and got it. It proved to be very productive and effective. Communication improved enormously, making the actors very happy because they felt supported. He has since become known as an actor's director, a reputation of which he is very proud.

The need to define the problem is critical, but solving the problem in human terms rather than mechanical is equally critical. For example, I once heard a director say to an actor who had just delivered a monologue that it, "Didn't have a build in it. It needs a build." The director was addressing a valid point but not offering a solution. The actor needed help to create the build through emotional logic and by raising the stakes, not through mechanical means.

Directors' instructions to their actors must also be imaginative. This is a complex issue, covered in full detail in Chapter 3, "The Actor's Language." Here we need to establish that actors need to be given "actable" instructions, rather than mechanical commands that are usually result-based. Asking for results is to tell actors the end product, when what they really need is help in how to get there organically. You'll learn to do this by giving your actors adjustments or tasks. But, to think of these, requires an active imagination.

In understanding your script and its characters, you can get down to its essence, which is all that actors want. They want the essence — the human element they can identify with — not a repetition of the given circumstances or the plot retold. If they become too intellectual, something dies, but experimenting and playing lead to lively behavior.

Directing isn't part of a critical studies course. Human behavior is actable, critical theory isn't. Human behavior is about what people want, what they do, what gets in the way of that, how they react, and what their conflicts are. Directing is about stimulating an audience's imagination by transporting them to a different time and place.

It's More than the Right Jargon

Remember, the appropriate language is more than the right jargon. Don't think that using the right term will guarantee good results. You can't throw just any formula at actors and expect magic to come out of the box. It takes more than theory or knowing the right terms. Instead, it's a question of empathizing with that human being in front of you, and defining very specifically what the problem is so you can call upon the appropriate remedy.

Over-Intellectualizing

Avoid over-intellectualizing and talking too much. There's a danger that all this talk about communicating will give you the impression that to be successful on the set, the director needs to intellectualize with the cast. Not so. Your cerebral work on a script should be your homework, not part of the way you talk to your cast. Many directors, particularly in theater, will go on and on about the theme, as if all this intellectualizing will bear fruit: not so! It can numb the actors and encourage them to stay in their heads rather than their instincts.

On the other hand, too many film directors — particularly young ones — haven't even thought about a theme or believe that plot equals theme. It doesn't occur to them that the writer may actually have a point of view about life and society.

Nevertheless, directors, in their desperate attempt to be helpful, keep reiterating the plot. But the actors read the script and probably know it better than the director does. If you find yourself reiterating the plot, it's because your thinking is not clear — and won't be — until you do the proper homework.

ADDRESSING COMMON PROBLEMS: SYMPTOMS AND SOLUTIONS

For the director, filmmaking is an exceedingly challenging experience, with roller-coaster ups and downs. Instead of cowering from the daunting demands of directing both your actors and the camera, embrace both and seize the unique opportunity to create memorable images and performances.

Up to now, you've done all the pre-production preparation you can do. The time has come for you and your actors to work together. But sometimes you sense that something is getting in the way. You can't pinpoint what it is, let alone know exactly what to look for. What follows is a synopsis of some of the problems you may encounter during the rehearsal process (or on set) and how you can solve them.

Physical Tension

Symptoms of physical tension are varied but obvious once you know what to look for. General anxiety manifests itself differently in different actors. Some actors get very nervous before a scene. They become physically tense, hyper, and unfocused. These actors need to physically relax in a systematic manner: contracting and relaxing the various muscles in their body that are tight, such as the jaw, neck, and the shoulders. Breathing deeply and exhaling completely several times helps center actors and puts them in touch with their feelings. These feelings, whether appropriate or not for the scene, should be released. By doing so, actors unblock their instrument and are open to their imagination, as well as to their fellow actors.

The reverse symptom of physical tension is a lack of energy resulting in numbness. In this case, actors should be encouraged to run, jump around, flail their arms about, and make sounds. This energizes them and allows them to release what is within.

Other manifestations of tension shown by actors include giving the same line reading over and over, regardless of what their fellow actors do. Various parts of their body may be tense: heels off the floor, shoulders up around their ears, clenched faces, perpetual frown, and so on. These are simple but very important clues. The more aware of them that you become, the faster and easier it will be to help your actors with simple but effective directives such as, "Lower your shoulders, relax your face, breathe," etc.

Emotional Tension

Emotional tension or "blocks" take longer to resolve but are equally possible to overcome. Encouraging actors to be aware of what they are literally feeling within and to express it fully in their own words produces the best results. This is known as "speaking out" (see Chapter 3, "The Actor's Language.") Another approach is to keep your actors moving physically: hitting a punching bag, shouting, jumping up and down, or running around the set. Such strong physical activity helps break through the defensive muscular wall that blocks freedom of emotional expression.

Vocal Tension

A high-pitched voice is another symptom of tension, especially in women. A high-pitched voice without modulation reveals actors are cut off from the center of their feelings. Fortunately, this symptom simply comes from bad habits and can be easily dealt with.

The key to this exercise is for your actors to think the word "low" rather than force their voice lower. Just thinking "low" relaxes the throat muscles and produces a centered sound. To understand it, try it yourself:

* Say "hello" out loud.
* Think the word "low" and then say "hello."
* Think the word "high" and then say "hello."

Notice the change in your tone as well as the feeling in your throat. A relaxed throat produces a full sound, while a tense one produces constrained tones. Introduce this exercise when necessary by demonstrating it separately from the dialogue. Once experienced, just calling out "think low" will serve you well. Once understood, this simple technique can have a remarkable effect on your actors.

Pushing and Indicating

As described in Chapter 1, "Understanding the Actor," pushing is when actors experience a germ of emotional reality within themselves but either don't trust it to grow or feel obligated to produce a stronger and more intense feeling by tightening their muscles to push it into being. Indicating is when an actor resorts to external, physical ways of showing what their character is experiencing without a germ of inner truth. The wise director immediately says, "Relax," or stops a scene when pushing and indicating occurs. Since obligation to a result is the primary culprit here, you must encourage your actors to drop all obligations and dare to do nothing at all if there's no impulse to express. This way you are cleaning the slate and leaving room for something real to happen. If that doesn't work, try the following:

* Sit your actors down and encourage complete physical and emotional relaxation.
* Then ask them to run their lines as neutrally as possible.
* If the same line readings or feelings repeat themselves, quiet them down to a neutral state again until they are truly listening and responding to each other.
* Suggest a new personalization.
* Keep insisting that they respond in the moment and to accept and express whatever they feel, regardless of the absence of any emotion.
* Encouraging this freedom from obligations leaves room for actors to become genuinely involved. Sharing the truth of the moment, no matter how it plays, is something audiences respond to.

Fear of Experiencing Painful Feelings

A characteristic of true actors is not only their ability to get in touch with the deepest of feelings, but their willingness to do so. They need to share their humanity with us — and we with them — or the theatrical experience doesn't exist.

Actors who have a solid background in the Stanislavski System are prepared and excited by the challenges presented by playing Lady MacBeth or Hamlet. There are other actors, however, who resist or refuse to enter such a painful place because it reverberates too closely to feelings they are afraid of experiencing. Compassionate directors back off, but sometimes at the cost of the role's total reality, which is unfortunate. Naturally, you can't force someone to "go there" and you shouldn't.

When faced with this dilemma, do all you can during rehearsal to gain the actor's trust. Often, private rehearsals of an emotionally demanding scene can be very helpful. Ultimately, you will have to settle for what you can bring forth from the actor or piece together the fullest moments during editing.

Some mature, professional directors may know how to make actors feel safe enough to go into deep waters, as well as when and how to pull them out. However, I don't encourage inexperienced directors to take chances with another person's feelings out of a slavish obligation to the story.

Actors Watching Themselves

One of the common problems you may encounter in rehearsal is when your actors begin to watch themselves instead of staying in the moment and paying attention to their fellow actors. You're in trouble the minute actors start to watch themselves. Instead of following their impulses and responding organically, they begin to act superficially as they try to create result-oriented behavior. Once you spot this problem, it's up to you to get your actors back on track. How you do this will determine whether they will move forward in a free, expressive way or tighten up. You are a mirror for your actors and if you've gained their confidence, they will trust your feedback. Again, free them to have fun, to dare to follow any impulse, to play a specific action fully, or fulfill a specific task so that there's no time to watch themselves.

When a Scene is Dead

When a scene's reality seems to die, it isn't necessarily because the choices are wrong or the personalizations have worn out. It can be the result of physical and emotional tension that disables the instrument's ability to respond, rendering the actor numb. In that event, use the actor's personal reality of the moment by having them "speak out" their — not the character's — moment-to-moment feelings and thoughts, rehearsing the scene without words or using the "repeat" exercise described in Chapter 7, "Resolving Problems on the Set." There are times when an actor may have just lost the incentive or the need to pursue their objective. In that case, reconnecting to a strong need or raising the stakes by suggesting a new consequence may be all you'll need.

There are also times when a personalization can dry up. In that case, suggest they reconnect to the object by focusing on different specifics. If all else fails, suggest a new personalization. Don't expect miracles the first time around. Keep at it and be patient until life is restored to the scene.

Switching Emotional Gears

An actor's self-discipline is usually unrecognized by others. Unless they have acted themselves, directors don't usually understand how difficult it can be to switch gears from one frame of mind to another. Yet, the actor's job is precisely that: to switch from their own emotional state into the character's emotional state. This takes extraordinary discipline that is made more challenging by the daily occurrences of financial difficulties, an illness in the family, a car accident, etc. Often, despite an actor's struggle to come into rehearsal relaxed and focused, they will come to work stressed or tense and not always in the frame of mind to create their performance.

Once aware of such a problem, you can help your actors switch gears. One approach that often works is to take actors aside privately and encourage them to express their feelings and frustrations: to "speak out" (see Chapter 3, "The Actor's Language"). Suppressing strong personal feelings will result in blocking their instrument. Without an emotional center for the scene, actors feel disconnected which, in turn, leads to more tension and keeps them from feeling alive on any level. This is an excellent time to use your actor's personal reality by having them vent their feelings through their lines.

Another good remedy for breaking through a block is for your actors to make strong sounds or to verbalize what they are experiencing in the moment until their real feelings break through and are discharged. If your actors are still feeling tense, encourage them to jump around and let their limbs flail like a rag doll. This playful and carefree activity can help them break through their wall.

Avoiding Predictable Behavior

One of the most important aspects of believable, truthful acting is that quality called "organic." It means that all parts of the human instrument — the mind, body, and voice — are expressing an inner state of being. An actor is successful in creating an organic performance if the audience understands what the characters are thinking and experiencing.

Unconsciously succumbing to predictability manifests itself in various ways. You'll sense something is amiss and either ignore it, hoping it will go away, or labor over it internally. Instead, be honest and discuss it with your actors. By unearthing the problem you'll know how to fix it.

While directing Act I of *The Effect of Gamma Rays on Man-In-The-Moon Marigolds,* I was blessed by recognizing such a problem early on. The actress playing Tillie, a gentle character, seemed to disappear even though she had many activities to accomplish during the scene. Since only the mother and sister were onstage with her, I knew it was not a matter of inactivity or being lost in a crowd. I stopped the scene and expressed my concern. The actor began crying and said she had very strong impulses to stand up to her mother but didn't because it seemed out of character. I encouraged her to follow every impulse and the result was fantastic. She had fallen into the "type trap" and assumed that a quiet person wouldn't stand up for herself. Wrong! Once this actor followed her impulses, this character became a gentle girl who was capable of standing up for herself. As a result, the actress was outstanding in the role because she brought a dimension to it that was not evident in the original play.

This story both demonstrates and reinforces many suggestions made in this chapter:

* Trust and encourage your actor's intuition and impulses, for they may be golden.
* Don't be too rigid in your own interpretation.
* Be honest regarding your concerns.
* Remain open and flexible to new ideas.
* Encourage your actors to take chances.

Even simple lines should not be taken for granted for they signify more than the actual words. As an example, while performing in Anton Chekhov's *Three Sisters,* I had to say to my sister, "Don't cry. I can't stand it when you cry." One would presume from such a line that my character was very moved by her sister's tears. Unfortunately, I couldn't muster up any sympathy for my fellow actor because I always felt she was pushing. I finally went with the truth of the moment. What emerged was my impatience with the falsity of her tone. The audience responded with amusement due to the familiarity of the situation; they too had been annoyed by someone's emotionalism. By being true to what I really felt, I not only avoided clichés, but touched on a personal note with the audience.

The major cause of predictability stems from actors sitting on impulses because of predetermined ideas about their character. The resulting clichés reduce the complexity of the character to a simple and boring stereotype. Acting is about uncovering truths and when your actors use themselves as the engine of creativity, they reveal the complexities of the human experience.

Mistaking Lifelessness for Relaxation

Another frustration for directors is when an actor appears to be relaxed, yet doesn't seem to have anything at stake. Rather than being emotionally invested in achieving the goal, the actor is mistaking lifelessness for relaxation. This state is very deceptive. The actors probably don't even realize they are deceiving themselves. But you shouldn't be fooled. There is no drama without conflict, and no conflict if your characters don't appear to care about anything. The remedy? Raising the stakes, shouting out the lines, and jumping around or punching a pillow — anything to restore and awaken your actor's instrument. As a director, you must be candid, supportive, and clear about what the problem is and why you are asking your actors to engage in such bizarre behavior. The result will confirm your instincts.

Lack of Connection

A lack of connection between actors also causes problems. You will often hear actors say that they can't make the scene work because the other actor isn't giving them anything to work with. This lack of interaction often results in frustration and undue worry. There are, however, two simple approaches you can use to address the situation.

The first approach is called "use it." This means that actors incorporate the frustration they are experiencing by injecting these feelings into their lines. This adjustment will restart an actor's stalled engine and, hopefully, help the other actors come alive.

The second approach is to surprise the unresponsive actor by suggesting a new and very strong action that can evoke a response from their partner. This, in turn, should feed your active actor and interaction will be restored. Your purpose is to encourage the actors to actively live in the reality of the moment — which is to arouse a response from their partner. In short, your complaining actor has to do some work. If you want somebody to pay attention to you, it is your responsibility to do something that gets his or her attention and provokes the desired response. This dynamic is probably going on with the characters' relationship anyway, though on a level much more subtle than the surface dialogue may suggest.

Restoring Energy to the Scene

When a director feels compelled to say, "Pick it up," it's because the energy in the scene is missing. Saying, "Pick it up," may solve the surface problem, but not the cause. The actors have clearly lost the "need" — that which gives them the fuel to pursue their objective. They have to reconnect to the need by raising the stakes or fantasizing on the consequences of not fulfilling their need. They can also create a new need. In this way, the problem is solved by human and not mechanical means.

Another cause of this lack of energy is when actors start to "think" rather than "do," or wait to make sure they are having a real response. Naturally, such self-examination not only takes the actor out of the situation but slows things down. Asking them to, "Pick up their cues," as mechanical as it may sound, can be very effective, allowing impulses and spontaneity to reemerge (if there was something there in the first place). That's because there is no time to turn inward. Their focus switches from themselves to their partners, resulting in active behavior.

Racing Through Lines

The consequence of speaking too quickly is not just confusion for an audience, but boredom as well. When racing, actors get too far ahead of their feelings. After slowing actors down, we either discover there is nothing behind the words or that the actors have an abundance of feelings and impulses but are going so fast that they have no opportunity to be expressed through the lines or activities.

By giving actors permission to physically relax, to breathe, and to slow down, you'll find the problem is on its way to being resolved. Impulses will start to flow again.

Switching from a fast to a slow pace may take a bit of adjusting, but not much time. Always encourage, coax, and guide actors into accepting what is happening around them and to respond freely. This active focusing helps reconnect the "racer" to their surroundings.

Vocal Inaudibility

The barely audible voice is more of a problem in theater than film, but I've been on many film sets where the soundperson couldn't even pick up the actor's voice. I have found this specific problem to be a symptom rather than a craft issue.

When actors are barely audible, it usually signifies that they are insecure about what they are experiencing and are unconsciously holding back. They are afraid that by using more energy to communicate, they are in danger of losing what they feel.

The only solution to the basic problem is recognition — on the director's part — that the actor is truly experiencing a very sensitive moment. Only by suggesting a specific and logical "action" can the director preserve the actor's inner life and solve the sound problem at the same time. Actors like this need to be brought out of themselves. Give simple objectives to play that force the actor to connect to the other person. Objectives could include: "Check to see if the other person really understands," or "Get them to hold you," or "They are hard of hearing. Shout." Suggestions such as these help actors get out of themselves by encouraging them to reach out to others in order to have an effect upon them. By putting life back into the scene through active behavior the audibility problem is solved.

Understandably, many of the problems I have described may seem similar and they are. Problems may manifest themselves as various symptoms but the causes are generally the same. The solutions offered are geared to work through the particular symptoms that interfere with the actor's work. With more experience, you will be able to create your own solutions.

USING REHEARSAL PROCEDURES

Pre-production is the period when directors shape their materials into a cohesive whole that will communicate their vision of the script. The rehearsal period is the most productive time to shape the actors.

The purpose of any rehearsal is for the director to guide the cast into exploring the text, the characters and their relationships, and — when needed — find the means to bring them to life. It is also the time when a modus operandi is established between the director and the cast.

Naturally, everyone goes into rehearsal excited, hopeful, and positive. However, the best intentions are not always a guarantee of success. Details of characters, events, and behaviors may not emerge as you had hoped, but new ideas you'd like to explore with your actors may come to you. Discussions will ensue but they may not produce results. It is at this point that rehearsal procedures will serve you well.

This structure helps bridge the gap between intellectual understanding (which tends to remain in the head) and visceral understanding (which leads to an emotional identification with the characters and events).

The most commonly used processes are based upon improvisation and sense memory (defined in Chapter 3, "The Actor's Language").

Imagination vs. Sensory Work

Imagination is one of the most important assets actors have because it taps their unconscious: their reservoir of experiences. Like inspiration, imagination may work very well at first, but might dry up or lose its power. Sometimes, actors can be so unconsciously connected to the circumstances that the scene works without their having to consciously substitute a personalization (the process of substituting something from our personal lives which corresponds to the specific demand in the script). Actor's intuition also plays an important part because it inspires an impulse that is totally spontaneous and non-intellectual. Lines alone may also evoke feelings and responses from actors. While an actor's intuition may create exciting impulses during the first few run-throughs, the magic can fade away as rehearsals or shooting continues. If this occurs, suggest that your actor call upon the sensory process to use a personal object that will create the necessary inner life and ensure their performances won't dry up.

Sense memory is a very controversial process and is sorely misunderstood. Critics sometimes argue that film, unlike theater, doesn't require personalization because actors only need to be inspired once, as opposed to being onstage where the performance must be replicated night after night. The argument is true if you plan to shoot one long take per scene, which is rarely the case. Most directors do multiple camera angles (set ups) to cover a scene and do more than one take per angle. This leads to the problem of fading inspiration. For this reason, sensory work and personalizations are vital in helping your actors connect with their character's needs. In fact, proper sensory work techniques open the doors to your actor's imagination, thus encouraging their instrument to behave spontaneously. The Stanislavski System and the Method help actors stay connected to their intuition and unconscious drives. Read Stanislavski's three major works, *An Actor Prepares, Building a Character,* and *Creating a Role.* In each of these highly creative and useful books, Stanislavski repeatedly stresses that the only reason to do sensory work is to free, not confuse, an actor's creativity.

There is a striking similarity between therapy and the Stanislavski System. The parallels are extraordinary. There are many exercises in sensory work that also occur in therapy. This includes putting people from your life in the room by sensory means and expressing your feelings about them. This is not to say that a rehearsal room should become an analyst's office or that actors be encouraged to use rehearsals for therapy. Quite the contrary.

Besides actors finding connection to the characters and events in the script, rehearsals are also the time to overcome barriers that can impede the creative process. Fear of taking risks, lack of commitment, the willingness to settle for habits and clichés, or self-delusion may be protective barriers but they are counterproductive in our work.

When you break through the barriers, you get a sense of truth that is needed to breathe life into a scene and a character. The truth of an experience, the truth of experiencing it in the moment, and the free expression of it — that's the sort of work we're looking for.

Recognizing truth can be tricky, though. As Lee Strasberg said, "You can be truthful and working from the core and still be generalizing." Bobby Lewis, another great teacher and a contemporary of Strasberg, once noted, "If all there is to acting is crying, then my Aunt Becky would be a great actress." This comment is right to the point, but the truth is still better than faking, indicating, and skirting the issue.

While sensory work can be helpful, guiding your actors through a sensory process should be a last resort. You don't need to be an acting teacher, but you should have a process to use when all else has failed. The exercises at the end of this chapter demonstrate this step-by-step process.

It's important to note that while you may assist an actor re-create a strong personalization, never ask what it is nor allow them to share it with you. Not only does this put you into the position of a therapist and wastes your time, but airing the memory will diminish its power.

Improvisation as a Rehearsal Procedure

We often read about directors who have developed an entire film through improvisation. Certainly, a few good films have resulted from working this way. But they are the exception to the rule. Keep in mind that, here, we are using improvs as a problem-solving device and a means of exploring certain specifics within a scene and not as an end in itself.

Improvs can be used in a number of situations: to free actors from a rut; to free them from patterns of vocal and physical mannerisms, from mechanical behavior, from emotional obligations; to deepen their emotional connection to the relationships and needs of their characters; to encourage emotional freedom; to discover how they would behave in similar situations and relate to the event on an intuitive and spontaneous level; to establish more specific and meaningful relationships; and to layer a scene with other values and colors.

Improvisations are greatly misunderstood, however. Although everyone knows the term, few really understand how to apply it. Improvs are not a panacea that can solve all problems. Directors need to guard against the lure of improvs unless they have a clear idea of what is needed. The term itself seems to suggest a magical remedy but it is not. Improvisations must be set up in a way that will serve your needs and not become an exercise in futility.

Understand that improvisations take time — which is always the bottom line in film and especially television production. Improvs can become expensive if not set up properly. In fact, improvisation might not be the most cost-effective way of working, since directors need to fix problems efficiently. Improvisation can be a circuitous way of working.

Improvisation forces actors to truly look and listen to their partners and react in the moment because they don't know what's coming next. An improv can and should be a very freeing experience that, when used correctly, opens the doors of perception and originality in behavior.

In life, we can't predict how people will respond or how events will turn out. Yet, actors and directors have read the script, so they know the outcome of a story. Therein lies the problem. This knowledge can diminish the actor's drive by affecting his or her investment in the circumstances. In order to get the most out of an improv, you must first be clear about the character's needs and objectives and what lies beneath the text. The needs and objectives must be in opposition to the other actor, or there is nothing for each actor to strive for (no conflict). Setting up a parallel situation that your actors can personally relate to is the next step, then let them go and see what happens. But be on the lookout for any tendency on their part to paraphrase the lines or use words as a crutch. Stop if necessary. Reinforce their need and try again.

Your last step, of course, is to return to the author's words and you'll find the scene filled with meaning and spontaneity. If things dry up again, don't despair. The problem lies in the fact that you and your actors did not examine the key that opens the door to their involvement. The success of the improv may have come as a result of the actors unconsciously finding a personal parallel. But if this is taken for granted, you'll most likely end up with the same empty scene. You and your actors must know what specific was discovered during the improv so that it can be used to supply the fuel needed for the scene. I cannot emphasize enough how crucial this step is if you want your improv to be of value.

Fundamentally, when any exercise or improv doesn't have a lasting effect, the difficulty may lie within the person applying it. I've already pointed out how the benefit of improvs can be sabotaged when there isn't a clear examination of what specific within the actor was ignited. Another problem can occur after the joy of having achieved a rich and meaningful response to the circumstances. Since it's only natural to want to achieve the same result again, actors may start third-eyeing themselves to make sure the same emotional peaks are being reproduced. This need to equal their original success leads them out of the situation and encourages an imitation of themselves. The underlying operative in these cases is a lack of trust in themselves. Remember that no one expresses joy, anger, or grief in exactly the same way, each and every time. Your actors must understand this if they want to keep their performances fresh.

Sometimes, an improvisation seems as dead as the scripted scene. This happens when actors are not really connected to the circumstances and are simply rewriting the dialogue. Worse yet, you may be seduced by the actors seeming free, only to discover when going back to the dialogue, that the issue is still the same. That's because they were merely paraphrasing. Actors who do this have no real idea about the nature of improvisations.

Being aware of potential problems makes it easier to prevent them. Make sure that your actors have simple and clear needs and objectives, that time is taken for them to key into personal parallels, and that you encourage their complete freedom.

Another form of improv is rehearsing a scene without words. Imagine a situation in which your actors are not emotionally connected to themselves or each other. The scene is dead, line readings are set in stone, the physical life is mechanical. What now? Everyone involved knows the objective and the relationship. So what is wrong? The actors need to escape from the tyranny of the lines and their dependence on them. Do this by taking away the dialogue. Don't allow any verbalization at all. At first your actors will think you're crazy and be absolutely miserable because you've stolen their crutch. Good! Wait till you see what happens — it can be wonderful. Encourage them and after a few awkward minutes you'll notice a dramatic change. They'll be interacting with glances and body language. You'll find that they are involved and interacting with each other, rather than leaning on the lines to do the work for them. The freedom, emotional connections, and spontaneity are rewarding. Once freed from the tyranny of the text, actors are forced to use themselves and their partner to make something happen. This does not take a great deal of time and should not be discussed *ad infinitum.* Just restate the need and the objective and ask them to, "Play the scene without words." This new experience opens them up to each other and to their own investment in the reality of the moment. After, they'll know what to do when they return to the text.

I recently witnessed a rehearsal of a scene in which we see a woman sleeping on a couch. She is then awakened by an unknown man offering her breakfast. We discover quite quickly that he had kidnapped her the night before because he loved her. Obviously, his objective is to bring her close to him. She, on the other hand, wants to escape from this terrifying situation. What we saw was a woman trying to understand who he is and why he kidnapped her. While she was reasonable with him, her attitude belied the circumstances she found herself in. It was hard to understand why there was no emotionally powerful conviction to her performance. It was suggested that she play the strong objective of getting out of the room — no matter what. She used her body to force the door open and that generated desperation more befitting the circumstance. Eventually, the need to escape faded and the rehearsal stopped.

Two very important points were made clear. As in "rehearsing the scene without words," the physical activity to escape evoked the logical needs and behavior for the event. One can describe what took place as working from the outside in. Yes, it can produce very good effects. However, since her need to escape faded away, we are forced to understand that in order for the "need" to sustain itself, the "object" one fears has to be created first. Otherwise, there would be no need to escape.

For the actor, the value of this rehearsal was in experiencing in her body — not her mind — what feelings she would have during such an event. It is not enough to just play the objective. One has to create the reason for the objective: the "why."

Creating Character Relationships

It's also important to develop relationships during the rehearsal period. I always joke that, "All is fair in love, war, and directing." You need to do all you can to create the characters' relationships through your actors. If the leading characters are in love, encourage your actors to find lovable aspects in each other. You can also use a personal substitution, which will evoke all the complexities of the actual relationship. The process, in this case, will be sense memory wherein the actor projects all the sensory specifics of their object onto their partner.

For a competitive or hostile relationship, you would do the same thing. One can also go to extremes by discouraging socializing by keeping your cast members apart, or by stimulating rivalries and resentments by carefully injecting something of a personal nature between actors. This last suggestion is tricky, however. I don't particularly recommend it because it can boomerang. You'd have to walk a very fine, dangerous line because creating such animosity may prevent your actors from being able to awaken more positive feelings inherent in the characters' relationships. The actors can become blocked by their feelings of distrust and hostility. I present this only to suggest what the consequences could be. Be careful. In Chapter 7, "Resolving Problems on the Set," I introduce another relationship exercise as a possible solution. All these exercises can be used in rehearsal, on the set, or both.

Coaching from the Sidelines

Rehearsal is also the time to establish a modus operandi with your cast. You can coach actors from the sidelines by suggesting various actions to play or adjustments to make. As both an actor and director, I find this very helpful. Naturally, you have to discuss this with your actors first, and once agreed upon, feel free. However, a word of caution: some actors may tend to look at you when you first address them. This is counterproductive because it weakens their focus on the event. Immediately tell them to simply listen to you but not to look. Whatever comments you make must be brief such as: "seduce her," or "mock him," or "frighten her." Anything longer will defeat your suggestions.

SETTING UP A REHEARSAL SCHEDULE

To those directors with an extensive background in theater, rehearsals are never in question. For film directors, it's another story. "What? Rehearse the actors? Without a camera? Never heard of such a thing." So, theater directors, bear with me since you already know the value of rehearsals but you can benefit from learning how to reduce a four- to six-week theater schedule into one week.

The amount of time that directors devote to rehearsing a movie varies. It depends on a multitude of factors including the budget, production schedule, the availability of actors, the way the actors like to work, the involvement of stars or other influential persons, and the way the director likes to work. Two weeks of rehearsals, while not unusual, are a luxury. While the amount of rehearsal time may be different, there are certain fundamental processes that should be followed. I have developed a one-week rehearsal approach to be used as a model when designing your own rehearsal schedule. Don't lose sight of the fact that the rehearsal atmosphere should encourage a sense of family — an ensemble — where the actors feel free to experiment and share their ideas (but not comment about someone else's work or role).

Day 1: The First Read-Through

On the first day of rehearsals, the director, cast, writer, cinematographer, and other key people will meet for the first time. This will be a first read-through of the entire script, followed by a discussion of the story and of the characters' relationships to the story and each other. As the director, you may share what you believe is the theme, what you consider to be the important elements in the story, and what you plan to emphasize.

As your reading begins, be on the lookout for a result-oriented reading. Insecurity may lead some actors into giving "a performance" or coming in with set line readings. You might diplomatically suggest that the actors just read, stay in the moment, listen to the others, and simply react. This will prevent the cast from developing patterns of behavior that will later become difficult to break.

Be aware of what your actors bring to your first rehearsal, either through their own homework or through their instinctive reaction to the material. Keep in mind that actors' instincts should be trusted because they often shed new light on the material.

On the second half of your first day you might reread the script and continue discussion, or begin improvisations based on some key scenes in order to discover the underlying emotional realities of the characters. Improvise on the scene before the scene (which doesn't exist in the script) or on the key elements of the scene.

Last, but not least, encourage your actors to find within themselves similar needs, experiences, and relationships to begin the process of meshing actor and character.

By the end of the first day's rehearsal, make clear what will be specifically explored the next day. Explain that the focus will be on how the characters feel about each other, what the dimensions of the relationships are in different scenes, and what the scene objectives are.

Day 2: Rehearsing Key Scenes

On the second day, begin the rehearsal by having your cast bring up questions they may have regarding their role or the script. Encourage them to share their ideas and feelings to maximize everyone's creativity and spark their imaginations. Once you start reading key scenes, encourage a genuine give-and-take, free of any preconceived ideas. This helps to establish a positive relationship between cast members.

During the rehearsal:

* Listen carefully and make note of your actors' instincts.
* Be on the lookout for acting and give your actors the freedom to follow all their impulses.
* Delve into the characters' biographies and backstories.

Find and discuss specifics of each character's state of mind and, if necessary, ask your actors if they have ever experienced a similar event, need, or state of mind. Don't ask for details but find a clue you can use as a trigger to capture an emotional response on the set. This type of questioning stimulates the subconscious to release certain memories that actors can use privately.

At this time be careful that discussing biographies, relationships, and backstory doesn't become a mere intellectual exercise. It sounds good and feels good, but does it bear fruit? Does it help find the specifics that can be used in creating a role? Does it bring you and your cast to a clear understanding of the situation and the characters? Make sure that it does.

Day 3: Connecting to the Characters

On the third day, suggest various adjustments or objectives to explore.

At this point you may also need to redefine and simplify the objectives: What do the characters want? Why do they want it? Phrase the objective simply. Watch and see if any verb actions result as a consequence of the actors being in touch with what their characters want and why. The "why" is essential because it allows actors to identify with the motivating force behind their objective. In the meantime, if the actors don't identify with the why/need spontaneously, encourage them to use personalization.

Don't forget that objectives aren't quite the same as needs. If my objective in a scene is to get you to demonstrate your love for me, the motivating force (the why) is the need. Do I need proof of your love because you have been unfaithful to me and I need reassurance? Or, is it because I've never felt loved in my life? Perhaps I need you to love me because my ego needs stroking today. Whatever the specific need is, your actors have to find it and create it within themselves. Then they have a real reason to behave. In other words, a character's actions won't have any subtext if the actor hasn't created the need: the "why." The actions might be to charm, to flirt, or to seduce. But without the "why," the actions will be general. The why/need affects how the action is played. If in the rehearsal you discover that an actor's personal substitution results in behavior that is not appropriate for that particular character or relationship, redefine the why, try other actions, include an adjustment, or point out their personalizations might not be appropriate or strong enough. Only through this process will you find the solution that best suits your interpretation of the material. Remember that before repeating the scene, the actors need to stay in touch with whatever they are using to ignite their inner lives.

If your actors are having trouble connecting to the event or relationships, guide them through a sensory exercise. However, only prescribe medicine for an illness that exists. Otherwise, you may kill the patient. In short, let your actors relate to each other on their own.

Keep looking for spontaneous dynamics in the scene. Make sure it's not being played on one level. Don't run the whole scene repeatedly to solve this problem because the danger lies in establishing a mechanical pattern. In contrast, examine the scene — beat by beat — and suggest various actions to play. By trying different tactics to achieve their goals, the actors will bring energy back to the scene.

Throughout your rehearsals, remember that this is a process of trial and error. Your actors need to try various objectives, actions, and personalizations until they find those that fulfill your interpretation. By allowing your actors to be in the moment and follow their impulses, they will discover exciting reactions and behavior. To recapture these moments, encourage your actors to examine, privately, what helped them achieve the results. Perhaps one actor was looking at his partner and thinking, "She has such beautiful eyes. I never noticed them before." Keep in mind that no one works in a vacuum. Whatever your actors do or express is motivated and guided by an inner need. Your task, when necessary, is to reflect back to them what seemed to create the desired reality. Since their inner associations occurred unconsciously, don't direct your actors to repeat the exact same behavior. Instead, suggest something new that will arouse a similar response. The behavior that emerges will then be real and expressed in a fresh way each time.

Day 4: Blocking Scenes

Most film directors know a great deal about composing shots and camera angles. They are often less skilled working with their actors. Because of this deficiency, these directors don't realize how much their actors can contribute to their staging. Once actors fully understand a scene's given circumstances and emotional logic, they will begin to spontaneously develop organic physical behaviors that the director would never have dreamed could happen. If you allow your actors to feel their way around the set, they will come up with activities and movement that you can build upon when blocking for the camera. This approach results in real behavior instead of sterile compositions. Smart directors use what the actors spontaneously bring to develop the camera blocking and compositions.

While directors plan complicated action sequences, many also recognize that pictorial compositions don't necessarily enhance the emotional colors and nuances of a scene and that simple behavior can tell us everything. For example, in the 1997 film *The Apostle,* directed by and starring Robert Duvall, there is a wonderful scene that illustrates my point. In this scene, Duvall confronts his estranged wife and asks her to come back to him. In the wide angle shot, we see his wife sitting on a couch while Duvall's character stands at camera left. Each time he leans toward her, she slides farther away until he must move to camera right to get close to her. The scene is an emotional firecracker and the wife's movements tell us everything. We instantly understand her resentment of him and her preparation to flee. Her acting, through body language, is as clear and specific as it gets. Instead of relying on fancy camera work or editing, Duvall — as director — let the actors' movements alone tell the story.

By giving actors the freedom to move around based on their instincts and intuition, you allow them to give you the reality of the scene in an exciting, fresh way. Of course, before they can create natural movement, you need to set up the terms of their given circumstances, allowing for a give-and-take relationship between people that will be expressed in movement.

On the fourth day, within the rehearsal space, arrange some basic furniture and hand props. Don't ask your actors to drink imaginary coffee or fake other such props; they will have their hands full just creating their emotional reality as it is. Asking them to work without the necessary props will split their concentration. Dress things up sufficiently to create the scene's sense of place. The more visceral stimuli you can give your actors, the more vivid their reality will become. In order to make a moment work better, give a simple reason such as, "Check the weather," or, "You are cold." This makes all the difference in the world. Not only does it fill the moment for the audience, it helps sustain a sense of reality for the actor.

Day 5: Your Rehearsal

This last day can be your rehearsal. Test your perception by finding quick solutions to problems and ways to keep your actors open. Think fast and decide quickly. Better yet (time permitting), go to the actual setting and allow them to become familiar with the surroundings they will be inhabiting for many weeks or improvise a key scene. You'll discover how richly actual realities will affect your actors in a scene. This wealth of detail also adds textures and atmosphere, which enhances your scene. It's another way of stimulating new behavior and responses.

A final note: don't be surprised if you don't progress as swiftly as this schedule suggests. Everything is relative. It all depends on your script, cast, and production obligations. In any case, the process will serve you well. Have fun with it.

Using Your Sets

You've prepared your cast, all production elements are settled, and you're now prepared to shoot. The props are in place, the lighting has been set, and a wonderful visual atmosphere has been created. The actors are on the set, yet the place seems more like a backdrop than a place the characters truly inhabit, because you're not utilizing what the location can offer. It can act as another character in the scene. Use the place, allow it to feed you so you can enrich your scenes. Again, behavior is worth a thousand words.

Let's take an outdoor environment, for example: say, the front of an apartment building late at night. Two people, on a first date, are saying the usual goodnights. How each of them uses the place will tell us more about how they feel than the lines will.

* Does she have her hand on the doorknob?
* Does she have a key in hand, ready to open the door?
* Does he stand between her and the door? Or, does he stand closer to the curb?
* How does she relate to sounds of fighting from within, to garbage in front of the building, or to loud music?
* Is it cold? Hot?
* Are they one foot or two feet apart?
* Does he try to take her key to open the door?
* Does someone else enter or leave the building?

All of these small activities and the actors' reactions create a more realistic visual environment. More importantly, they enhance our belief in the situation and the actors' belief in the circumstances. What can be less interesting than two actors just standing there, reciting lines?

Let's explore another setting. Let's say it's a restaurant.

* Is the music too loud?
* Are surrounding voices too loud, making it difficult to hear the conversation?
* Are the tables too close together, making a private conversation more difficult?
* How do the characters relate to others in the restaurant?
* Are they easily distracted by what is going on or not?
* Have they finished their meal or are they waiting for it?
* How do they relate to the menus and other objects on the table?

Create these specifics and encourage your actors to use them. How they relate to objects and outside stimulus creates a telling subtext that frees them from the tyranny of the lines. Their body language speaks to the audience on another level.

EXERCISES

The following exercises utilize the sense memory process that enables us to create any object, person, place, or thing to stimulate our imagination and emotional life. The purpose of these exercises is to both acquaint you with the basic sensory process and to show how it can be used to fulfill various dramatic realities.

The sense memory process has other benefits, as well. It induces relaxation and concentration by forcing you to focus on a specific outside of yourself. It also strengthens observation and insight. It opens the physical and emotional instrument that can enrich the imagination.

You can do these exercises alone or with someone who can ask the questions and later comment on what they observed. This personal experience will be beneficial when working with your actors.

Creating an Object With Your Senses

The following are questions you need to ask of each sense in order to re-create an object using your senses. Some of these questions may have to be adjusted according to the nature of the particular object.

First, choose one object that you can hold in your hand and that you find interesting or meaningful. Second, relax your body. Finally, focus on one sense at a time and ask each question with the actual object in hand. This requires careful exploration and concentration. When you have examined the object in detail, put it aside and ask the same question, looking for the answer on a sensory level. By experiencing the answer in this manner, the object will start to spring to life and become real to you. Be aware that continuing in this manner will arouse some kind of emotional response within you. If that doesn't occur, relax and keep going. Don't worry about it. The purpose here is not to be literally correct, but, rather, to experience the object in the here and now through smell, taste, touch, sight, and sound.

Sight (Keep your eyes open.)
  * Which parts of my hand and fingers cover the object?
  * How long, wide, and high is it?
  * What are its different textures?
  * What are the colors and patterns?
  * Is there any writing on it? If so, what are the specifics?
  * What kind of reflective finish does it have?
  * How does it reflect light?
  * What happens to the reflection of light when I move it around?
  * Are there any flaws? If so, what are the specifics?
  * Now put it aside and re-create it through sight.

Touch (Close your eyes to avoid visual distraction.)
  * How much does it weigh?
  * Which part of my hand and fingers cover it?
  * How much muscular tension is involved in holding it?
  * What is the texture? Is there more than one texture? What are they?
  * What is the temperature?
  * Does the temperature vary from one part of the object to another?
  * What is its shape?
  * Put it aside and re-create it through touch.
  * Once touch becomes alive, open your eyes and combine it with sight.

Sound (Close your eyes to avoid visual distraction.)
  * If I shake the object, does it make a sound? What is the nature of the sound?
  * Does it make a sound on its own?
  * When I hit the object with my fingers, what kind of sound does it make?
  * Does the nature of the sound change on different parts of the object?
  * What kind of sound does it make when I hit it with my fingernail and/or against another object?
  * Put the object aside and re-create it through sound.

Taste (Close your eyes to avoid visual distraction.)
  * How does it taste — sweet, bitter, or sour?
  * Does it affect my salivary glands? If so, how?
  * What effect does it have on my tongue and lips?

Smell (Close your eyes to avoid visual distraction.)
   * What is the quality of the smell: sharp, sweet, or bitter?
   * How does it affect my nostrils?
   * Can I also taste it when I smell it? If so, how does it taste?

Final Step: Return to Sight (eyes open)
   * Concentrate on one or two specifics of sight, touch, sound, taste, and smell, in order to create all aspects of the object.
   * Express through vocal sounds, not words, all you're experiencing.

Creating Meaningful Objects

The previous exercise was to acquaint you with the sensory process without attaching or expecting any emotional responses to the object.

The following exercises draw from one's personal background and should arouse specific and significant responses. The "place," for example, could create an overall sense of well-being, an enveloping discomfort, or a sense of total freedom.

While doing these exercises, don't anticipate how you will or should feel. Allow them to feed you and go with the flow. Directors should ask actors to employ meaningful personal objects when the actor's imagination does not evoke specific or deep enough feelings to fulfill the details of a place or person in a scene.

Re-creating a Place

Choose a place you are familiar with. Explore all the elements within the place.

   * **Sight:** (eyes open) What is the color of the walls, the position of doors, windows, and furniture in relation to you?
   * **Sound:** (eyes closed) Can you hear any extraneous sounds from outside — traffic, wind, voices, music, or animals?
   * **Touch:** (eyes closed) What are the textures and temperature of the objects closest to you?
   * **Smell:** (eyes closed) Can you smell food, perfume, dust, or fumes?
   * **Taste:** (eyes closed) Are there any flavors involved, such as food or drink?
   * **Open your eyes**, return to sight, and proceed with the final step.

Re-creating a Person

(Choose someone you know.)

Sight (eyes open)
   * Are they sitting or standing?
   * What is the color and shape of their hair, face, nose, eyes, and mouth?
   * What are the colors and textures of their clothes?

    * Are they wearing jewelry?

Sound (eyes closed)
    * What is the quality of their voice: low, high, or soft?
    * Do they have an accent?
    * How do they pronounce your name?

Smell (eyes closed)
    * What particular scent do you associate with them — such as cologne, cigarettes, coffee, toothpaste, or soap?

Touch (eyes closed)
    * What is the temperature of their skin?
    * What is the texture of their skin?
    * If you squeeze their arms or legs, do you feel muscle or bone?
    * Can you feel their density?
    * Touch their face and outline their bone structure with your fingers.
    * Proceed with the final step, then tell that person how you are feeling in the moment.

Using Affective Memory

As described in Chapter 3, "The Actor's Language," affective memories are not to be used casually. In fact, you may never need to use them. It's important to remember that this exercise creates a very intense experience.

Choose a very specific, intense experience you want to re-create, such as grief, rejection, terror, joy, or ecstasy.

    * Explore all the different times you have experienced such a feeling.
    * Choose one of these events and create the physical surroundings using your senses.
    * If applicable, create the important person in that place.
    * Once the event starts to feed you, use words, sounds, or text through which the feelings can be expressed. Don't anticipate what you should experience, just allow full reign to whatever feelings come up.

Using Personalizations and Substitutions

Personalizations and substitutions are used to substitute a personal object to create the required connection to a person, place, or thing in the script. The actor uses a personal reference in order to infuse the text with memory. It is particularly useful when one actor cannot find enough in the other actor to feed him, or through his or her imagination, to create the necessary relationship.

* Be very specific about the character's relationship so your actors can find a similar personal relationship.
* Relax — physically and emotionally — and stop any extraneous physical movements. Encourage relaxed breathing and sounds.
* Use all the sensory steps introduced at the beginning of this section to create the person. Place those sensory elements on the other actor, like a movie projector projecting the image onto a screen.
* Continue the sensory process until the actors seem relaxed and connected to their imaginary object. Then encourage expression of feelings through simple sounds. Have the actors say, "Hello," "Yes," or "No," until their voices are expressive of what they are feeling.
* Once the actors are open, emotionally connected, and free, have them segue to the text. Make sure that whatever they are experiencing colors the lines.
* Always be sure they are free of obligations or tension.

Using Fact and Fantasy

Just fantasizing about something isn't always enough to affect or sustain an actor's instrument. Nor does the use of a personal object carry with it all the different emotional links required by a scene. Therefore, a combination of the two is extremely effective. What we do have in common with the character is a basic relationship upon which we can build a fantasy to fulfill what the event calls for.

Using a personal object coupled with imagination:

* Select someone whom you have very strong feelings for and create the person using your senses.
* Imagine that person dancing alone, injured in a car, crying, with a rival, or anything else you might want to create.
* Once the image affects you, express your feelings through the text or your own words.

Creating a Physical Characteristic Through Observation

Earlier in the book, I recommended using imaginary tasks to create unique characters. Using other people's physical mannerisms is equally helpful, though it may take longer for the actors to make it their own.

To create a certain type of person and/or a particular state of mind:

* Observe a stranger's specific physical mannerisms such as posture, gait, how they use their hands, sound of voice, and their rhythm when they speak. Imitate each specific, one at a time. Don't try them all at once. Do this repeatedly until you are comfortable with each new physical behavior and then combine them. Notice the effect this has on your inner state.

* Once you are firmly in touch with this state, drink from a glass, make a phone call, change your clothes, etc. Be aware of how these simple physical activities are affected.

Using Place to Create Meaningful Behavior

Activities in any particular place are not, in and of themselves, interesting. Yet, how these everyday activities are performed reveals a great deal about a person's state of mind. The following exercise demonstrates this point.

Be aware of all the physical objects in the place and use them logically (e.g. kitchen: preparing vegetables for cooking; bedroom: making the bed; living room: cleaning and/or rearranging objects and furniture).

* Do a simple preparation before beginning by creating a "why" for the physical activity. Then perform the activity without lines.
* Now, use lines from a scene, making sure the physical activities and lines are affected by the "why." There should be a change in how these actual objects are handled.
* Now change the "why" and note how the same physical activity is altered. If it isn't, then the "why" is not stimulating the imagination. Example: Objective: to organize the room. Why: a new date is arriving or you are preparing to go abroad for a year.

These exercises have been included to familiarize you with how the various processes work. Once understood, it becomes a simple matter to apply them to complex material.

RESOLVING PROBLEMS ON THE SET

"If you're going to hire the best actors... their contribution on the set is going to be infinitely more interesting than your preconceived notions. So you'd better be flexible."
— *Bob Rafelson*

Several of the issues addressed in this chapter primarily occur on a film or television set and, thus, may not seem relevant to the theater directors. However, the reality is that sooner or later, most theater directors will try their hand at film directing. It doesn't matter whether actors are affected by the technology of film, by a long run in a play, or by whatever problems they may bring with them. The symptoms and solutions are the same. As a result, if you are a theater director, you will become acquainted with some of the problems a different media presents and will be forewarned about what can affect your actors. Either way, you will profit by recognizing the problems that can interfere with the actor's work, their causes, and what possible solutions can be applied.

While film and television sets are busy places, they don't have to be counterproductive environments for actors. Unfortunately, sometimes they are. Sets need to be built and dressed, lighting rigged and adjusted, microphones set up and tested, and cameras rehearsed. And the most immediate pressure on a director is the issue of time. Despite what you may have heard or read about directors taking months to film a project and spending hours on repeated takes, the reality is that time is usually very short. Most directors are pressured by producers to simply shoot the schedule and get the planned number of shots "in the can" by the end of the day — all without going into overtime. At the same time, the director is distracted by questions about camera placement, lighting, sound, wardrobe, etc. Even when these issues are all settled, the director is paying attention to how the image looks on camera. These elements require your attention and pull your focus away from the cast. Once everything is set up, actors are called in and the only rehearsal they may get is the camera rehearsal. Ironically, crews take all the time they need to get everything ready and then complain about the time actors need to become focused and relaxed. The needs of actors are overlooked simply because they aren't as tangible as equipment and, certainly, not as understood.

These aspects of filmmaking — blocking for camera, repeated takes, matching, multiple shots, and shooting out of continuity — directly affect actors. These technical issues can affect an actor's concentration and sap their ability to sustain emotional continuity. Whereas in the theater, technical issues don't demand equal attention during rehearsals. These issues are dealt with by the director and his designers — away from rehearsals. It is only during technical rehearsals prior to opening night that actors have to focus on technical matters.

THE EFFECTS OF PRODUCTION ELEMENTS ON PERFORMANCE

Without the technology in place there would be no film. Nevertheless, the impact of waiting on technicalities is very draining to actors. Non-actors and most directors have never experienced the type of discipline and concentration it takes to play a scene. Actors will have done an emotional preparation or some other task to create the life of the scene when suddenly the word "cut," is called out. They may try to sustain the emotional life they created, but for how long? Or they may drop out completely only to hear that the crew is ready for another take. This emotional seesaw can cause actors to dry up, lose energy, and cause confusion as to when they should or should not start preparing again.

Highly experienced film actors know how to conserve their energy and how to time their emotional preparations. Others may prepare too soon or too much and use themselves up until they go numb. Others may think they have more than enough time only to discover they are needed on the set immediately, which can lead to panic.

Being aware of how all these seemingly "little things" can subtly undermine an actor's work should encourage directors to keep the performer informed so they can pace themselves.

Blocking Issues

All film and television production requires camera rehearsal. This means showing the actors all the physical moves involved including where and when to move, where to stop, where to stand, and so on. If the camera is moving at the same time as the actor, timing becomes a factor too. The director may talk actors through the moves while a crew member marks the spots with tape or the actors may also use a set piece or a prop as a mark.

Many directors don't realize that doing this can split the actor's concentration. Actors have to master hitting their marks, not moving out of the frame, not casting a shadow on their partner's face, getting to the right place at the right time while moving at the required speed, and still give the best performance possible. Sometimes, it's like patting your head and rubbing your stomach at the same time. The more actors work in film or television, the less of a worry this is. The reality, however, is that most actors work irregularly.

Although a great deal of your time is spent waiting for your crews to set up, there's no reason not to use this time productively by making your cast members feel comfortable and secure. This is a good time to exchange ideas about the role and the scene. Experienced directors have learned to put this time to good use while younger ones tend to become too involved in the mechanics of the film.

Since the most common approach to blocking camera and actors is by having preplanned moves, some actors will go through this process methodically without any attempts to infuse the scene with feelings, while others try to sustain their emotional reality. A sensitive director accepts either approach while being alert to how the actors are affected. While this is all taking place, you may discover something that your actors are doing, or not doing, that you will want to work on before the actual shot takes place. Then again, you might not say a word until at least one take has been completed, because your actors will then be in gear and more open to suggestions. The point here is to avoid being passive simply because technical matters are being resolved. By remaining focused on the scene itself and on your actors, you may come up with some new ideas.

Another approach to blocking that's not commonly used involves asking your actors to use the set freely, unshackled from any preplanned blocking, and to follow their impulses. Directors who trust their actors and themselves know that any move or movement can be adjusted to fulfill the overall idea of the scene. The major advantage in staging a scene this way is that the moves will be more organic, spontaneous, and original. In this case, camera moves are determined by how the actors use the space. This is a natural consequence of their becoming comfortable in the "place" and in the circumstances.

Directors usually plan the blocking of a scene based on their visual composition of the shot. They are understandably concerned about where to place the camera to make the most dramatic statement. Blocking, however, should be an organic process. The placement of the actors should be a result of the characters' needs and conflict and not just a visual manifestation of these things. Allow actors to find their own moves in rehearsal and adjust what they come up with.

An example of blocking for effect came up in my class recently. In the scene, a woman is reminiscing to her husband of many years about a boy she loved when she was seventeen years old. He subsequently died. The scene was dull because there was no interaction between husband and wife. The director had the wife looking out the window — playing to the camera — and never once relating to her husband. This is a typical cliché depiction of reminiscing. It's not that she should have looked at him, but we needed to "feel" a strong need from each of them and it wasn't there. This vacuum rendered the staging meaningless. The director did not take into account that these people had a history together, even if there was no communication. He believed that keeping them physically distant would indicate to the viewer the distance in their emotional relationship. Moving people around symbolically does not create a relationship. In this instance, the scene was about two people who want to be close but are afraid. They try to reach out but fear of being rejected keeps them at an emotional distance. The problem was not in where he placed them but in the fact that there were no needs or fears expressed of trying and failing. While the director understood his characters and their relationship intellectually, the problem was in the translation of his analysis into their behavior.

Problems Created by Repeated Takes

Besides being aware of everything happening on the set, a director needs to recognize how the start-stop reality of film production can affect an actor's performance. Though it is true that some directors, such as Woody Allen, will shoot long scenes without cutting, the majority of directors shoot a scene in segments to get all the coverage they need.

Equipment problems, actors forgetting their lines, extraneous sounds on the set, shooting scenes from various angles, and needing to do take after take are all taken for granted by the people behind camera. It's all part of filmmaking for them, but it can be a big problem for actors.

Repeated takes sap an actor's ability to sustain emotion, dull their spontaneity and energy, and cause them to lose the impulse that made the scene work in the first place. Oftentimes, directors will repeat takes in the hope that they'll finally get the performance they want out of an actor but this repetition can backfire. Actors may fear they are doing a bad job or lose respect for the director because he doesn't seem to know what he wants or how to get it. This results in an inner tension that is counterproductive.

However, it is possible to help actors create fresh impulses by giving them a new stimulus. A new action may be suggested such as "flirt" rather than "seduce," or "tease" rather than "challenge." A simple task can be proposed, such as counting backwards from 99. In this way, the actor's mind is no longer focused on, "Am I doing this right? Am I hitting my marks?"

Such tasks help actors, thereby, making them far less self-conscious and freeing them from the obligation of repeating a line in exactly the same way, duplicating feelings, or hitting a predetermined emotional peak. Fundamentally, obligations can restrict actors and encourage them to program and police themselves.

If suggesting a new action or proposing a simple task doesn't work, try coaching from the sidelines. Tell your actor to, "Count the wrinkles on your partner's face," or "Find all the beautiful things about her," or "Listen to your favorite song in your head." Naturally, any suggestion that you make should always support what the scene calls for, the character's relationships, and the objective. The majority of actors welcome this approach. Remember, actors can't watch themselves and be spontaneously involved in the moment at the same time. They are aware, of course, but should not stand outside of themselves. That's why actors need your input.

At the same time, examine your expectations. Don't expect actors to perform a carbon copy of what they may have done in a previous take. Don't think, for example, that a line delivered angrily in a previous take must be expressed in exactly the same way the second time around. On the contrary, a moment's anger can be expressed in many different ways as long as the inner life is present. It is very, very important to recognize that no one expresses a feeling in exactly the same way twice. If your actors feel free enough to be spontaneous, consider yourself fortunate.

Finally, it's always important to trust your knowledge of the material. Do so and your suggestions will emerge easily. Should the scene have more tension? More sexuality? Implicit violence? Once you know how you want the scene to play, you'll dream up the proper adjustment to bring it to life.

Matching Physical and Emotional Behavior

In the past, actors were expected to duplicate every word and emotional moment from set-up to set-up to match previous takes. A script clerk would write down every move and remind them of every detail, such as raising the cup on a specific word or cocking the brow on a particular move. This can split an actors attention and divert them from playing the reality of the scene in order to fulfill technical obligations. Fortunately, today's directors are looser about such things.

Nonetheless, there may be specific activities that need to be duplicated. In that event, ask the actor to either rehearse the moment over and over mechanically, devoid of feeling, until it becomes second nature, or marry the gesture to an intention. This gives the gesture a specific motivation that will serve the reality and logic of the event. Be aware, however, that lapses in psychological and emotional continuity can occur because, as noted earlier, it is difficult for actors to maintain the exact state of mind shot after shot. They may not be aware that what they are playing has changed too much or that they are drying up. You can be a great help by being on the lookout for any such changes. Often, all that is necessary is a quiet reminder of the original motivation that propelled the way a prop was used or a movement was made. You may need to discreetly remind your actors of the intentions they were playing or suggest a new adjustment or task.

I make no secret that I believe Elia Kazan to be not only the most talented director in theater and film but also a genius in getting performances from his actors, far exceeding even their own expectations. Anthony Franciosa, one of the leads in *A Face in the Crowd,* told me Kazan never worried about matching. In fact, Franciosa said Kazan encouraged his actors to feel free to experiment. He never burdened them with technical problems. This is not to say, of course, that directors and actors should ignore these matters. Nevertheless, it's important to note that performance was everything to Kazan.

Shooting Out of Continuity

There is no better argument supporting the advantage of pre-production rehearsals than shooting out of continuity. Without a clear vision of a story's development and a character's evolution, the final product will be less than satisfying.

Shooting scenes in a nonsequential manner makes it very difficult to keep track of the character's arc: when they begin to reveal changes in their attitudes, personalities, their moral outlook, and whom they have become as a result of all the previous events and circumstances.

Having come to a mutual understanding of the character's development during rehearsals enables the director and actors to decide what aspect of the character needs to be revealed and when. Examples of character development include Russell Crowe in *A Beautiful Mind* and Sissy Spacek in *In The Bedroom*. Crowe's character battles internal forces while Spacek must face external circumstances.

Very few roles are as demanding as that of John Nash in *A Beautiful Mind*. The role required extremely specific choices to reveal how the character's psychological condition was taking over his day-to-day life. There had to be a slow and subtle manifestation of physical symptoms brought on by his inner demons. Take, for example, his right hand periodically brushing something away from his line of vision, his walk becoming just a bit more awkward, or the way he held on to his books. His emotional intensity became progressively more obsessive. Suffice to say, the physical and emotional demands of the role were awesome and were executed brilliantly.

Sissy Spacek's Oscar-nominated performance in *In The Bedroom,* although less demanding and complex, is a very good example of how a character, damaged by a personal tragedy, becomes another person. She transforms from an average wife and mother to a very hardened, cold, and detached woman. Her altered inner life permeated her entire body language from the way she looked at people to how she smoked a cigarette. The common trap of playing the victim was nowhere to be seen.

Traveling these roads requires insight, patience, and much exploration but the results are very rewarding.

RECOGNIZING WHEN ACTORS NEED YOU

Directors who don't understand the actor's instrument find themselves thinking that the cause of an acting problem is more complex than it really is. Or they fear that the actors haven't grasped what the characters and scene are about. In desperation, the director reiterates the facts of the story. Hoping this lengthy treatise has helped, the director has the actors rerun the scene again, only to find that nothing has changed.

At this point, some directors are at a loss to understand why there is no magic in the scene or why it has faded. Most of the time, the cause of the problem is very simple. The truth lies in the director not knowing what to look for or how to translate everyone's concept into active and alive behavior. The following should point you in the right direction.

Trust Your Instincts

Empathy — the ability to experience whatever is going on within a person, be it joy, grief, emptiness, physical tension, or an emotional block — is very important for directors. Trust your instincts because they will alert you to a problem. Paying attention to your own responses will lead to the actor's problem. Be aware of any physical symptoms in yourself such as:

* Physical tension: a lump in your throat, a stiff neck, tense jaws, pressure in your head, a knot in your stomach.

* Your thoughts wander to other issues which have no connection to the script: where to have dinner; phone calls to make, etc.
* Fatigue or boredom.

Unblocking the Blocked Actor

Once you have recognized the symptoms within yourself, begin looking for visible symptoms from the actor:

* Hollow, uninvolved, and mechanical behavior.
* Acting in a prescribed or preplanned manner.
* Lines delivered with the same intonation and rhythm each time.
* Lifeless performance devoid of any feelings or intentions; emotionally unexpressive.
* Unfocused performance; actor unable to concentrate, forgetting lines.
* Pitch of voice is high (see *Think Low* in Chapter 6, "Rehearsing the Cast").

After isolating the symptoms, ask yourself any of the following:

* Is the actor emotionally blocked?
* Is the actor pushing for results?
* Is the actor indicating?
* Is the actor watching him or herself?
* Has the actor gone numb from repetition?
* Is the actor bringing in outside problems?
* Has there been a lack of preparation?
* Is the actor no longer playing to the other actors?
* Has the actor stopped playing actions?
* Is the actor sitting on impulses?
* Is there too much physical tension?
* Are there extraneous physical mannerisms?
* Does the scene lack energy?
* Has the actor gone dry?
* Are the relationships alive or do they lack chemistry?
* Has the actor become one note? (Vocal expression, intonation, and rhythm are all on one colorless level and lack energy and variation.)

Having defined the nature of the problem, you are now in a position to help by applying any of the following suggestions (see also *Inner Monologue and Speaking Out* in Chapter 3, "The Actor's Language"):

* Have the actor make sounds and jump around to release the emotional block.
* Encourage the actor to express his or her moment-to-moment feelings through the lines, regardless of any logic.
* Speak out what the actor, not the character, is actually feeling in the moment between lines.
* Encourage the actor to feel he or she can do no wrong.
* Have your actor run lines without any obligations.
* Encourage your actor to open up and tell you what is really bothering him or her.
* Take a break.

Breaking Line Patterns

A frequent problem is that of actors getting stuck in a particular line reading in which the rhythm and tonality is always the same. The cause is usually a loss of belief in the moment. A useful tool to restore spontaneity and interaction is through the "Repeat Exercise." Although this process was designed by acting coach Sanford Meisner to train actors how to live in the moment and involves many steps, I'm condensing the exercise for our purposes. I've found the first step to be very effective in solving some of the traps actors fall into.

Start by having your actors seated, facing each other. Then have actor #1 verbalize what they notice about the other such as: "You have blue eyes," or "You're wearing a red sweater."

* #2 repeats the exact phrase.
* #1 repeats the exact phrase again.
* #2 repeats the exact phrase again. They continue this way until #1 or #2 has a strong impulse to say something totally different. Then the repetition starts anew.
* Continue this way until you feel they have become expressive by reconnecting to their partner. Once this happens, segue into the text. Look for in-the-moment freedom. Once the actors are comfortable and full of energy, start your scene.

The important element here is for the actors to respond to what they are picking up from each other and allowing their reaction to color the phrase they are repeating. By doing this, they get back in touch with the here and now of their partners and themselves which will restore vitality to the lines. Any of these exercises, if unfamiliar to your actor, may take a few minutes to employ effectively.

Releasing Muscular Tension

The actor's (and your) worst enemy is muscular tension. The symptoms of being blocked and experiencing muscular tension are very similar and are dealt with in similar ways. Essentially, one problem leads to the other. In life, we tighten our muscles in order to contain and deny our true feelings. This is usually an involuntary impulse but, occasionally, it's by choice. In acting, although it is involuntary, muscular tension can be eliminated by recognizing which part of the body is affected and dealing with it.

Symptoms of muscular tension include:

* Stiff physical bearing.
* Shoulders raised, jaw tight, and facial frown.
* High voice coming from restricted throat muscles that separates the voice from the seat of the actor's feelings.
* Breathing in an unrelaxed manner.

Solutions for muscular tension include encouraging the actor to:

* Relax his or her shoulders, jaw, face, etc.
* Jump around, make sounds, release all feelings.
* Use the "think low" techniques: thinking the word "low," the throat muscles relax, and the voice becomes centered again, allowing the vocal tone to be the true instrument of expression.
* Breathe deeply and let the air out.

Stopping Extraneous Movements and Mannerisms

Everyone has unique physical quirks and mannerisms but when they are unwittingly brought to a role, they can become a distraction when they don't suit the character or the event.

Extraneous physical movements are a symptom of an actor's discomfort because they are not following through on their impulses. Essentially, these strong physical impulses, requiring an outlet, manifest themselves as tics. Symptoms of extraneous physical movements are numerous but the most common include:

* Crossing and uncrossing of legs.
* Swinging a leg for no reason.
* Constantly tossing their hair.
* Toying with props in a meaningless way, etc.

Again, the solution is total physical relaxation so that your actors can become aware of what is inside of them. Once this is accomplished, tell your actors to follow through on all of their impulses — regardless of preconceptions. This should help them to center themselves, respond, and channel their impulses into appropriate behavior.

Preparation for the Scene

Before a scene begins, the actor's personal work must begin. Well-trained actors always prepare on their own because they know how much more effective their performance will be. Naturally, every scene puts different demands on an actor. If, for example, a character has just come from a successful meeting and is anxious to share it with her family, the actor must create that event prior to entering the scene. She may be able to identify with the author's facts or she may have to substitute something personal that will give her the same emotional life of the character. In this way she brings something to a scene that is real. How or what she uses is her own personal choice and is unimportant as long as she creates what the circumstances ask for. Otherwise, she may as well not enter the scene at all.

Conversely, a character may be entering a scene with the intent to end a relationship without hurting the other person's feelings or arousing anger. The actor's obligation then is not only to personalize the person they want to leave, but to rehearse what they are going to say "in their own words" prior to their entrance. This can be done with a personal object and is known as creating the (unwritten) "scene before the scene."

All scenes benefit greatly when actors improvise the moments that precede the actual scene. This is because it generates the emotional energy needed for the beginning of the scene. Creating the immediate history that precedes the entrance enlivens it in a very specific way, while at the same time helping the actor relax and focus on the objective.

The fact of the matter is simple: actors must become emotionally connected to the specifics of the event, either through their imagination or through their personalization. You must be clear about what you want to communicate through the scene so that, when necessary, you can remind your actors of where they have just come from and what they hope for in the ensuing minutes.

A final word of warning: when the end of a scene is quite emotional, many actors foolishly prepare for that ending. Be on the alert and stop it. The actors are unintentionally playing the end at the beginning without realizing it because they are fearful that they won't be able to fulfill that particular moment when they get to it. If this happens, the scene has no place to go. There will be no build-up to that intense moment. Keep in mind that the end of a scene is a direct result of everything that precedes it and not the other way around.

Finally, allow a few seconds to pass before you shout, "Cut." Just because the last word or activity has been completed doesn't mean the actor's motor has suddenly stopped. In fact, by resisting that final command, you'll discover the richest moments of all. Knowing the scene is finished, actors relax and at that moment — assuming they were emotionally involved in the first place — various emotional colors come to the surface. These golden moments can be very useful during your editing phase.

Creating New Stimuli

Re-stimulating your actor's imagination is one of the major tasks facing directors when actors have gone numb and dried up. It may be that their connection to the scene was inspirational but took them only so far. Now, when it comes to the actual shoot, the benefits it provided has long gone. Or, it may be that they are on the twentieth take and they have dried up.

As significant as this problem is, solutions are always at hand. Your understanding of the script will guide you to suggestions that will enliven actors in the manner necessary for the truth of the scene. You need not worry that all of these processes will slow down the shoot. Usually, all it takes is a suggestion from you and a moment of the actor's time to fully concentrate. For example, a man and woman meet in a coffee shop. They are coworkers about to embark on an illicit love affair. As a married woman, she fears being discovered. The actor's tasks would be to first create the sexual attraction for her partner and then create someone in the place by whom she would not want to be seen. To help her be more specific you might ask, "Where is this person sitting?" "What are they wearing?" "Are they staring at you?" etc. Such a suggestion can be considered a personalization, a fact and fantasy, or a "what if" exercise. They're all essentially the same.

For actors who can't be heard, understood, or who are not actively relating to the other actors, tell them the others are hard of hearing. Their loss of energy is symptomatic of having lost the need to fulfill their objective.

When you have a scene that requires a very strong subtext, one that is just the opposite of the objective, suggest other imaginary and sensory stimuli. For example: a man is proposing marriage. The woman is suddenly frightened by the idea but hides it. You might suggest there are insects crawling all over him or suggest there is an offensive odor emanating from him. But be careful. If she immediately recoils in fear or distaste, you may have an indicating actor on your hands. Not until she has created an object (using her senses) that affects her will she have something genuine to hide.

It's a given that an actor's instrument can eventually become desensitized to the same stimuli. This is an ongoing problem for both directors and actors. Actor Peter Falk, on the Bravo television series, "Inside the Actors' Studio," talked about needing to find a new thought for each take because, in his words, "thought precedes emotion, which precedes behavior." He related how he found that after many takes, he was experiencing nothing toward the other actor — until he started concentrating on the pores of the actor's face. This new focus of attention aroused thoughts and questions about how the actor took care of his skin, how long had the pores been large, etc. This specific new thought process enlivened his instrument and brought him back to a moment-to-moment state of responsiveness to his partners.

Falk recognized his own problem and took the initiative to solve it. Too often, however, actors are not as aware or skilled. This is the time to do any of the following actions:

* Rephrase the objective.
* Raise the stakes by having the actor consider what the consequences would be if he failed to achieve his objective.
* Do an improvisation based on "the scene before the scene" — one that hasn't been written.
* Suggest new actions or tasks, such as checking all the physical details that your actor likes or dislikes about his or her partner.

* Have the other actor surprise the numbed one by doing the unexpected. This is particularly effective for close-ups.

My own experience in film was similar to Falk's. One of my scenes opened with me hitting my grown son on the head with a newspaper. I used my own frustration as a catalyst because I hadn't been able to get the other actor to rehearse that morning.

Hours later, on his close-up, I had dried up and felt awkward hitting him until I came up with a new stimulus: a neighbor who was driving me crazy with his loud music. My partner, seeing the new look in my eyes, became frightened and asked me what I was going to do. When the director called, "Action," he received his answer from the way I used the newspaper. In this case, I not only used the reality I felt for my partner that morning, but a personalization later.

Developing Interaction and Relationships

Much of the time, cast members have never met prior to their first day on the set. In addition, many shooting schedules demand that some of the most intense or personal scenes be shot in the first few days of production.

How do you get around having two complete strangers play a love scene together or pretend to despise each other? If the actors don't find that for themselves, you can suggest trying a personalization or the following exercise.

* Explain that during the process they should never look at you but instead follow your instructions.
* Seat your actors opposite each other and ask them to relax.
* Begin by asking them to find answers to questions you'll ask by simply looking at each other. They are not to respond out loud but to arrive at the answers from what they see in each other. Being correct is not the goal. Ask such questions as:
* What kind of childhood did he/she have?
* Did he/she feel loved?
* Was he/she popular?
* Did he/she love or resent a sibling?
* Does he/she feel loved now?
* Is he/she capable of loving?
* Is this person someone you can trust?
* Is he/she insecure?

Keep asking meaningful questions that will arouse thoughts and feelings inherent in the characters' relationship. Continue until you feel that your actors are very connected to each other. If so, have them express what they are experiencing through one word back and forth. When you feel they are comfortable speaking and embracing the word with feeling, have them segue to lines. Be on the alert for any patterns of expression returning such as line readings with the same intonations, rhythm, and emphasis on certain words. If habits return, have your actors relax, speak out their personal feelings, and then go to the lines again.

This exercise helps create within (and between) actors the specific nature of the characters' relationship. The beauty of this exercise is that you can subtly steer their feelings in the direction you need by the type of questions you ask and by having them exchange simple words such as: "yes; no; please; don't; I need you," etc. You're understanding of the relationship will guide you toward the questions and words you suggest.

Creating Aspects of a Character

In Chapter 3, "The Actor's Language" and Chapter 6, "Rehearsing the Cast," a number of processes have been explained and exercises suggested that may be effective. Any of them can be utilized on a set, although some may take more time than you feel you can afford (which is why rehearsals are so important).

The principle behind any of the exercises is to enable actors to experience and engage in the here-and-now behavior of the character in the circumstance. In other words, find the character within themselves and behave accordingly. Oftentimes, employing a simple unrelated task can produce the desired result. These tasks can also help create a character's unique mannerism, essence, or a particular state of mind.

For example, tasks can generate the overall essence of a character that is revealed in their body language, posture, gestures, attitude, and vocal expression. These specifics communicate to the rest of us what kind of people they are and much about their background. As an example, suggest your actors balance an imaginary ball or crown on their heads and watch how it affects their overall essence. In turn, it will also affect their inner life. In so doing, we will see characters that are well bred, educated, polite, and so on. In this sense, tasks are not dissimilar from using animals to create a character but this is much simpler. Be sure, however, that this physical task reaches the soul of the actor. Otherwise, the result will be empty.

In the event that you wish to find some unique mannerisms or quirks for a character, the approach must be more singular. For example, suggesting an actor silently sing a quick tempo song to himself and keeping time with their head, a shoulder, or one finger is bound to produce a more positive energy and a specific character mannerism. A slow, sad melody would generate a different kind of energy. Another idea would be to suggest the actor is walking on very thin ice, a slippery floor, or very warm coals. At first, the actor may exaggerate, but the behavior must become subtle in order to be effective and this is where your guidance is important.

Finally, shy people usually find it difficult to make eye contact. In this case, rather than being general in your directions, suggest that your actor count all the spots on the floor or take in everything around the other person. A person anxious to please might touch people in order to ingratiate himself or be the life of the party. Observing people in daily life and asking what in them might cause their unique physical characteristics will supply you with a wealth of ideas.

Remember, you don't have to be right, just specific.

This is a good time to discuss that tricky job of being able to act drunk, which is a frequent demand in a script. What we often see, though, is cliché behavior rather than a unique individual. Remember, no two people behave the same way when they've had too much of one drug or another.

For our purposes, we will focus on the drinker. Alcohol relaxes the body of tension and lowers inhibitions. Each drink relaxes the muscles, which continue relaxing with each drink until, regardless of what demands an individual makes of their body, the muscles do not respond and the person becomes "falling-down drunk." If we set out to relax every muscle in our bodies — including the mouth, tongue, and eyelids — we will find that performing simple physical tasks such as walking, talking, drinking a cup of coffee, putting on makeup, and lighting a cigarette can be rather difficult depending on the degree of relaxation. Instead of trying to be drunk, the actor's focus needs to be on sustaining a certain degree of relaxation, while at the same time trying to complete these physical tasks. The results can be amazing.

The benefit of these exercises is that they can quickly solve problems and add texture and dimension to a character. In addition, they can help focus an actor's concentration and restimulate his or her instrument and imagination.

Helping an Actor "Not Act"

Acting that is indicated or pushed describes actors illustrating and/or faking an emotional or character obligation. There is no here-and-now reality. The causes may vary but the consequences are the same.

To help remedy the problem, the following examples suggest ways of preventing actors from playing the "idea" by supplying obvious realities for actors to respond to organically.

One way of helping an actor "not act" comes to us courtesy of actor Peter Falk. In shooting a feature film, a scene required him to struggle while putting on his coat. He was faking it all the way, which legendary film director Frank Capra found dissatisfying. Finally, Capra came up with a solution. Unbeknownst to Falk, Capra tied the inner lining of the sleeves. When, during the shot, Falk went to put his coat on, the struggle was immediate and totally real. Falk was prevented from "acting" (indicating) because it was an actuality. It is the director's job to recognize these problems and find solutions to them.

In another film, an actor played a character that discovers her dog has been slaughtered and left on her doorstep. After spending the entire morning attempting to get a genuine reaction to what she discovers, the director finally placed animal entrails in front of the door. Needless to say, upon opening the door, her reaction was one of horror. He finally got what he wanted and they were able to move on.

Remember, these processes should only be used when an actor is having a problem that could be helped by an exercise. They are helpful when you want to create a more specific behavior or add an additional dimension to a scene or moment. Don't make a big deal of it.

It's much better to quietly suggest, "Why don't we try . . . " and propose what you think will help. Be diplomatic, be specific, and be constructive.

Creatively Directing Extras

So far, we have focused on directing actors who are playing major roles. Yet, every film and television show incorporates extras and no one pays attention to these people, except as space fillers.

Extras can be used to create and support the tone of your production, rather than distract from it. Traditionally, extras often don't have a thought in their heads or a feeling in their hearts because directors and assistant directors don't ask anything of them. True, they are not actors but they can be given simple tasks that will provide you with useable behavior.

You may wonder why I speak of extras because, after all, they are not the core of a production. Yes, but what can be more distracting in a scene than "background" people walking in and out of shots like automatons? If extras are used to give a scene more credibility, it helps to engage them in meaningful behavior. It only takes a word or two to suggest specific tasks they can fulfill.

Using extras creatively can help establish any tone or atmosphere that will serve your production. Let's use the opening scene of a script that addresses the dehumanization of man by the corporate structure. Let's assume that this is not a satire but a film that is meant to portray corruption, betrayal, and tension.

The first scene introduces us to the lobby of a huge corporate building at 9:00 a.m. Hordes of people are entering. This first scene should set a tone of tension. With this in mind, a group of mindless and unexpressive neutral people serves no purpose at all. However, giving various individuals specific tasks to accomplish will help to establish the sense of intensity and urgency that is inherent in the script and would set the tone of the film.

To get the desired emotional response, ask the extra to imagine that he is late again and in danger of being fired. You might suggest to another to rehearse how he is going to ask for a raise because his wife needs surgery, or suggest that two women share an actual tense event in their lives.

The basic idea is to have your extras engaged in tasks in the here and now in order to create the tone you want. If a woman were typing a report due in five minutes it would be quite different from a woman typing a love letter. The key is to have her actually type four pages in five minutes or write a letter to her loved one.

What you're doing is creating human behavior. People don't walk around like empty vessels. If you give your extras specific tasks, it engages them in the moment and contributes to the scene rather than taking away from it.

Watching Dailies

This is a tricky topic. Some actors gain a great deal from watching their scenes in dailies. It serves as a guide and checklist. Others are afraid of becoming too aware of their acting and how they look. These actors are in danger of becoming too self-critical and tense, thereby losing spontaneity. To be on the safe side, I would discourage having your actors view the dailies (particularly less experienced actors). They must trust your judgment and know that if something is wrong with a scene or a moment, you, as director, will note it and take care of the problem.

EXERCISES

Using the same scene you have analyzed and rehearsed for Chapter 4, "The Director's Preparation," and Chapter 6, "Rehearsing the Cast," shoot the scene using a camcorder.

* Rehearse your actors according to Chapter 6, "Rehearsing the Cast."
* Plan your shots and close-ups from various angles and then shoot.
* During the shoot, observe your actors closely. Detect any tension, loss of energy, loss of an inner life, lack of commitment, concentration, or believability.
* Look for any behavioral problems such as lack of spontaneity, not playing the objectives or actions specifically, monotonous line readings, and no give and take between actors.
* This is also a good time to experiment with creating unique character behavior and note how it plays on film.
* Finally, edit your takes and look for physical and emotional continuity.

The idea of this multi-layered exercise is for you to develop faith in your instincts and your ability to diagnose a problem and create a solution — under the pressure of a camera. Don't be afraid to say, "Cut," if any of your actors or extras are not involved and spontaneous. As you know, the more actors repeat their behavior, the more entrenched the pattern becomes and the more difficult it is to change it.

A final reminder: I've stressed the importance of analyzing your scripts and characters so you'll have a solid foundation from which to work. You may be justifiably proud of your analysis but don't impose it on your cast. The danger lies in putting your actors into an intellectual straightjacket. Even useful terms such as an "action" could backfire by insisting that the same action be played each and every time. You need to know what "actions" are possible and suggest them when necessary. Remember, one doesn't always have to arrive at a destination in the same way. We have to trust that all the work you and your actors have put in has seeped into their subconscious. Now all they need to do is look, listen, and react in the moment.

DIRECTOR'S NOTES: ON THE WATERFRONT

8

> "At the beginning of a project, I make a notebook about what I'm trying to get out of the whole picture, what the picture means, and what each scene contributes to that."
> — Elia Kazan

I selected the screenplay *On the Waterfront* to serve as an illustration of how a director's notes might read. Naturally, the ensuing analysis reflects my interpretation of the material and the social and moral issues it raises. To me, the paramount issue is of humanity's capacity for evil and the consequences of not taking responsibility or action against negative forces.

My decision to use *On the Waterfront* was based on several factors. Most importantly, it lends itself well to the analysis of a script as described in Chapter 4, "The Director's Preparation." And, as a classic it is readily available for viewing. In addition, the script has a very strong story that could be relevant in any age, as well as a clear and definite point of view about our society. Finally, it is character driven and deals with the complexities of human nature and morality: universal themes.

The film itself earned twelve Academy Award nominations and won Best Director for Elia Kazan, Best Story and Screenplay for Budd Schulberg, Best Actor for Marlon Brando, Best Supporting Actress for Eva Marie Saint, plus Academy Awards for Best Cinematography, Best Art Direction, and Best Film Editing.

As a note of caution, it may appear that I have made more than one choice for the theme. The reason for this is that there was such an abundance of interlocking issues that it was impossible to overlook them. Consequently, I decided they all belonged together as sub-themes. Doing so enabled me to be more specific and allowed me to find and focus on the script's additional social and moral points of view. This creates additional layers. For example, I found the character of the priest to be quite representative of many leaders in our world who, though using the "correct" words, do not follow through with action. While the priest does change, I find his early character extremely relevant to our times.

As a model for the scene breakdown, I chose the first private conversation of the story's two main characters, Terry and Edie, which takes place in a local bar. The place (environment) and its patrons, the newness of their relationship, the very lively subtext, the characters' objectives, as well as the sexual tension and the clash of moral values between Terry and Edie afford a vast opportunity to demonstrate how all these elements can be used to enrich a scene.

It is important to understand that a rich script allows for various interpretations. In dealing with substantive material, the possibilities are endless. Is Hamlet weak because he can't make up his mind as to whether to avenge his father's murder? Or is he indecisive because, subconsciously, he is aware that his real problem is his mother marrying his uncle rather than devoting herself to loving him only. Either choice would hold up.

It is also important to keep in mind that there are various actions that one must play to achieve an objective. Any one of these actions may be played at different times. The actions and beats I chose for these notes are not the only possibilities. Remember, when actors are emotionally connected to the circumstances, they will spontaneously play different actions at different places in the scene in the pursuit of their desires. They should not be forced to follow a road map. That will only breed sterility. However, if your actors lose their way or dry up, be prepared with active actions they can play at different times (beats) to reinvigorate their instrument.

After I had written my director's notes, I watched *On the Waterfront* again after many years. I found that the scene in the film plays quite differently from the ideas I had. Neither is right or wrong, but, rather, simply different ideas. If dealing with an already-produced script, avoid seeing any previous production of it. It will stifle your own creativity and cause you to doubt your instincts and choices. Strive to be true to yourself, rather than become a copycat.

THE SCRIPT

Begin your director's notes by dissecting the script. Delve into all areas of the story, overall theme, climactic moments, the setting, and your goal in bringing this script to life.

The Story

On the Waterfront takes place on the loading docks of the New Jersey harbor and revolves around the abuse of the dockworkers by their union's corrupt and ruthless leader, Johnny Friendly. By keeping the dockworkers divided through intimidation, fear, and even murder, Friendly has managed to build his own empire.

He has one young dockworker, Jimmy Doyle, murdered before he can cooperate with the police. It's also a warning to others in this waterfront ghetto. Jimmy's sister, Edie, determines to break down the union members' self-protective "code of silence" and becomes the catalyst for events leading to the destruction of Johnny Friendly and his corrupt cronies.

The story centers on Terry Malloy, an immature, uneducated former prizefighter whose brother Charley works for Johnny Friendly. Terry, who has no life direction of his own, is essentially a gofer for Friendly and Charley. He is drawn into the crossfire when he meets and falls in love with Edie. At this point, he begins to examine what his life has been about and the plight of the suffering dockworkers.

His moral struggle between his loyalty to his brother and his benefactor versus his compassionate awakening to the dockworkers plight arouses within him the heroic conscience needed to destroy the evil forces within that community.

Revealing how fear and the basic need for survival makes cowards of us all, the story is about men driven to complicity in their own self-destruction. It teaches how, in order to right the wrongs, one must be willing to make sacrifices and risk dying by standing up against evil. The story also indicts some aspects of our society: communities willing to let evil flourish rather than take action, and those elements in the Catholic Church that choose to hide behind pontifications rather than committing themselves to change.

The Theme

There are several interconnected themes in *On The Waterfront;* each a direct consequence of the other. These themes include:

* Corruption starts at the top. If one sees it and doesn't stop it, one is part of that evil.
* The unwillingness to risk leads to one's own self-destruction.
* Without principle an individual is corruptible.
* By hiding behind platitudes, paragons of our society, such as clerics, are equally guilty.

The Climax

The climax of the script begins when Terry is refused work again as retribution for testifying against the union bosses. He confronts Friendly and his cohorts who end up beating him mercilessly. The dockworkers watch the beating but do nothing to stop it until a few refuse orders to get to work on the ship. This is their only means of survival but they are hesitant without Terry leading them. Terry, despite his physical condition, manages to stagger toward the ship alone, while the men watch in confusion, fear, and awe. Will they follow his lead or allow him to be killed? By recognizing his courage to stand alone, one by one they find hope and courage within themselves and follow him to the boat to reclaim their right to work free from tyranny.

The Setting

The dangerous, harsh atmosphere of the New Jersey shore loading docks and the barren, concrete working-class neighborhood from which its inhabitants — the dockworkers and their families — cannot escape. The cold and gray setting of the film is the physical representation of their lives.

The atmosphere of the community is one of fear, which leads to the unspoken code of silence. A definite sense of camaraderie exists within the neighborhood, even though the dockworkers are pitted against each other. Deep down, the men know that a house divided has no strength.

The only free creatures in this setting are the pigeons Terry Malloy raises on his rooftop. They symbolize love, freedom, and nature as a buffer against the asphalt jungle.

With a plain, documentary-like visual style, the film creates a gritty sense of place. It is a dangerous, grim environment that underscores the harsh reality of bare necessity on the docks.

The Director's Goal

As director, my goal is to not only awaken the conscience of the audience but to remind them of the cost being silent can exact. By not only underscoring the social and personal issues in the story, I hope to have audiences recognize how evil can permeate all aspects of our lives if left unchecked.

CHARACTER ANALYSIS

As discussed in Chapter 4, "Director's Preparation," you must intimately understand each of the characters in your script. In order to guide your actors, you must be familiar with the characters' backgrounds, super objectives, inner conflicts, character developments, character arcs, and the relationship between characters. Your notes will be the foundation upon which you draw inspiration throughout production.

Terry Malloy
Background
   * Late twenties but emotionally immature.
   * Didn't finish school; still reads comic books.
   * As a boy, he and his brother Charley are sent to an orphanage, from which they escape.
   * Charley, 10 years older, becomes his protector.
   * Terry grew up on the streets where he learned to fend for himself.
   * Became an amateur boxer a couple of years before and showed promise.
   * Has no personal goals (passive).
   * Raised with values of the street, "Don't ask. Don't answer."
   * No sense of himself.
   * Always takes the easy way out.
   * Content to stay a boy; has no responsibilities.
   * Capacity for love and tenderness showered on his pigeons.

Super-Objective
   * To gain the approval of those he is dependent upon — at any price.
   * Events change his super objective to being his own person, going against the grain by standing up for his own beliefs — no matter what the cost.

Inner Conflict

* Guilty because he set Joey Doyle up to be killed by Friendly's gang.
* Difficult to accept that he was used.
* Having to choose between two evils — informing on his friend, Friendly, and endangering his brother, Charley, versus listening to his conscience and defending the community. He knows he will lose either way.
* Incapable of ignoring his conscience.
* Filled with shame for throwing his life away; recognizes how he participated in his own self-destruction.
* Giving up his old lifestyle versus taking a stand against evil.
* Torn by loyalty to his past relationships and his new relationship with Edie.

Character Development

* Begins with Joey Doyle's death.
* Guilt sets in when he realizes that by not questioning Johnny Friendly's orders, he contributed to Joey's death.
* Doyle's death starts his new awareness; puts him at war with himself.
* Realizes he's been betraying himself by always doing Charley's and the boss' bidding; participating in his own self-destruction.
* His philosophy of "Look out for #1" is because he always had to.

Character Arc

* Starts out with simple needs and goals.
* Events awaken him to values he never examined: betrayal, responsibility, a conscience, and personal inner pain versus his previous happy-go-lucky lifestyle.
* Grows from a blind kid to an aware man who is willing to take risks.

Relationship to:

Charley Malloy

* Feels protected by his older brother.
* Dependent on him and impressed by his position with Friendly.
* Willing to be the court jester for Charley and his cronies.
* Feels Charley always has his best interests at heart.
* Would do anything to please him. Feels he owes Charley and even threw a fight for him once.
* Can't admit to himself that Charley shouldn't have asked him to throw the fight.
* Likes that Charley still looks out for him. He is impressed by his powerful connections; makes him feel more important. He respects his efficiency and admires his power, the way he dresses. He is grateful that Charley stuck by him. He admires his elegant style and ambition.

* Is devastated by Charley treating him like a kid.
* Feels Charley is too private about his business life.
* Is still hurt by Charley having asked him to throw a fight.

Edie Boyle
* Different from other girls; he is impressed by her education.
* Impressed by her willingness to fight for her beliefs.
* Finds her purity compelling and moving; she is a "good girl" to him.
* Feels she is too good for him.
* Feels protective of her and yet is drawn by her strength; is assertive with her.
* His guilt over her brother's death spurs his maturity.
* Teases her to hide his awe of her and maintain a masculine superiority in his own eyes.
* Very guilty about setting up her brother's death; torn because he should have known what the boss was up to.
* Realizes he needs to be a man to deserve her; knows he really isn't "man enough" because she encourages him to look at himself as never before.
* Her stubbornness frustrates him, her advanced education intimidates him, and he fears her purity.

Johnny Friendly — the Boss
* Boss is his benefactor, protector, father figure.
* Offers him many special favors.
* Impressed by his confidence, power, and money.
* Enjoys being his pet.
* Respects him and never questions his actions.
* Needs his approval and support.
* Always stays on Johnny's good side because he feels grateful to him.

Edie Boyle
Background
* Sent away to Catholic schools.
* Loyal, good girl with courage.
* Has been sheltered from the realities of her community, therefore not caught up in the "code of silence."
* She is drawn into the struggle by her brother's murder.
* Her convent education has not only developed strong principles but a fearless determination to uncover the evil that killed her brother and still degrades her father.
* Even though her superior education was to encourage her to leave the neighborhood and its self-defeating ways, she remains out of love and loyalty to her father and brother.

* She is effective because, as the outsider, she has a fresh perspective and is not bound by community rules.

Super-Objective
* To seek and speak the truth at any cost, remaining true to her beliefs.

Inner Conflict
* Her relationship to Terry is one of inner conflict.
* Loyalty to her family and principles clash with her love and desire for a man who is unable to take a stand against evil.
* Very attracted to him in the beginning, but feels he is too crude.
* When he does take a stand, she fears for his life.

Character Arc
* Edie's character does not change dramatically but, in addition to her brother's death, she witnesses the degradation of her father and that fires her determination to explore the evil behind it.

Relationship to:
Terry
* Charmed by his boyishness but also confused by his cocky, tough, crude behavior versus his tenderness with his pigeons.
* Senses his naiveté and need for a strong woman to help him feel worthwhile.
* Affected by his protectiveness of her.
* Touched by his need but frustrated because he is unable to take action.

Charley Malloy
Background
* Parents died young and he became Terry's "parent" in and out of the orphanage.
* College educated.
* Vain man who needs instant gratification and power. Meticulous and ambitious.
* Very self-serving and without a conscience.
* Works for Boss Friendly as corrupt union official extorting money from the union members.
* No scruples, capable of betraying Terry for monetary gain: "Business is business."
* Quiet but shrewd.

Super-Objective
* To achieve power and stature to make up for his father's life of struggle and lack of dignity.

Inner Conflict

Charley's inner conflict is revealed in the "Taxi scene."
* "Taxi scene" reveals there is a decent core in Charley when he frees Terry.
* Objective: to persuade Terry to do Friendly's bidding.
* Why: to save his own neck.
* Inner conflict: knows he is putting Terry in danger.

Character Arc
* Takes Terry's loyalty to him for granted until the "Taxi scene."
* He undergoes major changes when he admits his betrayal of Terry's talents as a boxer. At this point, his love and restored loyalty to Terry makes him realize he cannot lead his brother to his death by forcing him to do Friendly's bidding. He is totally aware that he will pay for this decision with his own life.

Relationship to:

Terry
* Paternalistic and very protective; truly loves him.
* Enjoys Terry's defending of him — a cross between love and power.
* Doesn't take him seriously; still sees him as a kid and easily manipulated.
* Uses Terry's passivity to his own benefit.
* Does nothing to guide him toward a life of his own.
* Appreciates Terry's skill as a boxer, his loyalty to himself, and boss Friendly.
* Has no respect for Terry's lack of ambition, being a hanger-on, his softness, he has no respect for his passivity.

The Men

I see the men who work on the docks as one character because they are all locked into a way of thinking that has sealed their fate. Their desperate need to survive and their unstated but understood, "code of silence" unites them. They need each other's support but by being pitted against each other are deliberately kept weak. Fear of hunger enslaves and weakens them, rendering them helpless. The script does individualize their personalities but they operate as one. They all know the codes: "keep quiet," "don't make waves," and "be deaf and dumb — don't rat on anyone."

Character Arc

Through the courage and inspiration of one man, Terry Malloy, the defeated men recover their dignity and refuse to live as victims any longer. They are shaken out of their fear to stand up to the evil force of corruption. Their shame of having lost their manhood makes them join Terry.

The Priest

I find this character most interesting. To me, he represents the ivory tower existence that is of no use if it keeps you detached from reality.

Super-Objective

* To remain pure through the Church by detaching himself from any mortal realities.

Inner Conflict

* The Priest grew up in this community, yet deserted the neighborhood by hiding behind his clerical robes. Inside, he knows he has deserted his sheep. I would intensify his moral struggle (his inner conflict) through most of his scenes — doing the right thing versus upholding his interpretation of his priestly role.

Character Arc

* The Priest's development starts when Edie accuses him and the Church of hiding behind empty and useless platitudes rather then seeing the world around them. He, too, is guilty of avoiding reality. His conversion comes when he is shamed enough to become part of the community, rather than stand above it.

The Pigeons

* The pigeons are a symbol of innocence. When they die, it is the death of Terry's innocence.

SCENE-BREAKDOWN: BAR SCENE IN ACT II

Theme of Script

Corruption starts at the top. If you see it and don't stop it, you are part of that evil.

How the Scene Furthers Theme

Terry begins developing a conscience by slowly realizing how he contributed to the murder of Edie's brother. He starts to realize his contribution to evil was in not having questioned the favor Friendly asked of him. The germ of a conscience begins in this scene as he realizes the destructive consequences of his act.

Super-Objective

* **Terry:** To gain the approval of those he is dependent upon, at any cost.
* **Edie:** To find and nourish the best in everyone so that they can live better lives.

Scene-Objectives

* **Terry:** To sell himself to Edie. To make the girl want him. Why? Because she has class and she makes him feel better about himself.
* **Edie:** To experience Terry on an intellectual and spiritual level - the emotional level is already there. To make him an ally. To check out his beliefs. Why? She needs to be protected.

Conflict Within the Scene

* **Terry:** Wants to impress Edie with his macho-tough attitude.
* **Edie:** Wants to uncover a kindred spirit.

Inner Conflict

Terry

* Guilt over the murder of Edie's brother.
* Doesn't feel worthy of Edie.

Edie

* Too attracted to Terry.
* Terry is confusing to her.
* Needs Terry's help but she isn't sure of his principles.

Actions to Play

Terry

* Show her off to other customers in the bar.
* Impress her.
* Encourage her.
* Teach the "little woman."
* Get support.
* Apologize.
* Take the upper hand.
* Make light of it.
* Challenge her.
* Make her suspicious.
* Teach her the reality of the streets.
* Lighten her up.
* Apologize or make amends.

Edie

* Cover her discomfort.
* Play along.
* Encourage him.
* Shame him.
* Challenge him.
* Reassure him.
* Plead to him.
* Dismiss subject.
* Escape.

Obstacles: Internal and External

Terry

* Men ogling Edie in bar.
* Fear of Edie discovering his role in Joey's death.

Edie

* Bar atmosphere.
* Loud music.
* Smells of place.
* Dizzy from drink.
* Lack of privacy.

Relationship in the Scene

Terry

* Finds Edie very desirable.
* Impressed with her style and vulnerability.
* Admires her emotional strength.
* Intimidated by her education and sense of purity.

Edie

* Finds Terry charming and sexy.
* Attracted by his vulnerability.
* Disapproves of his tough philosophy.
* Feels he could protect her.
* Moved by the hurt in his eyes.
* Enjoys his smile and exuberance.
* Attracted by his "macho," yet gentle manner.

Relationship to the Place

Terry
* Feels at home.
* Feels respected and accepted by the owner and customers.
* Feels like a man there.

Edie
* Is uncomfortable by the stares, smells, and sounds.
* Intimidated by macho, primitive atmosphere.
* Feels self-conscious, yet free.

The Actor's Preparation

* **Terry**: Actor needs to first connect with all of his shortcomings. Then, focus on the one person or thing that can validate his self worth. For his relationship with Edie: Use partner or substitute a woman whom he finds exciting, yet is afraid of.
* **Edie**: Create loss of a loved one and then an intense attraction to the wrong kind of person.

The Director's Goal

To emphasize the the conflict between Terry and Edie's incompatibility and their intense attraction to each other.

THE BAR SCENE FROM *ON THE WATERFRONT*

------------ BEAT 1 ------------

INT. SALOON LADIES' SIDE NIGHT
Perhaps a sign can emphasize *Ladies'
Entrance*. As Terry leads Edie in, a tipsy
Irish biddy is noisily protesting her
enforced departure.

           WOMAN
  I'm only after havin' one more wee bit —

           BARTENDER
  You and your one-mores. Now beat it.

As Terry and Edie reach the bar, the radio
blares a baseball game. A roar goes up
from the speaker. Bartender nods to Terry. In
the corner a small, well-oiled longshoreman
sings, "I'll Take You Home Again, Kathleen"
in a plaintive, cracking voice.

           BARTENDER
    Well, what do you know —
      Jackie just stole home.

           TERRY
  (glancing at Edie with a mischievous
      wink at the bartender)
  I wouldn't mind doing that myself.

SHOW HER OFF

The bartender grins. Terry guides Edie to a
small table.

------------ BEAT 2 ------------
IMPRESS HER WITH GOOD MANNERS

        (to Edie)
  What're you drinking?

Edie hesitates, obviously not knowing
what to ask for. A customer at the bar says,
loudly —

> SINGER OF "KATHLEEN"
> Give me a Glockenheimer

> EDIE
> (it could be root beer for all she knows)   COVER UP YOUR DISCOMFORT —
> I'll try a — Glockenheimer.   PLAY ALONG

> TERRY
> (to bartender)
> Likewise. And draw two for chasers.   BE A BIG SHOT
> (to Edie)
> Now you're beginning to live.   ENCOURAGE HER

> EDIE
> (as the drinks are poured)
> I am?

Edie picks up her glass, sniffs the contents
with some distaste and then sips it
tentatively. Terry watches with amusement.

> TERRY
> (still swaggering)
> Not that way — like this.   TEACH THE LITTLE WOMAN
> (holds glass up)
> Down the hatch!
> (gulps it down)
> Wham!

Edie takes her drink and does likewise.
She gasps and her eyes pop.

> EDIE
> (with soft amazement)
> Wham . . .   HUMOR HIM

TERRY
(grinning at her)
How you like it?

EDIE
It's quite —
(gulps)
— nice.

TERRY
How about another one?

EDIE
(already feeling this one)
No thanks . . .

TERRY
(to bartender)   ----------- BEAT 3 -----------
Hit me again, Mac.

BARTENDER
(as he pours drink)
See the fight last night? That Riley—
both hands. Little bit on your style.

TERRY
Hope he has better luck.

EDIE
Were you really a prizefighter?   FLATTER HIM

TERRY
(nods)
I went pretty good for a while, didn't I, Al?   GET AL'S SUPPORT
But I didn't stay in shape — and —
(a little ashamed)
—I had to take a few dives.   APOLOGIZE

EDIE
A dive? You mean, into the water?

TERRY
(laughs harshly)
Naw, in the ring, a dive is —

TAKE THE UPPER HAND
----------- BEAT 4 -----------
TEASE HER

He stops, shakes his head and with his
finger draws an invisible square in the air.

EDIE
(mystified)
Now what are you doing?

INSIST

TERRY
Describing you. A square from out there.
I mean you're nowhere.
(draws it again)
Miss Four Corners.

MAKE LIGHT OF IT

EDIE
(smiles, but persistent)
What made you want to be a fighter?

----------- BEAT 5 -----------

INSIST

TERRY
I had to scrap all my life. Figured I might as
well get paid for it. When I was a kid my
old man got killed, never mind how.
Charley and I was put in a place — they
called it a Children's Home. Some home!
I run away and peddled papers, fought in
Club smokers and —
(catches himself)
But what am I runnin' off at the mouth for?
What
do you care?

TEST HER

EDIE
Shouldn't we care about everybody?

CHALLENGE HIM

TERRY
What a fruitcake you are!

LIGHTEN HER UP

EDIE
Isn't everybody a part of everybody else?

GET THE RIGHT ANSWER

TERRY
Gee, thoughts! Alla time thoughts!
(then)
You believe that drool?

CHALLENGE HER

EDIE
(deeply shocked)
Terry!

TERRY
Want to hear my philosophy? Do it to him
before he does it to you.

JUSTIFY YOUR VIEW

EDIE
(aroused)
Our Lord said just the opposite.

SHAME HIM

TERRY
I'm not lookin' to get crucified. I'm lookin'
to stay in one piece.

REASON WITH HER

------------ BEAT 6------------

EDIE
(flaring up)
I never met such a person. Not a spark of
romance or sentiment or — human kindness
in your whole body.

SHAME HIM

TERRY
What do they do for you, except get
in your way?

GET THROUGH TO HER

EDIE
And when things get in your way — or
people — You just knock them aside — get
rid of them — is that your idea?

CHALLENGE HIM

TERRY
(defensive — stung)
Listen — get this straight — don't look at me
when you say them things. It wasn't my
fault what happened to your brother. Fixing
Joey wasn't my idea.

GET THROUGH TO HER

------------ BEAT 7 ------------

EDIE
(gently)
Why, Terry, who said it was?

CALM HIM DOWN

TERRY
(lamely)
Well, nobody, I guess. But that Father Barry,
I didn't like the way he kept
looking at me.

BLAME FATHER BARRY

EDIE
He was looking at everybody
the same way.
Asking the same question.

REASSURE HIM

TERRY
(troubled, not convinced)
Yeah, yeah . . .
(suddenly)
This Father Barry, what's his racket?

MAKE HER SUSPICIOUS

EDIE
(shocked)
His — racket?

TERRY   .
(trying to regain his bravado)
You've been off in daisyland, honey.
Everybody's got a racket.

WAKE HER UP

EDIE
But a priest?

With his finger he again describes a square
in the air and then points through it to Edie.
This time it angers her.

------------ BEAT 8 ------------

EDIE
You don't believe anything, do you?

SHAME HIM

TERRY
Edie, down here it's every man for himself.
It's keepin' alive! It's standin' in with the right
people so you can keep a little loose
change jinglin' in your pocket.

TEACH HER REALITY OF STREETS

EDIE
And if you don't?

TERRY
If you don't . . .
(points downward with a descending whistle)
Keep your neck in and your nose clean and
you'll never have no trouble down here.

EDIE
But that's living like an animal —

REJECT THE CONCEPT

Terry seems almost to illustrate this by the
way he drains off his beer and wipes his
mouth with his sleeve.

TERRY
I'd rather live like an animal than
end up like —

DEFEND

(He hesitates.)

                    EDIE
        Like Joey? Are you afraid to mention
                  his name?

                                              PROBE

                                              ----------- BEAT 9-----------

                    TERRY
            (challenged—defensive)   LIGHTEN THE MOOD
          Why keep harpin' on it?
          (looks at her unfinished beer)
        Come on, drink up. You got to get a little
        fun out of life. What's the matter with you?
                (nods toward jukebox)
              I'll play you some music.

He starts toward the jukebox. She turns with
him. Suddenly something cries out in her,
almost as if she didn't know she was going
to say it—

                                              ----------- BEAT 10-----------

                    EDIE
            Help me, if you can —   REACH OUT
          for God sakes help me!

CLOSE ON TERRY
For the first time the edge is knocked off
his swagger. He feels the purity of her grief.
He'd like to help — that's his immediate
reaction. But there's his brother Charley and
his steady work and his loyalties to the mob
and its code. All this runs through his mind,
confusing him, tearing him.

CLOSE ON TERRY AND EDIE
Terry turns back to her,
with a helpless gesture.

TERRY
I — I'd like to, Edie, but —
(shakes his head)
— there's nothin' I can do.

APOLOGIZE

Edie feels subdued, ashamed at breaking
down. She rises, and in a low voice says—

EDIE
All right, all right . . .
I shouldn't have asked you.

DISMISS THE SUBJECT

TERRY
You haven't finished your beer.

EDIE
I don't want it. But why don't you stay and
finish your drink.

ESCAPE

TERRY
(swinging off the stool)
I got my whole life to drink.

As if magnetized by her, he follows her out.

CUT

9 CONVERSATIONS WITH DIRECTORS AND ACTORS

"... we look to artists to feel for us, to suffer and rejoice, so
that we can enjoy them from a safe distance and get to know
better what the full range of human experience really is ...
we ask artists to fill our lives with a cavalcade of fresh sights
and insights."

— *Diane Ackerman, A Natural History of the Senses*

At this point, it's probably clear that getting *the* performance — at the expense of everything else except the script — is of utmost importance. Some in this business may claim that a director doesn't really need to understand the actor's instrument. After all, directors aren't supposed to be acting teachers. That much is true. That would be like expecting every driver to be an auto mechanic. However, if you want the best performance from your vehicle, you must learn how to drive it and familiarize yourself with the machine.

Yet, without knowledge of the actor's language and mindset, how can a director dream of inspiring and capturing the truth of a performance? Herein lies the key to successful directing.

To shed further light on the subject, it's valuable for you to read how a few very successful directors deal with the same issues. Also included are conversations with three fine actors. It's rare for actors to share what they feel about directors. Their comments — from the actor's point of view — are quite interesting.

BURT BRINCKERHOFF
Director/Producer/Actor

Burt Brinckerhoff, a well-known television director, produced and directed the successful television series *7th Heaven*. He has directed nearly 50 television shows, including episodes of *Touched by an Angel, Beverly Hills 90210, Magnum P.I., Moonlighting, Remington Steele, Alf,* and *The Bob Newhart Show.* He has also directed numerous miniseries and movies for television such as *The Hamptons, Steambath, Cracker Factory,* and *Brave New World,* as well as the pilots for *Three's Company, PBS/Two Hour Specials,* and *PBS Playhouse.* A former Broadway and film actor, Brinckerhoff appeared in the classic film, *The Goddess.*

DS: *What's the most important thing to understand when working with actors?*

BB: Understanding the difference between objective energy and subjective energy. Understanding that there are two energies at work in the relationship between the director and the actor. The objective energy comes from the director and the subjective should be encouraged to come from the actor. If directors can get that clear in their minds, they will be able to move to the next part of the process, which is interpreting a map — the vision. The vision is what the writer puts on paper and what the director — if properly in tune — should do, as well. The director becomes a creative midwife who turns the vision/map into vivid and, hopefully, irresistible territory. Directors aren't the creators of the vision but have the responsibility of bringing a living creation into our experience. Therefore, it is necessary that a director have an explorer's senses — not just a way of looking at things. You need to feel that you are capable of guiding the actors' very strong, subjective energy and the art director's strong visual style.

DS: *One problem that often comes up for actors and directors is that of matching business (activities executed by the character/actor, such as setting a table) and emotional continuity. This is a problem actors are acutely aware of. Marlon Brando has told directors that he's going to do it the way he wants and the rest is their problem. But then again, there is only one Brando. The rest of us have to take these technical realities into account. What do you do when you have an actor who is having trouble matching emotional and business continuity?*

BB: If you established trust, the actor will not have any trouble with emotional continuity. They appreciate your decision regarding how their energy enters the scene. From there you begin to let them know how to move from the entrance into the scene and how you envision them exiting. This has to do with the continuity of the arc of the character. If you have good eyes and ears for your actors, they will be able to see why they are entering the scene — emotionally and physically — at this point and why you are suggesting they exit the scene at another point. It also has to do with when the camera will enter and exit the scene. This has to be given to actors in such a way that their subjective and emotional characterization isn't interrupted.

If you are a good midwife, the actor will appreciate guidance towards a continuity of character. Once you are let into the actor's psyche and you sense the "Wow, I get to do that," you have found that trusting relationship. Then they will, in most cases, come back to you with, "Hey, what about this? Can I get away with this? Is that too naked? Is that too scary? Too big?"

DS: *What do you say?*

BB: If I trust them trusting me, I will say, "Hey, let's try that." Interestingly enough, they might try it and realize they are pushing harder against the obstacles than the obstacles against them, in which case they've brought too much to the relationship and should save some of it for later. Otherwise, they are going to roll over the other energies in the scene, at which point the audience begins to lose track and, therefore, trust, in the actor's ability to carry them along. They just sense something's wrong. Then directors are put in the situation of having editors attempt to save the scenes.

DS: *The idea is to leave something to the imagination.*

BB: Jack Nicholson constantly did that in the role of Joker in *Batman*. As a result, my children were totally confused. I had to go back and connect the dots for them. I find that irresponsible and it's not Nicholson's fault. It's the director's fault. Nicholson brought more than the director dreamed of. If you're not a strong director — or a good midwife — you're not going to be able to guide the energies into the dynamic that makes the film irresistible and makes the audience go, "Oh, I hope so-and-so wins" when the protagonist and antagonist come together in a death struggle.

DS: *Many actors feel stifled by the necessity to match business from shot to shot for the sake of physical continuity. As a director, how do you make it comfortable for an actor?*

BB: In terms of physical continuity, as a director I'm certainly not going to complicate their lives. If they can't drink a cup of coffee and talk at the same time, I'm not going to have them do it. If I think coffee is important to a scene, I'll find another way to do it.

Smoking and drinking become mere crutches. They don't have anything to do with the real dynamic of either the human being or the continuity of the scene. They may look good, but they don't really help.

If business is not important, then you have to find connectors in some other way. Elia Kazan was really a master at that — at putting opposing energies together and encouraging each one to be strong enough to give the other a real obstacle. Once that happens, then you lose activity as just business. It becomes a dynamic part of the scene. If you're blowing smoke in somebody's face, that becomes an obstacle. The other actor can now think, " I love you blowing smoke in my face because now I can do what I want. I want to reach across the table, grab you, and throw you against the wall. That's what's going to happen at the end of the scene, "so blow more smoke in my face." That's a very cliché example, but it works.

DS: *It's a simple, uncomplicated solution.*

BB: If you can spill the coffee, then make that part of the dynamic of the scene (the obstacle of the scene). If you can spill it on somebody's lap and now they have to react to being burned by a silly cup of coffee, this becomes a whole other thing.

DS: *The spilling of the coffee has to come from one character's relationship to the other and what he is trying to accomplish. The character may want to punish him and get his attention.*

BB: Yes, but you can't insist if your actor is not trained enough to do the business well. Spilling cups of hot coffee and making that work, either comedically or seriously, is tricky. You have to be very careful.

DS: *Yes, but the way to make it easy for the actor is to make the act an extension of the feeling he has for the other person.*

BB: Sometimes they are not capable of doing that.

DS: *What if it's essential? It's in the script and part of the story. Then what do you do?*

BB: In that case, I say to the producer, "Look, this actor can't spill coffee. I want the money and time to train this actor to spill coffee effectively for the scene. If you don't give it to me, I can't guarantee you that moment." It takes experience and strength. You can't let people stand around thinking, "Okay, take 16 and he still can't get it right." Then everybody looks bad. You, as the director, will look particularly bad.

DS: *Now, what about preparation time? Some actors don't like to rehearse at all.*

BB: I'm not sure I would even say that that person was an actor. He might have the most wonderful, scary energy that ever walked on to a set, but now I'm challenged to use that energy.

DS: *When you say the person's not an actor if he doesn't take the time to get into the mindset he*

needs to start the scene, is that something you encourage, or do you let him do what he wants to do?
BB: It depends on how much I trust the actor. If I give them time and they come on and nothing's changed, I'm not going to trust them. I can't afford to. I will then use my charm to encourage them to take the plunge and come right in. I say, "You don't need an hour. You are fine. Let's go." That's seducing the child. There is no question about it.

DS: *By doing that, you are really building up the actor's confidence.*

BB: But I won't lie to him. A director must never lie to an actor because the actor's antenna is always functioning and once you lie to them: forget it. Don't expect their trust.

DS: *Sometimes there are those actors who are so insecure that they will take a compliment and think, "Oh, he just said that to make me feel good."*

BB: That's okay, but I'll never pay the compliment unless I can back it up.

DS: *You mentioned Kazan and his ability to pick effective actors.*

BB: That's the art of Kazan's understanding of subjective energies. Subjective energies tend to be broad and deep and are sometimes searching and unfocused. A good director is not afraid of the actor's energy, and will start to focus it by telling them, "Go, go. Follow that choice. It's going to cause sparks."

I try to encourage actors by having them understand that this is a human relationship. This is about human beings. The audience is always interested in human beings and I want them to always understand that. Currently we've got a lot of animation films going, but the audience is interested in the dynamic of the voices because that is something they can understand. Actually, we've lost a lot of the art of listening, and yet that's the basis of communication. We have to listen before we learn to speak.

DS: *Let me clarify. When you say "listening," you don't mean listening to the words, but to the vibrations, to the tone of the voice that communicates what is really going on.*

BB: I go and work in schools and the teachers and administrators stand up and say, "We're going to teach communication," and they talk about speaking and listening. I say to them, "Excuse me, it should be listening, then speaking." They look at me as if I'm crazy. They don't understand that they're putting the cart before the horse. And yet, almost every teacher I talk with says, "It's so tragic today, the children just don't seem to listen." Well, that's because we're not teaching listening. We're teaching talking. We're teaching noise, and our society is filled with noise. Communication between humans is something else.

DS: *Empty words do not really communicate anything.*

BB: True. I call it noise.

DS: *"It's full of sound and fury, signifying nothing."*

BB: We always go back to Shakespeare, in this case, *Macbeth*. He was the best.

DS: *When you have an actor who becomes emotionally blocked, how do you handle it?*

BB: Well, I certainly don't let him know that I think he's blocked.

DS: *But he knows it, he feels it. The more blocked you feel, the more frightened you become. The more tense you become and the worse it gets.*

BB: In that case I try to tap the child directly through humor. Most children respond to a sense of humor.

DS: *Through laughing at themselves?*

BB: Finally, we get to that. I'm really the one laughing at myself first, to show them it's okay to laugh. If you can get to that place, then the key can usually be slipped in and you go on from there.

DS: *Before you go to the humor, do you try anything else?*

BB: Most times they're trying to do more than they need to do.

DS: *Well, they become emotionally blocked when they feel they are not able to meet the emotional peaks and depths they think they should. How do you release them from their self-imposed obligations?*

BB: I tell them that we are probably going to use all of it eventually. Somewhere we are going to couple all of this together — where they are in their character arc, their relationships, where they came from, and where they are going. I don't tell them, I ask them: "Hey, wouldn't it be fun if you did this at this point?"

DS: *What do you do when your actors have developed a tremendous antagonism toward each other and yet their characters are supposed to be in love?*

BB: I find that if they are good actors and trained at all, they create a wonderful substitution from their own lives and bring it to the scene, while not letting anyone know that's what they're doing.

DS: *Do you encourage the use of substitutions?*

BB: Yes, but it has to be personal substitutions. I can't give them substitutions. I can only encourage them to find it in themselves.

As a professional director, you will find yourself in situations where you are given energies — sometimes arbitrarily and sometimes for financial reasons — and you have to make them work. That's part of the responsibility of being a director. Sometimes, when you are working with two stars, you end up being a traffic cop. Interestingly enough, if you have two really good stars with irresistible energy, they will find their own ways with each other because they are both such wonderful professionals.

DS: *People in theater make a big to-do about styles of acting for theater versus film or television. Do you think there is a major difference between the mediums? What would you say is the difference?*

BB: The difference is that with a stage production, you are creating an immediate dynamic energy that has to be repeated each performance — and the only really big change is the audience. You need people who understand that. If they are going to have a satisfying and rewarding experience, they have to be aware of the immediate dynamic with the audience every night. If they lose that, they might as well not come back for Act Two. In a film, we can put together three or four different moments from three or four different takes. We can print all of them and, later on, in editing, we can see which one is the better dynamic.

There is nothing less important in the theater than a director on opening night. Whereas, once you have completed the photography on a film, the director becomes more important during the process of putting that film together.

DS: *But the energy the actor brings, the way that he expresses himself on stage versus in front of a camera, is always in question. What is the difference?*

BB: I saw Sir Laurence Olivier play *The Entertainer* in New York. Olivier's ability to be irresistible from the stage was awesome. I then saw the film, which he also starred in. Well, he was Marlon Brando with style. In each situation, you're going to find the key. You're going to create the dynamic energy.

You have to understand the material. You have to understand the space that you're doing it in. You have to understand the dynamic of the camera and the relationship between the camera and the actors. Some of it is instinct; some experience. There are no rules, only basic principles.

As I said, in films someone comes to you and says, "You have so much incredible energy, but let's save part of it for the next scene." In theater, it's probably the opposite problem. You drop the connection and the audience will probably be lost. As a director, make sure that the actors keep their energy up. It's like an electric current going between them. Each has to know when to receive and when to give in order to keep it going.

DS: *I attend the theater regularly and the thing that always disturbs me is that at least 85 percent of the performances are mannered, not because of style but because there is such emptiness behind the words. That's considered theatrical behavior? I'm never moved because I'm always aware of the actor performing.*

BB: The only thing I can suggest is that they are doing it for themselves, not the audience. If, as a professional, you are not really interested in communicating with your audience, you are doing it for vanity.

DS: *When the performance is not there, I wonder how the director let those actors get away with what they're doing. Then you finally realize the director's focus was on staging only.*

BB: You're talking about a traffic cop. A traffic cop and a director are two different energies.

DS: *When you have a camera rehearsal to show actors their relationship to the camera and vice versa, do you use that time to help the actor work out certain problems he may have with the role?*

BB: It depends on the actor. Some actors are capable of combining the two elements and some actors prefer not knowing anything about the technology. They just want to live a life in front of the camera and prefer to keep focus on that. They don't want to know if they're in the wrong place at the wrong time, if the microphone is to their right or their left, where their key light is, etc.

There are certain things that are necessary and I try to make it easy for the actor. You know the expression, "Hit the mark." Well, for the actor to be captured by technology, they'll need to hit the mark now and then — whether they like it or not. I don't put that mark out in the middle of nowhere. If they want to knock that chair down to get to a mark, that's their business. If they can make that work, if they're Robin Williams and they can make it work, that's okay. I'll just say to the camera operator and the people lighting the set, "This guy is a comic genius and he might knock the chair over, so be prepared, because I don't want to miss that moment." If it's going to happen in a spontaneous way, then we can build from that energy. On the other hand, in most cases I'll say to the actor, "Okay, stop at the table. Stop at the chair." I'll put those real elements in the actor's way and then go from there.

DS: *Instead of chalk or tape?*

BB: Absolutely. A lot of people assume it's okay to stop an actor midair, that he will adjust and even appreciate it. Having made my living as an actor, I can assure you the assumption is uneducated.

I just had an occasion to talk with a British journalist who is doing a book on Natalie Wood. One of the stories I tell is that she had a very, very emotional scene where she is in a hospital bed and goes berserk.

I had gotten multiple cameras to capture this moment. I didn't want her to have to do it again because I knew it would be difficult. We were all ready to go and we called her back in. She came through the door of the hospital room and I was right behind her. She stopped right in the door, so I couldn't get past. She stood there for 30 seconds at least. I thought, "Oh, she's preparing," so I calmed everybody down. In about 30 seconds she turned around, looked me directly in the eye, and said, "My slippers are in the wrong place" and went and got into bed. I learned so much from that. I realized that somewhere in the past she had gone through an entire emotional acting experience only to find that her slippers had been in the wrong place.

I never had a moment when I felt that she was going to be lacking. All I could do was give her the obstacles she needed to create moments and helpful energy that comes from good composition in the technical areas.

DS: *When actors encounter problems on the set, it becomes your problem. What immediate solutions do you come up with?*

BB: If you carefully watch your talent enter the space, the way they enter is certainly going to give you a lot of help. You always want to let them explore the space. Find out what makes them comfortable and what makes them uncomfortable. You can tell this immediately if you are sensitive.

DS: *Let's discuss blocking for camera versus the actor finding his own blocking.*

BB: Most actors appreciate being given a map of the scene.

DS: *You tell them where they will move throughout the scene and where they exit.*

BB: I'm encouraging the actor to trust me because I have thought about this. I'm only saying that this is the life I think the character is leading and I'm trying to lead you to that. Now, I want you (the actor) to help me fill it because your energy, ultimately, is what's going to fill it.

DS: *If a movement feels false to an actor, do you adjust the camera?*

BB: It depends. I never let the actor think that I already know where the camera is going to be. Not at first. Some actors like to know where the camera is. I don't impose that on the first go-round, though. As a matter of fact, when they walk into the location space I make sure that I've talked to the director of photography about how it should go. It's very important that we agree so we won't be working at cross-purposes. I don't want to suddenly go to the director of photography and say, "Okay, let's hang the camera off the wall up here." They would look at me as if I were absolutely nuts.

DS: *Do you pre-plan your blocking?*

BB: I pre-plan the life I think is being led there and put myself in their living space. I have the advantage of having earned my living as an actor and, as a result, I put myself there and think about it. That's the reason you have to understand human relationships. If you're going to impose yourself on other people, God help you if you don't understand the people you are trying to guide. I try to understand what makes women comfortable and uncomfortable. I don't impose my maleness. Sometimes women appreciate that and sometimes they are suspicious, which is interesting. They may think I am trying to be tricky. But I'm getting good at it — I don't often let them catch me at it because what I do is put myself in their position. Think about it, women like to be seen differently than men.

DS: *What's the difference?*

BB: I don't know that I can sum it up in so many words. Women have a different dynamic as human beings. They like to receive something before they give something back. Very often, they know that they are expected to give before they receive and this makes them suspicious. So I always like to give something to a woman on the set before I expect her to give back.

DS: *What would you give?*

BB: Just awareness that I understand who she is as a person, and as a character, and that I have very trustworthy eyes and ears. Usually they appreciate that. Now men never want to appear weak. As a result, I always give them the sense that they are action. They are in action, doing something, and that's the reason that they enter this way or do something that way. There are actors who always want to enter and have something to do. There are others who are, as you say, empty vessels. You take their hand and guide them to the kitchen sink or whatever it is that is going to give them a life they didn't bring. I also think there is a big lack of trust in our industry between females and males. I am sensitive to this and I try to put myself in the position of the female, as well as the male. That doesn't have anything to do with crossing a room. It has to do with who you are when you enter that room and who you are in terms of the character's relationships. I treat each person and situation as sensitively as I am capable of and have the time to do. I can't put a milk bottle with a nipple in every mouth and expect to get something done. I don't do that, but I never lie to the actor either.

DS: *Tell me more about the dynamic energy?*

BB: What you want to do is create such a "preponderance" of positive energy that you, as a director, can stand back and let them go. Once they're playing wonderfully together and are creating irresistible energy, let them go because that's really what you want.

DS: *That's the kind of thing Kazan does, and does very effectively.*

BB: Kazan usually does it individually. He doesn't say it openly so that everyone hears it. He takes a particular moment in a scene and makes a suggestion to one of the actors so that the next time through, another spark goes off.

DS: *Yes, and the first actor is unaware of what the second actor will do. Did you ever work with him?*

BB: I never worked with him, but when they were casting *Tea and Sympathy*, Kazan called me in to audition. I came out of the wings and walked across the stage to the center where he was sitting down with a couple of other people. He said, "How are you Burt?" And I said, "I'm fine Mr. Kazan. Thank you." Then he said, "I'm sorry you can't play this part." I said, "Excuse me?" He said, "Look. You walk like an athlete. You can never play this part." Then said, "And, I don't think you are big enough to play the role of the athlete, but thank you very much. I hope we'll see you again."

DS: *He was just looking at your body language.*

BB: I learned more from that than if I'd been given the part.

DS: *Finally, is there any advice you'd like give directors?*

BB: There are no conclusions to be drawn. Each new experience is a living adventure. Enjoy!

TODD HOLLAND
Director

Todd Holland has won three Emmy Awards for Outstanding Directing for a Comedy Series. Three for *Malcolm in the Middle* (for which he is also co-executive producer) and one for *The Larry Sanders Show*. In 2002, he received the Directors Guild of America (DGA) award for Outstanding Directorial Achievement for Comedy Series, *Malcolm in the Middle*. He has been an Emmy nominee several times in this category. Holland is also a six-time DGA nominee for Directing Comedy Series and a five-time Cable Ace Award winner for Director of a Comedy for *The Larry Sanders Show*. Other television credits include: *Felicity, My So-Called Life, Tales from the Crypt, Twin Peaks, Vietnam Stories,* and Steven Spielberg's *Amazing Stories*. Holland has also directed the films *Krippendorf's Tribe* and *The Wizard*.

DS: *Where did you find that wonderful woman in* Malcolm in the Middle?

TH: Jane Kaczmarek plays Lois, the wife and mother, in *Malcolm in the Middle*. I worked with her on *Felicity*, where she played Felicity's mom. Jane came in and read for the part of Lois when we were casting for *Malcolm*. Lois is based on the mother of the show's creator, Linwood Boomer. It's no secret. But he had a terrible time casting an actress to play his mother. Jane read, then left the room. Linwood said he wasn't sure. I said she was the only one who made me laugh and the only one to present a cohesive character who was believable: someone with dignity and reality, who wasn't looking for laughs. A week or two after that session, Linwood kept saying we didn't have anybody. I kept saying Jane Kaczmarek. I kept repeating her name; defending her name. When we finally went to the network auditions, Jane totally came up to bat. She gave a great reading and everyone knew she was it.

Comedy is an accident for me. I always feel, "How did I get here? This is totally a mistake. I'm not a comedy director." I think I mistrust comedy, so I work very hard. I don't assume anything is funny. It sounds terrible, but I don't like comedy that much. I love suspense. I did *Amazing Stories, Tales from the Crypt*, then *Twin Peaks*, which was weird horror-comedy. I find humor in all truthful human behavior. I would be directing something scary and say, "Hey, here's a moment that's organically funny." Hollywood doesn't understand that tone. It's either scary or funny. They didn't know how to market something in the middle.

When *The Larry Sanders Show* came along, it was biting and cynical, but not dark. My mother thought it was a loathsome show because they said the f-word. She asked if all the characters were meant to be so hateful. I said, "Mom, if I hadn't believed that those characters loved each other, I couldn't have done the show for six years." *Larry Sanders* was a comedy that came completely from the character, not jokes or situations. We would approach every scene by asking its purpose. Why is actor Jeffrey Tambor entering the room? Why is he leaving the room? What did he get in the scene? If it didn't serve a dramatic purpose, we would say that the scene was wrong. Garry Shandling would say, "You're absolutely right." He's "Mr. Story." Garry's brilliance is that once we had the story, he could find a way to twist the scenes to make them riotously funny and human. A comedy unfolds when you have a cast like that, an amazing supporting cast with clear intentions. *Larry Sanders* was a drama where everything people said was funny. Yet everyone had a clear intention, purpose, something they wanted. No one ever came in a room, just told a joke, and left.

DS: *So you started on a premise of reality? It was your solid foundation.*

TH: Right.

DS: *You never thought about the form? The style? You dealt with simple, human logic?*

TH: Absolutely.

DS: *You said Sandling would know how to twist something in a scene to make it very funny. Give me an example.*

TH: For instance, Jeffrey's character, Hank (who is essentially Ed McMahon) would go to Garry Shandling, who is Larry Sanders (Johnny Carson). He would open or close the door in a ritualistic pattern. They had all these little counterpoints and ritualistic behaviors in everyday life. We incorporated a great deal of our actors' human behavior, and their very human bad behavior became entire episodes. I'm not sure the actors ever identified their bad behavior. You don't always see your behavior when it's mirrored back to you.

When I was reading *Malcolm in the Middle,* I thought that it was funny and smart. I called Linwood, the creator, and said, "This has a lot of heart. Is that an accident?" I'm used to people who want laughs, laughs, laughs. I just worked with a guy who said, "Funny is money." If I ever hear the word "funny" used like that again, I'm going to choke myself. Comedy, for me, is all about character. If you are ever up against a wall with nothing working, look at what you're doing on a character level. Most likely, you've lost the path of the character.

For the first time in 20 years, in the spring of 2000, I had the chance to do a pilot that was suspense driven and it was scary for me. Three days into it, I realized I was in a trap. I missed things because I presumed the genre would permit certain behavior. As a result, I was not as vigilant with my questions of characters and motivations. I thought, "This is a scary movie, and this kind of stuff happens in a scary movie." I realized I was messing up. The actor in the pilot was acting as if he knew it was scary. I missed it the first day and kept thinking, "Something's not right here." I was so in love with the suspense genre, I didn't catch it at first. In comedy, I'm very skeptical. "Okay, that's not funny. That's false. I don't believe that behavior. Let's go back and find something real." I always tell people when I interview for jobs, "I'm not good at physical comedy. I didn't grow up on it." But the people who are good at it have a library of shtick on their brain.

DS: *Like Michael Richards of* Seinfeld.

TH: Yes. Those falls, stumbles, and bits. I've had people hire me for character comedy. I show up on set and that's not what they want. They want shtick.

DS: *What do you do when that happens?*

TH: I fight. I fight to keep the character comedy vivid. Only one comedy film sticks out as great — *Tootsie.* It made me laugh and taught life lessons. Insightful and true to the entertainment industry in which it is set. But there is also shtick, like when Charles Durning puts his arm around Dustin Hoffman, who misunderstands the gesture and slaps his hand onto his own breast for protection.

I've only done one true sitcom, *Friends.* I loved it, but it is as broad a comedy as I want to do. Usually, situation comedies are just about characters and situations. Less character, more situation. Lucille Ball was the "founding father" of sitcoms, and she played this brilliant character. She had pathos and generated enormous empathy from her audience.

We had successful writers from other shows write for *Larry Sanders.* Their episodes looked, sounded, and even read like a *Larry Sanders* show. But it was just the jokey shell, not the meaty core or the fight for humanity beneath it all. There's darkness and pain behind the characters. Those writers that could show depth and character stayed around for the most part.

DS: *Look at* All in the Family. *There aren't enough people who can write like that. It's easier to write a joke.*

TH: Which is the problem with any genre. My complaint is about people who do science fiction or horror and say, "Oh, who needs characters?" It's one film in fifty that actually spends time on character and becomes a classic. Look at the original *Alien* with Sigourney Weaver and Ian Holm. They never played the horror. They were real people caught in extraordinary situations. Same thing with *Malcolm.* It's a hard show to do because it happens at a fevered pitch, compared to *Sanders.*

At its best, *Malcolm* is a strange show that has enormous reality. You can play incredibly broad if you remember to anchor the characters in reality. If your characters are false, your comedy will be false and there will be nothing. I don't laugh at the false. I'm not good with stand-up comedy because of the set-up and the punch line. I go, "This is where they expect me to laugh." You have to surprise me. I'm not going to give you my laughter. You have to earn my laughter. Comedy is ultimately about surprise — a twist you didn't see coming that tells you about the character. It is unexpected, but believable.

DS: *Is Malcolm shot live?*

TH: No. It's single camera.

DS: *And what about Sanders?*

TH: *Sanders* was unusual because we had three cameras, but four-wall sets and no audience — except for the talk show. The behind-the-scenes stuff was shot in a room like this: four walls, three cameramen, and the actors. We would shoot a five-page scene like a theater scene — start to finish, no stopping. The actors loved it. We'd get our coverage simultaneously.

DS: *Is it more expensive?*

TH: It is actually very affordable. It works like a faux documentary, so you end up locked into certain stylistic choices. It has a roughness in the style, but in *Sanders* it served the overall tone.

DS: *What about rehearsals? Did you do a lot of rehearsing?*

TH: *Sanders* was a weird hybrid. A sitcom typically has three days of rehearsals. Thursday is camera blocking. Friday night is the shoot. On *Sanders,* Monday was a table read, then rehearsal Monday, Tuesday, and Wednesday with no official camera blocking. We'd create the form as we went along. Unofficially, camera blocking was Wednesday night. We'd shoot all day Thursday and Friday. Because it was multiple camera, it was more complex so we'd shoot for two whole days. We'd have a good two full days of rehearsals. Because Garry Shandling was creator, producer, writer, and actor, he was not frequently available to me as an actor. Garry had this strange process where he would sit as a writer at the table and read the scenes with absolute dead-on bull's-eye intuition. As a writer he could do it just like that. But, suddenly, when he had to do it as an actor, it was a much more painful, agonizing journey. He demanded an absolutely clear, intellectual understanding of all his character's obstacles and intentions. And when he didn't do his homework, he'd be completely lost — all that fantastic instinct was useless to the *actor.*

DS: *Then, I presume he'd start watching, doubting, and judging himself. Being judge, jury, and executioner of your work is the kiss of death. You said you'd actually have three days of rehearsal. For most of this time, are you actually working on characters and events or spending a lot of time blocking for the camera?*

TH: Actually, very little time was spent on fitting actors to the camera. On *Sanders,* the camera chased what was organic about the blocking. *Malcolm* is different. It's a higher-pitched, visual comedy. In *Malcolm,* you design the shot and then put the characters into it. It's a whole different animal. And it's kids. You really don't let kids run wild. I tried that once on my first movie and it was a disaster. Kids have the unique ability to be able to stand on a mark and be absolutely real. You have to let adults find it. With kids, you can just tell them the blocking and they'll be real. They're good actors. Kid actors are amazing.

I worked on a movie with Fred Savage and he was amazing at age 12. I put marks down and he would just be dead-on. One time I decided to let the kids find their organic blocking and it was a nightmare. Kids don't intellectually perceive themselves in space. They think, "Where do I feel comfortable?" As 12-year-olds, they don't think, "What is my organic blocking?" If they are good, they are good at being real. Period.

DS: *Directing children is of interest to many directors.*

TH: *Malcolm in the Middle* has a lot of kids. I find the most important thing for them is respect. The kids in *Malcolm* are uniformly brilliant, even though they are very different. One is 14, one is 15, and the other one is 9. Frankie Muniz, who plays Malcolm, is very cerebral. The whole first season, his character had enormous speeches and physical bits, and I kept thinking, "Oh my God. If Frankie wasn't so smart we'd be sunk." I would say, "Okay, Frankie, you are dancing with the camera at this point in the comedy. The camera is going to swish onto you and, as it swishes, take a step off, but don't speak till your second step because it will feel right with the camera." He says, "Okay okay okay." And then he gets it all and isn't phased in the least.

But Frankie is also an actor, and part and parcel of Frankie's amazing ability is his perfectionism, which can be a very cruel master. In our first season, whenever Frankie felt he wasn't dead-on he would send himself into a spiral of self-recrimination. You have to understand that every actor has his or her unique approach to their craft and deals with each differently. Frankie needed a lot of encouraging that first year. Whereas, Justin Berfield, who plays Reese (the second-oldest bother) has this amazing ability to mess up, and when you say, "Try it this way," he'll just do it again. When he starts to go south, he never turns on himself. He just does it again. And again. For whatever reason, he never gets in that shame cycle.

DS: *Shame is really inhibiting.*

TH: It really shuts them down. You spend all your time and energy as a director saying, "No, you are not bad. You are doing fine. We wouldn't move on if you weren't good enough. You can't always expect it to be in one take. You might not feel it, but you have to trust that I'm not moving on unless I know it can be cut to feel real and organic." I've had this conversation with Frankie before.

Erik Per Sullivan, who plays Dewey, is 9. He has a whole different energy. He's very bright but, being the youngest, he's easily distracted. My job with Erik the first season was to keep him focused. With Eric I always stay right next to the camera. He needs to feel my intensity, and then he follows direction.

We have a wonderful acting coach, Mary McCusker, on *Malcolm*. I go to her with, "What are we going to do?" and she says, "We need to give him something to preoccupy him. He's not having an inner life." With children, you often give them something to eat or something to do. You give them another activity on top of what they are doing. It's really straightforward and it doesn't matter if this activity had nothing to do with the scene. It will make them alive and real. Don't let them just sit and try to be. Kids are not good at just *being* on command. Give them crayons at the dining room table or a truck to play with during the scene. If you don't, they're going to look awkward, because they have three lines in a five-page scene. I give Erik really strong intentions, such as "I want you to draw a spaceship on Saturn. Show me what the ground looks like there." So his job in the scene is to draw this and show it to me after we cut. You have to give them rules and you have to make it fun for them.

DS: *It takes his mind off himself and frees him to be spontaneous. I do that with adult actors, as well.*

TH: Ok, if he misses his cue you just go back and pick up his line. You talk him through until you get a reading you like. In the master, he is real. He is alive and he is involved in his own story.

I once did an anthology show with a very successful comedic actor and I refused to let him do his persona. He has this very specific persona that he does, like Dana Carvey. What happened was that this very successful comedy actor with great timing — because he knew it was horror/comedy and not straight comedy — abandoned every comedic instinct he had until everything became leaden. It was heavy and uninspired because he wasn't doing his thing. I didn't see it coming. I can actually understand what he was thinking. "If I'm not doing [the persona], then I'm letting all of it go," instead of, "I'm not doing the persona, but I'm going to keep the instincts, the timing, and the energy that supports that persona."

DS: *How did you get him back on track?*

TH: It was a tough one — take by take by take and working through it. I had to lead him back so he could trust his instinct. It turned out to be one of my favorite pieces of work. It was interesting to see how difficult actors can make life for themselves when they perceive themselves as taking a big detour in their professional life. The most brilliant dramatic actors will laugh inappropriately or cry at the wrong time. Inappropriate behavior is so human and so real.

DS: *That's the surprise element.*

TH: It's in all the great James Brooks movies, such as *Broadcast News* and *As Good As It Gets*. He has a great handle on brilliant and human behavior that is unexpected. Just because an actor considers a show to be drama doesn't mean that he has to abandon his comedic instincts.

It doesn't mean people aren't making a ton of money doing it the wrong way. I read scripts and I turn them down all the time. I say, "I think you should give this to someone who laughed when they read it." It's actually a very genuine response. If it's not funny the first time, it's never going to get funnier than that.

Either it amuses you, you find spark in it, or walk away . . . because the journey just gets harder from that first read.

DS: Election *exemplifies what you're talking about. Director Alexander Payne has a tongue-in-cheek tone that comes through consistently. But it's played for real.*

It's a good example of the stakes in comedy having to be twice as high as they are in drama.

TH: In drama, you get to some sort of reality that is truthful and living, and then you have a real living moment. And it works. It plays. Great comedy has to be all that... plus. That's why the stakes need to be twice as high in comedy. People tend to think, "Oh, I'm being funny." No, keep your stakes. Keep your intentions.

DS: *Do you prefer directing drama, comedy, or suspense?*

TH: Suspense would be my choice. I actually put comedies last — unless it's just that right kind of comedy. *Malcolm* is an unusual piece. It's a great opportunity for a director, because it's a very smart comedy. It has razor-sharp writing. It's emotional. And, it's visual. That's something television comedy has not been in many years. It's never cinematic.

The problem with comedy directing is that you typically never get to show that you can direct camera, whereas in suspense the camera is as large a character as the actors are because a lot of suspense is not vocal. We once tried tightening the close-ups on Larry Sanders to get a cinematic feel and it wasn't funny. You have to see the actors in the physical space. Comedy is about the relationship of people in physical space. You have to have a wide enough frame to see them relating to each other in the space. Drama, suspense . . . they take place in eyes . . . in details: the hand on a railing, feet on steps. Suspense is withholding information. Comedy is letting you feel as unmanipulated as possible. We're talking about surprise. The audience has to discover what is funny about it and not feel that you're directing their attention to it.

DS: *How do you conduct your auditions?*

TH: I really work to make actors comfortable. I'm an honest person, not a manipulator. I've never been one to put actors through headtrips to get a performance. It's just not my style.

If you're stuck with an actor who is really not up to the task, then you are in a bad place. Every actor has a different language. You have to learn everybody's language.

DS: *That's a tall order when you're working with an actor for the first time, how do you do that?*

TH: I learned a lot doing episodic television. I did one show where the actors were very resistant and suspicious. They were afraid I was judging them. I never gave them the impression that I was judging them, but what I didn't do was say how wonderful I thought their work was. I never made that mistake again.

I went to do some work up in Canada and I sent each actor a note letting them know how pleased I was to work with them, how I was glad we were doing this project together. This is something directors don't do in Hollywood. I worked with actress Ellen Burstyn once and wrote her a note after the show saying, "Thank you for your wonderful performance. It was great to work with you." She wrote back, "Your note sent me back to the days when actresses wore white gloves and directors wore hats and ties on the set. Thank you so much for your unexpected civility." Nobody sends thank-you notes anymore.

This is an awful story: my very first job was on *Amazing Stories* and I was so excited about this job that I literally had thank-you notes custom printed with every cast and crew member on them. I handwrote individual notes on the back. I had this huge construction foreman come up to me in tears because almost nobody had ever said "Thank you." Wow, it's easy to forget that in this business. I don't have time anymore to make custom notes for every episode. But I try to always let my cast and crew know I respect and appreciate them.

DS: *At one time, stars of a big movie always bought expensive gifts for the cast and crew as a thank you. I don't think that happens anymore.*

TH: No, it is very unusual. Companies don't buy the crew jackets. I have bought crew jackets for my crewmembers a number of times. I've been the instigator in getting producers to split the cost when the studio is not buying them. In this industry — theater and film — there are long hours and a lot of sacrifice. You can get more out of people with goodwill than any sort of coercion, badgering, or negative energy. You can't goad someone into doing his or her best work. You need to encourage it.

DS: *When you have a difficult and resistant actor who resents what you say or doesn't agree with you, how do you deal with it?*

TH: I immediately take it back to their childhood. "How was your relationship with your parents?" My father was very difficult through my childhood so it takes me back to that dynamic. With difficult actors and difficult producers, I've been called tenacious. I very quietly just keep pushing. I am not good at getting results from direct, violent confrontations. I'm not good at tantrums. I can see that some tantrums are a brilliant tool to use, but I'm not good at using them. I've had it backfire. Then the studio thinks that you are irresponsible and out of control.

Some people are very brilliant at tantrums. I've worked with a few difficult actors who refused to accept direction or input — and, in a few cases, I've literally just stood back, given them a lot of freedom, and let them hang themselves, if that is what they have chosen to do. I just make sure I know I can get around what they're doing in editing.

A lot of difficult actors are people whose careers haven't gone the way they hoped: an actor with a big series in the 1960s who never got a hit again. They think I am just this arrogant little snot who has been given everything. One actor said to me, "Oh, one of Spielberg's boys is here." I'd never met him before and I was very shocked. He had researched me and didn't like me even before he met me because I had worked for Spielberg. He was extremely difficult. It was really tough getting any sort of pace out of his performance. He had this tendency to do a bogus French-Canadian accent, and he would say, "I . . . keeled . . . her . . . weeth . . . thee . . . peelow." What you do is you cut away from him and cut off all the dead space. So, while you are looking at the other person in the scene, you hear him saying off-scene, "I keeled her weeth thee peelow." I'm actually a good editor. He got shot in the piece and he wanted to do this, then that, etc. He would never take any direction. At a certain point I said, "Okay. Let him do it." As a director, you have a plan in your head. You think, "I can get out of that. I can cut to them." Or, you can negotiate. "Okay, we'll do it my way first, then your way."

DS: *Your saving grace is that you deal with it technically, in the editing room. But, on a one-to-one basis.*

TH: Some actors are a nightmare. My most difficult actor was a star who was very good at direct verbal confrontation, like a battle of wits. That's not my strength. I am very intuitive and have discovered that I come to intuition first and intellectual realizations second. So when people confront me intellectually, I have to go through this whole process of, "Okay, how did I get here?" and go back to the situation to find the logic. He didn't like me from the get-go. If there wasn't a problem, he would create one. If there wasn't a problem with the scene, he would find a way to create a problem with the scene. Everything had to be torn apart. There were two-hour rehearsals for every scene, and he wouldn't do the scenes as they were written. He wanted to get me into huge philosophical arguments because he is a master at it. I knew I couldn't win, so I would bring up the story: what are the goals, what are the intentions in the scene? It was 52 days of shooting and I didn't think I was going to survive it. Maybe I should have taken him to the parking lot and knocked his lights out. It might have been better personally, though not intellectually.

DS: *It would have been faster, too.*

TH: And, probably less painful for everyone around. It becomes about survival at that point. It's one of the reasons I love working with young, unestablished actors. They are really just there for the journey. There's nothing more joyful than seeing Jeffrey Tambor's work on *Larry Sanders*. He is just a wonderful, brilliant actor. He was so much fun. Jeffrey would be the one in independent scenes with our young cast and we would just play and rehearse. I called it play. I'd say, "Let's try it like this . . ." "Maybe we could do it like this . . ." We would play.

But that playtime becomes more and more difficult to protect when a show becomes successful. Careers that are heating up pull people's focus in many disparate directions — publicity, hiatus projects, feature opportunities — so "playtime" dissipates. That's why I love young actors. The cast of *Felicity, My So-Called Life,* the pilots I've done — any of these shows that aren't really established when I join them are the most fun to work on. These actors are thrilled that they are acting. Young casts are such a brilliant gift. Because they are young, you are able to have a great deal of influence over their minds.

DS: *They have nothing to hide — no image to protect.*

TH: They are also incredibly talented. I did *My So-Called Life* a few years ago with actress Claire Danes. At fifteen, as an actress she intimidated me. I said, "Oh, Clarie, the scene is about this." And she would answer, "Oh yes. It's about this, that, this, that, and this," and I would think, "Oh my God." She has an awareness of every dynamic happening. I was in the presence of something incredible. She's sweet, too. Keri Russell, who played the lead role in the television series *Felicity,* is like that. Keri is an amazing actress. And Frankie Muniz from *Malcolm.* Incredibly smart. Keri would be doing a scene and notice the focus-puller having problems. She'd ask, "Are you okay?" They'd say, "Oh, I'm good." "Okay" and boom, she is right back in character. She is aware of the world around her — the entire process. We used to ask her, "When do you want to direct?" Her talents were just so obvious.

You'll find that some actors are so generous. You'd ask them to step one way a little bit for the camera and they'll say, "That's great. What do you need?" It's just a statement about their craft, their professionalism. Film is one of those things that is absolutely collaborative. It has to be.

I've had a ton of fun in television; I'm determined to carry that joy to movies. But the few I've made so far were incredibly difficult. Features seem so fraught with ego and Machiavellian intrigue. Television never feels like that. Television is trench warfare, but it's also truly intense collaboration. In TV, you are not going to anguish your decisions to death. In features, everyone has too much time to second-guess everything. And comedy is fragile; it rarely survives intellectual scrutiny.

I'm famous for calling everybody back to one without saying, "Cut." The cast has spent so much time thinking about their work that the first take will often not be clicking so I am forced to yell, "We are going back to one. The camera scrambles, the actors grab their props and run for the doors, and everybody resets. And, the second I yell "Action!" again the actors let go of all the intellectualizations and planning. It's like giving an actor permission to forget all the directions and just live it.

It is very hard to get the filmmaking machine to understand. I've had my director of photography say, "No, no, the light!" And I yell, "I don't care about the light!" We are rolling!" If you don't have life in the scene, who cares if the light is beautiful? You either have a beautiful life happening, or you've got pretty pictures.

Sometimes, when you are hitting a wall with an actor you ask, "What is your choice? Because something is not lining up between your choice and what I think your character should be doing."

I did a pilot in Canada and the actor was totally missing the mark. We kept thinking that he was just bad. When we asked him what his choice was, we discovered he'd based his choice on something I had said in passing — that his character had already been on this job for six months in Washington, but the actor heard that as meaning that all of it was now old news to him. We had to see that every day is brand new, that every day is Christmas. That choice was hard for him; the world-weary approach was easier for him. Energy, effervescence, enthusiasm, and freshness — those were real acting challenges. Until I asked him what his choice was, I just thought he was bad. There was no charisma, no life.

DS: *You try to find out what his mind is telling him.*

TH: Listen! You have to listen. Listen actively because you learn by what they say back to you. It's hard sometimes because you are under pressure, but it makes life easier in the long run.

DS: *Because he feels you paid attention to him, he'll respect you.*

TH: I get a lot of compliments from actors. It's a hard job and I wouldn't want to be an actor walking into an audition.

I learn so much about the characters from adjusting and working with an actor in an audition — and learning from him or her, getting their energy, and feeling it in my body. I think, "Oh, that is an interesting aspect to the character that I hadn't thought about." The audition process is critical for the director.

It's an individual thing with each actor. For instance, take a femme fatale. On one pilot I did, no one seemed to hit the femme fatale. I needed the kind of presence which says you own your body, you own the room, you own everything in there — a Barbara Stanwyck kind of classic cinema energy. Nobody can do it these days. There was a woman in an acting class I saw, we brought her in and she knocked the casting director and me for a loop. We cast her in a big part because she knew how to hit that power. Then we had to work on the colors. We had to bring the humor, the humanity out of her.

DS: *What did you suggest?*

TH: I said, "You have all the power this character needs. Now I need to get the sense that you have some empathy for the persons you are talking to." Or, "Now let's focus on listening, enjoying the person." It's an individual process with each actor and how they communicate. You listen to each person as an individual. The worst thing a director can do in an audition is to stop listening. You have to keep listening.

DS: *Todd, would you like to add a closing statement?*

TH: You know, Delia, I was never able to get into your class when I was at UCLA. So when Steven Spielberg hired me right out of graduate school, I began my professional career with a confidence about how to use the camera to tell a story but felt woefully unprepared to deal with actors. So, I made that my focus. I desperately wanted to be helpful to actors. So I took acting as an actor — doing scene work, putting myself in front of an audience. Putting myself on stage gave me enormous empathy for what actors go through — the incredible vulnerability, the danger of approaching roles that challenge your innate self-perceptions. It takes immense courage!

And I leaned what kind of communication reached me, and what kind missed. I learned to find something positive to say as I began an adjustment: "That was a great moment when you smiled. I loved that reaction to such and such." It's such a vulnerable thing to act that approaching an actor from a positive place makes a world of difference. I try to take responsibility for the performance. I often say, "Okay, this may be totally wrong, but let's try this-or-that adjustment. If it's wrong, we'll learn something." I try to give an actor permission to take a chance. That's what I've tried to carry into all my later work: respect for the courage of the actor. The only thing I never had the courage to do was go in and really audition for a role with somebody who didn't know me. I urge anyone planning to write or direct to act!

The greatest compliment I get now is when an actor says, "You've done a lot of theater directing, haven't you?" I love that! I've never done any theater, and I'm thrilled that I confuse people into thinking I have!

ALEXANDER PAYNE
Director/Writer

Alexander Payne directed and co-wrote *About Schmidt,* a comedy starring Jack Nicholson. He has won numerous awards for his screenplays and directing. His second film, *Election,* won the Writers Guild of America Award for Best Screenplay based on Material Previously Produced or Published; the New York Film Critics award for Best Adapted Screenplay; the Los Angeles Film Critics Award for Best Adapted Screenplay; the Independent Spirit Awards for Best Feature, Best Director, and Best Screenplay; and an Oscar nomination for Best Adapted Screenplay. For his first feature film, *Citizen Ruth,* actress Laura Dern received the Best Actress Award at the Montreal Film Festival.

DS: *How do you select a casting director?*

AP: I met casting director Lisa Beach on *Citizen Ruth* and I liked her a lot because she makes actors feel comfortable. She respects the work and the preparation with which they come to the interview. If they don't feel comfortable, they can't do their best and I lose.

DS: *Do you insist on her having the same perspective on what the script is about?*

AP: The whole creative team I've been fortunate to have assembled all have a similar sense of humor. So, I think when she reads it, Lisa gets it. I have to add, though, that I have two casting directors. I have one here in Los Angeles who helps secure the stars and I have another, John Jackson, in Omaha who casts the smaller, but no less important, parts. He understands the verisimilitude that I am trying to achieve — the sense of genuine reality in the films. In making a film, I want it to be about life and based on life. So John works with me to get that because I like to work with non-actors to mix it up. *Citizen Ruth* opens with Ruth having sex with a very low-life fellow whom we found in a bar. It's a sizable speaking part and the casting assistant, who is a regular at this bar, knew him.

John Jackson is also an actor. He was once onstage at a dinner theater in Omaha and, from the stage, saw this woman in the audience. As soon as the curtain went down he ran out into the audience and grabbed her. She is now a one-take actress. I also put her in *Election* and I will put her in anything else I shoot in Omaha. I have to have her in them because she is so good.

As long as you don't need them to carry a long take or play someone very different from who they are, non-professional actors or non-actors can bring a great sense of reality. Sometimes you see acting in a movie that strikes you as bad acting and, after a moment, you think, "No, no, that's not bad acting. That's just how people really are off stage, in real life." Also, I think it's fun to put stars with real people. I think it makes them both look more real.

During auditions, I visualize the actors with various wigs and costumes. I hear them changing their voice. I am really using my imagination to see them. Often I will say to actors in an audition, "Look. This is unfair to both of us. All I'm asking from you is a pencil sketch of what may be, later, an oil painting. And, we may throw away the sketch. I'm just trying to get a general sense of how you occur in space. I'm just trying to get a general sense of you." I really want to liberate them in that moment, I want them to be liberated later on set. I was thinking how awful it would be to be directed by a really prestigious director whom you fear or who intimidates you. It would be awful to be an actor and be directed by someone who, either because of his stature or energy, closes you off in such a way that you don't risk.

DS: *Conversely, some actors can make it difficult for directors by being very, very resistant and difficult.*

AP: Sometimes you just want to say to difficult actors, "I'm sorry, didn't you become an actor because you wanted to be liked?"

DS: *So many young directors have a strong desire to use non-actors and my advice to them is, "Use at your own risk."*

AP: At your own risk is true. It has backfired on me a couple of times. I've had to make compromises in a film because the actor was good at the audition but choked on the set.

DS: *But back to the audition. The actor enters. Do you let him read the scene first or do you insist on talking to him first?*

AP: I think talking is very destructive. They're coming in. They're thinking. They rehearsed the night before. They woke up that morning thinking about it, looking in the mirror, being very vulnerable, and then they wait. I try to keep waiting to a minimum. If we ever get backed up, I personally go out to the waiting room and apologize because it is just discourteous. By offering themselves to be in the film, they're doing me a service. They come in and I say, "Do you have any questions?" If they say no, I say "Okay. Let's go." A lot of people think they should chat the actors up first to foster a relaxed atmosphere.

After that, I like to throw a direction out. I let them do whatever they came in doing and then, either because I want to see more of what I was thinking about, or because they are doing it too much like I was already thinking about, I like to drop one more idea and see how well it will ripple through the rest of the reading or the take. For a director, it is thrilling to give an actor an idea and see how it alters the entire landscape of the take. If the actor can really carry it through you know you have a good one.

DS: *Do you tape your auditions?*

AP: Yes. I have noticed that sometimes auditions can be voluminous and I am present at so many that I forget. It's nice to watch later and think, "Oh wow, they are really doing something interesting," or "You know what? I thought they were good, but now they are not so good."

DS: *Who reads with them?*

AP: Casting director Lisa Beach will read with them or I will read with them. After one reading in the audition, I sometimes give Lisa, not the actor, the direction.

DS: *For example?*

AP: I'll say, "Be harsh, be soft, try to draw him in more." I hate it when the casting director is too speedy. I'll say, "Slow down. Let him have it." She'll know to say one line, let the actor respond, and wait a beat to see what else is going on. Other times, I read with the actor.

DS: *Why do you do that?*

AP: Then I can control what the actor is being given. I can direct myself and see how he reacts. If I suddenly get more intense, I can see how the actor responds: if he becomes more intense or recoils. It's like getting in the ring and sparring. A lot is dependent on whom they are acting with. You don't act alone. You act with someone. It also allows me to look directly into their eyes. I can look at them and try to pretend I am a camera and see what their eyes give me.

DS: *Do you have rehearsals before production?*

AP: I haven't had that luxury. For my first two films, I rehearsed about five days — and not the whole day. The good thing, though, is that making a movie over 50 days means that you only do three pages a day, at the most. You're doing microsurgery. Each day is a rehearsal for the next. What you might discover one day, during those 12 hours of rehearsal and shooting, are dimensions that you can apply to the next day and to the rest of the shoot. In a way, then, you have 55 days of rehearsal. I do try to structure it so that the easier stuff is up front.

Throwing a scene up on stage like famed directors Sidney Lumet or [Akira} Kurosawa — really making a stage, a room and going through it... I haven't had the luxury to do it and I don't know if I'd be very good at it. I do what I can, however. During the week of rehearsal I might drive the actors to the locations and tell them, "This is the house where you live." It's important for them to have a pre-existing relationship not only with one another but also with their environment. On *Citizen Ruth* we did some improvs in the house. You know, "Take out the garbage." "You don't want to take out the garbage?" "Tell her to take out the garbage." It's the simplest thing in the world.

Some people seem to get really fixated sitting around the table and reading the script.

DS: *For the first time through?*

AP: What do you mean, "first time?"

DS: *When key people are there and actors are meeting each other for the first time, there is a sense of sharing and discovering together, which helps create a bond. They just read it and get a sense of what it sounds like. It is very productive.*

AP: Personally, I haven't gotten much out of it. I guess that part is great. But, in terms of the screenplay, using a reading to change lines and really see if the script is good — I've never gotten anything out of that.

DS: *That's the problem when you're a writer and a director at the same time. Who's going to be the captain of the ship? But it does give you a sense of bringing everything together to see how it all melds, to see what the chemistry of this company is. Sometimes actors will do things that you had never thought of in a scene or a line at the table reading. Those are wonderful surprises. Gifts. It's not a matter of rewriting the line, but getting a different stance on it.*

AP: I love engaging the actors as partners. Sometimes I'll arrive and say, "You know what, I have no idea what to do with this scene. I'm just not sure how to shoot it."

DS: *You don't go in with a storyboard? You and the director of photography just set up the camera?*

AP: Then we play with the scene for a couple of hours and it starts to take shape. I might have some idea, like a final ending shot with someone over another actor's shoulder, and I think, "How can we get there?" But most of the time, because of a low budget and time constraints, I pre-block and say to the actors, "I'm sorry but I'm short on time. Here's the blocking." Another thing I do is go to the set before the actors, before anyone, and act out the scene we will do that day. I act out all the parts for myself, thinking, "Where would I go? What would I do?" That way I have some idea of what the their processes will be. Also, because I've written the scene, I have a strong sense of the characters. Then I bring the actors in.

DS: *What kind of problems have you found on the set with actors? I'm talking about actors losing a connection with the role because they dry up or they keep going blank.*

AP: The only problem that irritates me is when they don't know their dialogue.

DS: *That can be caused by fear and tension.*

AP: Or laziness. One actor really made me suffer. It was our first day working together with no rehearsal and he had a big speech but couldn't get it out. Rather than having it in one take, I had to chop it up and piece it together in editing. I do not benefit by cutting away just because the next word is flubbed. The movie does not benefit. I benefit from cutting away when it's emotionally correct, and I want to be able to do a very long take because it leads to a good movie. Then, everyone benefits.

DS: *Sometimes actors forget dialogue because they are tense. They may just need to relax.*

AP: I've called out, "You know what? Twenty-minute break. Let's all just take a walk." One time this happened with an actress and we just walked around the block and I told her, "We all have trouble, so don't worry about it. You're fine. We can make mistakes. That's why God invented editing."

But I love actors who know their dialogue and can say it word for word, take after take, and respond easily and subtly to direction.

I make comedies but the acting is always for real. On one set I needed an actress to really cry. It was late at night and we were all waiting quietly in this little bedroom at the location. Then we heard this little "tap, tap, tap" on the door, which meant she was ready. She was weeping as if she had gone to a very dark and personal space inside of her.

When I needed one more take, she got a little upset. She was like, "Uh, didn't you get it?" I said, "No, please just try one more." She was drained but by the time we wrapped she was exhilarated. Talk about results!

Thinking of myself as an actor, sometimes if I am given a result it allows me, as the actor, to use my own process. What I'm trying to say is that I don't think giving result direction is always bad. What I might say specifically to the actor may not totally harmonize with what he or she is already doing but it could actually take him somewhere else, somewhere wrong. So, I have to find the right action.

DS: *Right. That's the actor's craft. That's why you hired him.*

AP: As a result of your class, I am somewhat conversant in the actor's process. But often, as a director, you just have to give more result-oriented direction. I tell the actor, "Here's the scene and at this point I need this result." Later, the actor is on his own. How he does that is his craft. He knows the character and what feels right vis-à-vis what he and the character have in common.

DS: *Do you coach from the sidelines?*

AP: Yes. I talk a lot during a take. "Do that again!" "Don't let him get away with that!" It makes it hard for the script supervisor and the editor because I don't cut a lot. When the scene is over I will often say, "Don't cut. Do it again, but start from where you are now." There is a momentum that you get, but when you cut, everybody relaxes and in two minutes the momentum is lost. I like to just keep rolling and keep the momentum up. That's how time is well spent.

One other thing, too, about doing takes: I like to do about one too many. I like to do it when the actor starts to get stale because there might be something more — even if he already has it. I like to be thorough. I'll do the first take just to see what the actor has brought to it. And only then will I say something. You find little veins of gold in a take that you can then encourage the actor to exploit. That means that Take Six might be much more focused and much more refined, because it is based on what came out in Take One or Two. Shaping a performance over five or six takes is like sculpting a work of art.

DS: *What is your normal shooting ratio?*

AP: When I do a shot and performance is involved I do three to six, four to six, and seven every once in a while. Sometimes one.

DS: *What do you do when the actor's impulse seems to belie the logic of the character? Do you embrace it?*

AP: It depends. Federico Fellini had a great quote, "I always begin a film thinking I'm going to direct a film and then I see that the film is directing me." You're only there as the witness to a film giving birth to itself. It's only somewhat in your control. I didn't know it was going to be overcast that day. I didn't know the actor was going to be slow that day. I thought he was going to be fast. I didn't know that scene was funny. I always thought it was serious. Or, I didn't know that scene was serious, I thought it was funny.

DS: *So, do you incorporate these things?*

AP: There's this Zen of controlling, but not controlling. It's like your child. You give birth to this thing and think you are going to mold it. But you can do so only to a certain extent. Your child is its own thing. I wanted him to be a doctor but he wants to be a welder. So, I'm going to push him to be the best possible welder.

DS: *What about dailies? Do you mind if actors watch their dailies?*

AP: It's fine if the actor can take it and isn't going to become too self-conscious or shocked. On a personal level, it's the one time I don't have to say, "Darling, you're wonderful," etc. I want to be able to say to my editor, "That take sucks." It's my only time with my editor. I stroke the actors the whole time I'm on set, but now it's my time. Sometimes, though, if an actor is overacting, it is good to have them go to dailies. You shoot a big close-up and you have him come to dailies.

DS: *You know who you are going to end up being?*

AP: Director Otto Preminger?

DS: *Maybe William Wyler or one of those directors who was really tough with his actors.*

AP: They say Wyler shot 60 to 70 takes without knowing what to tell actors. All he had was an instinct for what was good and what wasn't. Famous actors — Laurence Olivier, Bette Davis, Olivia de Haviland — would say, "What was wrong with that take?" "I don't know. Just do it again." He'd drive them crazy, but more actors won Oscars under Wyler than any other director.

DS: *You know what can happen under those circumstances? The actors become so drained that they finally stop acting and just start being. They are out of their heads and what emerges as a result of their fatigue, depression, and discouragement is true and in the moment. When Reese Witherspoon didn't want to do that last take in which she was crying, was the take any different from the others?*

AP: I think it was because it was a challenge. That was a very specific case because she was crying her eyes out.

DS: *What could have happened was that in becoming more frustrated she gave you that truth. She might have thought, "Damn it," and you might have gotten her tears of anger. Or tears from a sense of failure and frustration. All of this could have come out of the exchange between the two of you. These are the things that happen when actors are drained.*

AP: One joke is that off-camera acting is the best acting. They've already done the scene and now they are right next to the camera feeding lines and they are unbelievably good. They're not acting.

DS: *They're not under pressure to deliver. Now they are free to be.*

AP: I even feel it in myself. The moment you turned on the recorder for this interview it became my job to give you raw material to edit later. I felt a shift in myself, that I was performing for this session that, after time went by, I was able to forget about it and do what I am actually doing now, engaging you as if the recorder weren't here.

When that camera is on them, good film actors become more real. Well, they lie less than they might in real life. They know they can't lie to the camera, because it shows the real them and they share with it like they do with a friend that maybe they don't even have in real life. I don't even think it's an achievement. It's just a thing you have or don't have. For actors and models, it's just a relationship. It's an honest-to-God interactive relationship with the camera.

Kurosawa, very often, shot with three cameras, especially later on in his career. He believed that when the actors didn't know which camera was on, they acted more naturally.

DS: *In* Election, *Reese was so intense that it was one notch above what we would ordinarily expect, yet so rooted in reality, and that's what made it funny.*

AP: My work was, both in directing and editing, to keep her from teetering into caricature. I want type sometimes, but not caricature. My comments to her between takes were to keep it pumped up without falling into caricature.

DS: *She ended up being mean because she was so determined. That determination was other-worldly, but it never felt as if she was commenting on the character. It was a woman who was bigger than life with as much sincerity as she could possible have. You never doubted her ambition for one minute. Having Matthew Broderick laid back in the beginning was such an incredible contrast. It was perfect.*

AP: It was a lot of luck too.

DS: *It was casting.*

AP: *Election* was Chris Klein's first film (he played Reese Witherspoon's rival for class president). He's lucky. He got a career off that. But I'm lucky, because I found the perfect guy.

DS: *I think you were instinctively looking for the right person, and that is more than luck. It's perseverance and not giving up or compromising your vision. That's not luck.*

AP: Lisa Beach showed it to someone who was high up in casting at Paramount and her comment was, "Oh, he doesn't pop. He doesn't come off the screen. You shouldn't cast him." But he did, didn't he?

DS: *Our discussion here has underscored the importance of trusting your instincts. You could have had your pick of actors for that part but you didn't just settle. The same thing applies to your direction. You never compromised and remained true to your vision of the subject and its tone and that's why it worked.*

MARK RYDELL
Director/Actor/Producer

Mark Rydell is an Academy Award nominated director, a classically trained actor, and known as an "actor's director." Nine of Mark Rydell's twelve feature films earned twenty-six Academy Award nominations and won five Oscars, including Best Performance by Katherine Hepburn and Henry Fonda in *On Golden Pond*. He directed Bette Midler, Sissy Spacek, and Marsha Mason whom the Academy nominated for Outstanding Performances in a leading and or a supporting role. His films have received 30 Golden Globe nominations, including a Best Actor nomination for James Franco, and Golden Globe awards for Best Actress for Marsha Mason and Bette Midler.

His TV film *James Dean* earned eleven Emmy nominations and won the Best Actor award for James Franco in his role as James Dean. In 1973, his company's film *Scarecrow* won the Cannes Film Festival's top honor: the Palm D'Or. Rydell continues to direct, produce, and act and appeared in a leading role in Woody Allen's film, *Hollywood Ending*.

MR: I find very few directors know or understand the process of acting, and those that do have a more compassionate view of how to work with actors. Directing is often like gardening. You try to create an atmosphere in which things can grow. You hope that by planting seeds, nurturing them, and, sometimes, giving physical touches, they can grow and reach fruition.

DS: *When did you decide to go into directing?*

MR: When I was a musician, I wanted to be a conductor. I left music because I discovered I had started too late to reach the goals that I wanted. At New York University, I became friends with a woman who felt I should be an actor and sent me to Sandy Meisner of the Neighborhood Playhouse. He gave me a scholarship to study with him and that was the beginning of the rest of my real creative life. I knew from the beginning that I wanted to direct. I like gathering the right people together and setting the tone for everybody. A director is a man with a high-powered rifle, shooting for a bull's-eye, and only one chance to get it. In order to direct, you have to love people and love the objective that you're going for — to share it with people, to nurture them, and get them on your team with everybody going in the same direction. I enjoy that work.

DS: *What was the first thing you directed?*

MR: The first thing I directed was at the Actors Studio. It was a one-act play about two primitive blacks on a South Carolina dock, selling clams to passing motorboats. They are describing the agony and horror of their friend's lynching. It was an incredible experience. I remember the first words Lee Strasberg said: " We have watched the birth of a director today." Molly and Elia

Kazan were also there. It was a fabulous moment for me, and I never looked back.

DS: *What was your theater training?*

MR: All my training was with Sanford Meisner, Bobby Lewis, Harold Clurman, Elia Kazan, and Lee Strasberg. They were my teachers.

DS: *What was the first film or television show you directed?*

MR: Sydney Pollack, a close friend, recommended me for an assistant position on the *Ben Casey* TV show in Los Angeles. I took to it very quickly and a couple of months later, they gave me a script to direct. I prepared and worked hard. I believe in training.

DS: *Is the lack of proper preparation and training on the director's part a problem in today's industry?*

MR: In fact, I think that respect for craft and training has diminished over the years. You have a lot of people, for example, directing films who are from MTV or commercials and who know nothing about the human experience. They have a lot of photographic dazzle, but I think art in the industry has suffered. I have a feeling that we are watching the disintegration of our culture.

DS: *What do you feel is your greatest responsibility to an actor?*

MR: To protect them.

DS: *From?*

MR: If they're really talented and really good, they expose themselves and become vulnerable to circumstances and relationships. They let things affect them and they become easily injured. I think it's the director's responsibility to create an atmosphere where actors can do the kind of work they want without being worried that people will judge them harshly instead of encouraging them and looking for the best in them. That's the automatic responsibility of the director.

DS: *As a film director, what do you consider the single most important element besides the story?*

MR: Sandy Meisner used to say that the defining characteristic of excellence in art is the artist's sense of emotional rhythm. Someone who can say, "Now this happens" and "There's the climax," and "That's where that goes." Those are talents I don't think you can teach.
DS: *What do you look for when you interview casting directors?*

MR: I want a partner. I want to make sure they love the theater, love acting, and love actors. Many casting directors don't love actors and are impatient with them. I have no tolerance for that. I worship actors and I want to find a casting director who appreciates the goals of acting, maybe understands acting themselves. I spend a lot of time talking about the characters with the casting director. I want them to understand what I'm looking for. How do you cast? You look at a piece of material and you ask, "What is the most demanding moment in this material for the actor?" Then you look for an actor who has the equipment to handle that most demanding moment.

DS: *When you say, "demanding," are you talking about emotional range?*

MR: Let's say an actor has a scene like Brando at the coffin in *Last Tango in Paris*. On the surface of things, you might say I need an actor who can make love to a girl, but the really deep moment in that material is in the scene where he has to grieve over his wife's coffin. Well then, you want an actor who has that equipment and can handle it. The rest will fall into line.

DS: *So, your final choice always rests with the emotional courage of the actor, his talents, his willingness to go into all kinds of waters. It's never the type.*

MR: Never. Never. What I describe is the determining factor. Types can be adjusted. You know a writer will write a lengthy description of a character that is usually superficial, that has to do with the way he walks, his eyes, the type of glasses he wears, or is slightly fat. All of that is useless. What we want to know is who is the character and how do you find character? Character is determined by how a person responds under pressure. So you look for the moments in the material where the character, or the actor, is under pressure and see how the actor responds. What do they do in these circumstances? Then you find somebody who's sensitive to those values. That's casting. Casting never has to do with type, except in a small way. A very small way where you need someone to come in, make a quick impression, and leave. Sometimes you need a physical type, such as a gorgeous girl. She enters a room, everybody looks up, and then she leaves. There are no big acting requirements for that. She has to be beautiful and have a sense of herself. Those are the exceptions — these small roles that you can identify immediately.

DS: *What qualities do you look for in a casting director?*

MR: How talented they are. Are they perceptive? Do they know what's good and what isn't? I try to get casting directors who were actors. If I see a casting director pick up a script, bury his face in the script, and send a cue line to an actor during a reading, I correct the casting director, not the actor. Generally, I don't like to read actors because there are actors who know how to read very well but can't act to save their lives. Acting is the creation of behavior. Reading is another talent entirely. I know many actors who are brilliant readers who can't act, and then there's the opposite, actors who are brilliant actors but cannot read. So, I always hire an actor to read with the actors. I hired Barry Primus for *James Dean*. He is a giver and that mobilizes an actor's talent. Then you can see who they really are and whether you can use them or not. News broadcasters know how to read the news. They read well, confidently, with a kind of intelligence, but are rarely involved. You're hungry for Walter Cronkite to cry, as he did when John F. Kennedy was assassinated. You're hungry for something humanizing. There are all kinds of handsome and meticulous star readers, but you want feelings and interpretations — someone saying, "My God what happened today was unbelievable." That's what you want. Anyway, I only read actors if I'm forced into it. I like to have a conversation with my actors, find out who they are, who their parents are, where they grew up, where they went to school. "Do you have a sister? What is she like?" And all of a sudden people stop all the anxiety, because you're talking to them about stuff they can answer better than anybody else. "What's your mother like?" And suddenly they start to reveal themselves, which is what you're trying to find out. I have conversations with them, walk them around the block, and have a cup of coffee to learn who they are. Then I know what equipment I have to work with. Actors come into auditions automatically anxious because they're being judged. Sometimes they come in trying to be the character, which I don't like. They need to bring themselves. That's who I have to work with. It's who they are. The character may be far away from you, but I believe that most actors can play most characters. What you do is take certain elements of your personality, exaggerate some of them, and repress others. Suddenly you have a character. That's coming from you. It's not anything the writer wrote. It's you.

DS: *When you're auditioning then, do you sometimes direct them?*

MR: Yes, I do. Sometimes I'll suggest a way of going into the scene. "What do you think of this idea," I'll say, and they answer, "Well, supposing so-and-so and so-and-so." I see them light up, which is what I'm trying to see. Are they going to be responsive to me? Are they listening? Are they terrified? Are they closed off? Are they willing to embrace new ideas? Are they elastic? I'll suggest something new which excites them and suddenly I'm having fun with the actor and he is having fun with me. When he leaves I hope he's thinking, " God, I wish every director was like him." I rarely cast wrong, which comes from understanding actors, loving them, and understanding they're under tremendous pressure when they walk into the room to meet you for a part. Chances are, they're starving and they need the job so desperately. Everything is involved, which interferes with their ability to be who they are. The first thing you do is relax them.

DS: *Do you ever tape some of these auditions?*

MR: Casting directors do. I don't look at them. I let them say, "Here's ten people I think I like," and I say let's bring them in.

DS: *What about pairing people up when you are considering actors for two roles who will have scenes together?*

MR: It makes sense to do that. Although I tell you, I don't read very often. But if I do read, chances are I'll pair somebody up with someone else which gives them the opportunity to act with somebody, instead of against somebody who's holding a script and not looking at them. There is a scene in *James Dean* where Jimmy goes to read for Billy Rose, the theater producer. Jimmy DeStefano played the stage manager, and I said "Play it like all those shitty stage managers who read the cue lines, so when Jimmy Dean comes back to re-read the scene, he hands the stage manager a pretend plate of food. Jimmy DeStefano, as the stage manager, was completely thrown by somebody interrelating with him. This dramatized the agony of what it is to read for a Broadway play.

DS: *Unfortunately, most directors, particularly coming out of film school, haven't a clue.*

MR: It's insane for anybody to choose the responsibility of being a director and not understand acting. It is like somebody deciding to be a conductor and not understanding music, not understanding what a musician does. A conductor should know the range of every instrument, how difficult it is to play a flute, what the difference is between a flute and a piccolo, and what's its range.

DS: *Do you like to have pre-production rehearsals?*

MR: I always have them.

DS: *How long for a feature?*

MR: Two weeks at least, and we almost never get up from the table, because you don't want people up on their feet before they know what it's about — before they start connecting. I encourage that kind of connecting around the table, nurturing relationships into existence. Then, usually by the second week of rehearsal, I take them to the place that we're going to shoot. So they see, "Ah, this is the street," or "This is where I walk down those stairs," and they embrace what the experience is.

DS: *Don't you find from an economic point that it saves money and time?*

MR: It does, but you have to convince the studio of that. I insist on it, and it's always a money saver, but they don't see that. They say, "Oh my God, you want the actors for two weeks? I have to pay salaries, rehearsal salaries." Generally speaking, they don't want to do that.

DS: *Moving on to the set. Do you block the camera for the actors or do you block the actors for the camera?*

MR: The first thing I do is bring the actors to where they can move wherever they want. I'm just sort of standing around. Then an actor may turn to me and say, "That window would be great. Could he move toward the window?" And I'll say, "Go get some air, lift up that shade," and he goes to the window, which becomes an opportunity to light them well, but it's ostensibly from the actor's point of view. In the meantime, because of my experience as a visualist, I know where I'm trying to get them or how I can move them. But I rarely make them move to a place without giving them a reason. You know, "Go raise the shade a little bit. The air is great out there, isn't it?" Now I've got them by the window, the light can come in, and I can get something beautiful. So you work with them both.

DS: *Many directors just stage for the shot.*

MR: Listen, I just finished a Woody Allen movie called *Hollywood Ending*. One day, we had a four-and-a-half page scene to shoot — just the two of us in an apartment. He's in one spot sitting in his chair and I have to move the chair because he's not seeing well and I have a lot of activities to do, a lot of things to accomplish: go to the kitchen, get sandwiches, get stuff from the refrigerator, while the dialogue is going on and the camera is panning back and forth. I get a couple of beers and bring them over to the table. I'm all over the place right? No rehearsal, none. "Ok, let's roll," said Woody and I said, "Holy shit." Suddenly, it was like the theater. If you fuck up, you fuck up! Of course, I'm experienced and I enjoyed it. It was a challenge, but there was no rehearsal. I had to trust my instincts. I hope it worked out well, but it was the opposite of the way I love to work. Allen said to me, "You know, I'm not a good director, but I'm a great caster and a good writer." He knows how to write, he knows how to cast, he puts people in a room and then lets them go.

DS: *Fortunately, he has a good cinematographer.*

MR: He has somebody who is watching what he does. I'm telling you, we did four and a half pages in two takes and it was over. No coverage. None. Not even a close up so we can cut from one master to the other. I said, "Woody, supposing the first part of this master is good and the second part of the other master is good. If you have close-ups then you can go to a close-up and then cut to the other master. 'Nah, it's too much trouble,'" he said. He likes to get what he gets.

DS: *When you work on a script, do you have a conscious sense of what you're trying to say? In other words, do you articulate a theme for yourself?*

MR: I think it's critical. Sometimes you work on a script as if you're going through the rubble, hoping to find something. Maybe something will be there if you dig deeper. When you analyze material, it takes time to understand what it's really about. Very often I find that writers do not know what they have written. They are instinctive. They're wonderful, but they can't articulate everything. That's your job as a director, to distill the essence of the material so that you can handle it in a paragraph, a statement, or a sentence. Once you know what the material is about, it will tell you what to cut, what's not relevant, or what doesn't agitate from the essence of the material. But, it takes a long time to get to that. Sometimes it takes me months and months.

DS: *Do you share that with the actors ever?*

MR: Yes, it's not necessary to keep secrets from the actors unless it interferes with their performance. You have to tell different actors different things — whatever it takes to mobilize their talent. There is a famous story about the gravedigger scene in *Hamlet*. A famous actor of the time had played it in many productions. When asked at a dinner party what *Hamlet* is about, he said, "Well, there's this gravedigger." From his point of view, *Hamlet* was about the gravedigger and that is correct for the actor. He needs to know about digging up the skulls and such, from his point of view. The director, unfortunately, has to know the whole shebang. How can you guide everyone towards the common goal if you don't know who they are? And, I find every actor is different. Some actors are stimulated by understanding what the overall thematic ideas are. If they're stimulated by it, give it to them. If they're inhibited by it, keep it from them because the objective is to get them to really live under these imaginary circumstances. That is what acting is about.

DS: *When you have an actor who becomes emotionally blocked or dries up, how do you turn them back on?*

MR: It's a complicated problem. You have to find out what the block is. It takes almost analytic perceptions to draw out of the actor what the problem is. There was an actor that I had in a picture once who told me from the beginning that he didn't like a certain scene. "Something is wrong with that scene," he told me. "Well, we'll work on it," I said. We're shooting, everything is fine, and then we get to this scene which is scheduled for 8 o'clock the following morning. This actor, who was extremely responsible and punctual, showed up at 11:30, bearded and red eyed. I said, "What's going on? You know we're all sitting here waiting." He said, "Something is wrong with the scene. I can't do this scene. I don't know why, but I can't do it." So, I took him for a walk. It was my job at that moment to find out. I shouldn't have waited until the day of the scene. I should have talked to him about it before. The scene was about him claiming a child as his own and he couldn't play it for several deep reasons that emerged during our conversation. "Well, that's why you're having a problem with the scene," I said and his eyes lit up. He was able to do the scene because the block was gone. Unconsciously, he was resisting claiming the child in the scene because of his own personal experience.

DS: *What about the ones who dry up emotionally?*

MR: Sometimes you can't do anything. I remember a screen test where someone played a very emotional scene and after she did it twice, she couldn't get any of the feelings back and there was no time to walk her around the block, so to speak. When an actor dries up it's a problem. It's usually because they have some resistance. You have to fish around to find the problem in order to turn the motor on again.

DS: *But sometimes the drying up happens because you have to repeat a scene over and over again.*

MR: I don't do that. For example, I made a picture called *The Reivers* with Steve McQueen and Rupert Cross, who was a very well trained actor who would be good on the second take, better on the third, and really good by the fifth take. By the ninth he was sensational, but he was playing opposite Steve McQueen, who only had two takes in him. Steve McQueen was a very intuitive actor. He didn't want to study his lines. He just kind of knew them and he didn't want to walk around the set. I was faced with a problem, because they were playing scenes together. If I waited until the ninth take, by the second take Steve would be finished or bored while Rupert would get better and better. I thought, "I can't go through the whole film like this." I solved it by acting the first eight takes with Rupert myself and when Rupert was ready, I brought in Steve. You have to do what you have to do. Steve died six months after the picture was released. Rupert Cross was later nominated for an Academy Award for his performance in that picture.

DS: *Before shooting, some actors take time to prepare on their own. Others may not, and yet a preparation is probably called for. What do you do when your actors don't do it on their own?*

MR: Sometimes actors don't know how to prepare, so I prepare them by talking with them. Get them stoked. I'll talk about the circumstance of the scene and nurture them into the place I want them to be.

DS: *Like a coach on the sidelines?*

MR: Exactly. First of all, you have to have their confidence, and you will once they feel you know what you're doing. I did that with Sissy Spacek one time in *The River.* Sissy is a brilliant actress, but she would get to a moment where she would say "I can't cope," and I would look into her eyes, talk about the moment, and in a minute she was crying and went into the scene. In *On Golden Pond,* Katherine Hepburn had a scene where Henry Fonda comes back from being lost in the woods and confesses to her on the porch how castrated he felt in a sense, because he couldn't find his way back. It was a helpless moment. She comes in, sits down, and tells him not to worry, that, "we're going to get on the horse and we're going to go, go, go... and we'll do it." She was doing it very big and broad. I said, "Put it in his ear, plant the seed, but do it very, very quietly." She was so thrilled with that piece of direction that she went right over to him and whispered to him. It was a highlight moment in the picture. Because she was all over the place and doing it very broadly, she needed a vision she could understand, which was "put it in his ear." You do what's necessary.

DS: *Many actors resist pre-production rehearsals. What is your opinion about that?*

MR: They have to rehearse with me. If they want a job, they have to rehearse.

DS: *I'm talking about big names.*

MR: Well, you try. You do your best. As for rehearsing, there are actors who don't know how to rehearse. Or, they are afraid they won't be spontaneous if they rehearse. When I'm directing, I try to train actors to rehearse.

I once got into a tremendous argument with Richard Chamberlain because he wouldn't come out to rehearse a scene. I was a beginner, directing my second or third TV show, and had everyone out there. I called for him and the assistant director said, "Richard doesn't want to rehearse." I said, "Get him out here." In front of the whole crew, I told him, "The other actor needs you, his acting depends on you. You must rehearse." And he said, " I didn't realize." By the way, I never did the show again.

DS: *Did he rehearse?*

MR: He rehearsed because I pushed him into it. I've made many stupid moves in my life, and that was one of them.

DS: *But ultimately, you were right.*

MR: I was right, but sometimes right doesn't get you anywhere. I was too young and I didn't realize who was the real boss. I thought I was the boss.

DS: *Well, there goes that illusion. Do you ever coach your actors from the sidelines, while the camera is going?*

MR: Sometimes. For example, I've shot a trial scene and now I need to shoot the judge's close ups. But because it involves another actor who is not there, I'll have to talk him through it. I try not to. I do my best to avoid that because not every actor wants to work that way.

DS: *I've been coaching Geena Davis on her latest project. She told me once about shooting a close-up. The other actor was off-camera, of course, and he started saying things to her that were not in the script and absolutely unexpected and it blew her away. As a result, she had all sorts of spontaneous responses and said it was one of the best close-ups she ever had.*

MR: Yes, you do that. There's a scene in *James Dean* where Kazan says to Jimmy during Raymond Massey's close-up, "Curse. Curse. He hates that." That, of course, angered Massey. This spontaneous response fed right into the conflict between the father and son.

DS: *What do you find to be common problems for actors on a set?*

MR: Time. Movies are so expensive. There are so many people being paid that it can cost $100,000 a day. Very rarely do people who are involved behind the camera recognize that actors are a sensitive instrument and need time. They have no patience, which is often the problem.

DS: *Do you use improvisations in rehearsals and on the set?*

MR: I do. I do it more in rehearsals than on the set though.

DS: *And you always have specific things that you're working towards?*

MR: I find general improvisations useless. You need to recognize, for example, that you may need a certain intimacy between two people having a conversation and work for that. One time, I sat on the floor with a couple of actors and told them to tell each other their most private secrets and then left the room. When I returned they were into a really intimate connection, which was what I wanted. Sometimes people will sing together, share a song, whatever it is that will bring them together.

DS: *What about when you have actors who dislike each other intensely, yet their characters are supposed to be in love?*

MR: I've never had that situation because I cast people who like each other. But, if the chemistry doesn't work — even between brilliant actors — it's not going to be helpful.

DS: *Do you discourage your actors from watching dailies?*

MR: I find that some actors are perfectly okay with dailies. There are others, though, whom you allow to see dailies and suddenly the next day, they walk in and their chin is way up and I say, "What the hell is going on?" and they answer, "Well, when my face is down . . . " So, you can't let a person like that go to dailies. Generally speaking, I don't invite the actors to dailies, and I explain to them "You have trust my taste and I don't want you to be self-conscious." If an actor says to me, "I insist on going," I let him or her go once or twice. Then the actor sees he can trust my judgment.

DS: *When you moderate at the Actors Studio, you emphasize the playing of objectives and behavior. Do you use those terms on the set?*

MR: No. I rarely ask, "What is your objective?" I'll say, "What do you want? What are you trying for?" I try not to make it literal. I'll say, "See if you can get him excited. Flirt with him."

DS: *What do you think the difference is between film acting and theater acting?*

MR: Movie acting has to be much more real than stage acting. When a movie camera looks at you and you're on a forty-foot screen, you can see fragments of loss of concentration. In the theater, you can't see that. In the theater you know what you're doing in each scene. You have the beats laid out and you can do those things whether you feel lousy, your mother died, or you just got a great new job. If you really do those things, the performance will work. Movies demand a much deeper reality of the experience. Movies won't tolerate exaggeration.

DS: *In terms of performance, is your approach as director different with each actor?*

MR: You have to be sensitive to the needs of every single one of them. You can't set rules because each one relates differently. It's part of your job to understand with whom you are working and to give them what they need. Everybody has a different instrument, different sensibilities, different ways of approaching things — even if they're all trained the same way. There are different things that will turn them on; different things they're responsive to. Some people like certain things and don't like others. You have to be selective.

DS: *You really have to be a student of human nature.*

MR: I think so. I think that's a reasonable observation.

DS: *It's not something that can be taught. You either have it or you don't but it can be developed.*

MR: You have to be interested in how people respond, what they're going to do, and how they feel about something.

DS: *Do you have a final comment, for directors in particular?*

MR: Directors often make the mistake of thinking the words are everything. On a number of occasions Elia Kazan has said, "Dialogue is decoration on the skirts of action." What you have to do is find out what you are doing in the scene and many, many directors don't know about that.

DS: *It's so important for directors to understand this.*

MR: Directing is one of the most glorious professions. It's so great to be involved in art. It is, perhaps, the highest matriculation of human evolution and at times like this, when it seems as if the world is tumbling down around us, I find the way to handle it is through art.

DS: *In art, we can make things happen and, hopefully, better.*

MR: That's the nobility of our profession.

BRAD SILBERLING
Director/Writer/Producer

Brad Silberling is a director, writer, and producer of film and television. At the time of this interview, Silberling had just completed *Moonlight Mile* starring Jake Gyllenhaal and Academy Award winners Dustin Hoffman, Susan Sarandon, and Holly Hunter. The picture was released by Buena Vista in September 2002.

Silberling directed the critically acclaimed, box office smash *City of Angels,* starring Meg Ryan and Nicolas Cage, which grossed over $200 million worldwide for Warner Brothers Pictures. He earned a Masters of Fine Arts from the University of California, Los Angeles in 1987.

Silberling's extensive television directing credits include — among others — multiple episodes of Steven Bochco's *NYPD Blue, L.A. Law, Civil Wars,* as well as *Brooklyn Bridge,* and the pilot for *Judging Amy.*

He directed an episode of *Brooklyn Bridge,* which caught the eye of producer Steven Spielberg. The two forged a bond which resulted in his backing Brad on his first feature, *Casper,* which grossed more than $300 million worldwide. In addition to capturing Spielberg's attention, the *Brooklyn Bridge* episode garnered Brad and writer John Masius the 1992 Humanitus Award for Dramatic Series Television.

DS: *How important is it to match emotional and/or business continuity?*

BS: What I value is an emotional life within myself and what I can impart to others through the business of making movies and directing. So, I think emotional and business continuity is important. To enjoy my professional life, they have to be tied. If I don't have a handle on the emotional life of a story I'm going to shoot, I'm lost.

DS: *In other words, you have nothing to say if it's not coming out of your heart?*

BS: Exactly. I was fortunate enough to have had director Marty Ritt as a teacher while he was a visiting professor at UCLA film school. He chose me as one of the three or four students that he wanted to work with. He chose solely by reading my screenplay. He didn't meet the students first — just read a little pile of thesis screenplays. This was to his own credit and observation because without having met us, he knew the filmmaker within these stories. He said to me, "Where are you in your story? If you can't answer that question — if you don't know where you are in your film — then it's a travesty and you shouldn't be making it." He had a great phrase about talent and "dumb-fucking luck." He said, "Don't get an ego about it. If you've got it, you're blessed. If not, so what. But the real question is: what will you do with your talent? It is a matter of not demeaning it by getting into work that you can't find yourself in."

DS: *How lucky you were to have had him.*

BS: He's still with me today. It's just so typical and so great — the best instructors are the ones who just say, "Well, here's what I know" rather than the ones who say, "I'm going to teach you the world." He always said, "I don't know what I can teach you." But, in the end, there was so much there.

DS: *Working with actors is intense. Do you encourage your actors to take preparation time to get into the role before you start a scene?*

BS: What I try to gauge, from my first meeting with every actor, is a process. Where have they come from in their lives? Training? How have they evolved? And, in their varying previous outings, what has worked and not worked for them? Of course, the interesting thing is that you always get different instruments. On *City of Angels,* the most intuitive, non-schooled, non-process-oriented actor was Nick Cage. Meg Ryan, who is quite the opposite, is a smart girl and has a much more intellectual process than a specific craft process of emotional preparation. At times, I would encourage her to do something I thought she would be less comfortable with. We would be very specific, track the journey of the scene, and track beats. In those instances, Nick's desire was usually not to participate in a discussion like that because he was afraid he would get into his head.

DS: *That's a legitimate fear.*

BS: I love to find out — as fast as possible — what the actor's processes are in order to establish a language we can use to work with. And, you might have varying ones.

DS: *Nick Cage is very intuitive and he learned to act on the screen. If you were to use certain terminology with him like, "What is your objective?" would he resist that or would he go with it?*

BS: The good thing about Nick was that you could really talk about the emotional journey of the character in the entirety of the film, as well as the emotional journey within a scene. Beyond that, in terms of getting technical moment-to-moment objectives that shift within the scene, that's when you would find him checking out. He would respond more to one big, beautiful objective for the scene, which is: "just love her. Find a way that, at every moment, even though she can't see you, she is feeling your absolute and unconditional love so she will go to bed happy." He's a romantic figure as a person, so it actually cracked him open.

DS: *Then he would find his own beats.*

BS: Exactly. And he might say, "Wow, I don't know what just happened." But that's when I knew he was responding to what was coming at him.

DS: *Know where those beats are. Know what the potential actions are. If the actor is really stimulated, he will find his own way and be liberated from the plan.*

BS: From the homework. Exactly.

DS: *If actors understand the emotional relationships and what the arc is, that will feed their instrument.*

BS: In many cases, that discussion starts early for me. If I'm shooting on a Tuesday afternoon with a particular actor, we meet between shots and I'll, in a casual way, introduce a discussion about tomorrow morning's scene. What we're really talking about are those objectives. "What is his attack in this scene? Isn't it great that he gets to come in through the backdoor so that she doesn't see it coming?" You start to plant the seeds, as every good director wants to do. Start to plant the seeds and get the discussion going so that, come morning, you're not suddenly walking in and people with makeup bibs on are saying, "Where are we?" Instead, it's, "Oh, we've been looking forward to this."

DS: *Do you give your actors a few minutes to make sure they are not distracted before a scene or work with them before the scene starts if they can't get there (emotionally) on their own?*

BS: Yes. Again, depending on who the actors are, I will find ways. I like to create a certain atmosphere. I don't love a noisy set, but I'm very affected by music and I'll use it at times if the actor is comfortable with it or it helps them in a scene without dialogue. If it encourages an emotional journey. If it doesn't supplant it, but actually elicits it, then I love to do that.

DS: *Actors are always burdened with the technical problems on the set: constant repetition, takes from different angles, a partner who can't remember his lines. That will impact the emotional and business continuity — particularly business such as, "Pick up that cup of coffee on that word." How do you deal with that? How important do you feel business continuity is?*

BS: I try to free everybody up as much as possible in terms of not coming in already committed to my homework. Boy, in television you see many directors — because of the time constraints — walk in and say, "Okay, you're crossing stage on that line. You're grabbing the cup here." That's why they're called traffic cops and the actors become marionettes. That's when the actors say, "Sure, it's show number 22. I'm tired. Tell me what to do." But then, you'll get a non-connected performance. I always come in with my homework done but I try to reduce it to what is the emotional story I want to tell in this scene. And though I have thoughts as to how this can be brought to life with business, I don't impose it if the actor, thankfully, discovers something better.

DS: *When do you notice that he may have come up with something new?*

BS: Oh, from the first time we discuss the script. I'll kick everyone off the set and build this sort of sacred time. Usually, we'll all just sit on our butts and just throw the words around without commitment to make sure that everyone feels like, "Okay, we got that." I might supply the barest technical direction such as, "You're going to be coming through this door." Then, the first time we run the scene on its feet, something may happen that is smarter and more intuitive than anything I could have said. I start to encourage and say, "Whether it was conscious or not, that was a beautiful, evasive move."

DS: *You're really being in your actor's skin, then giving back.*

BS: When I start to rehearse, I try to see what's going on and keep things loose from take to take. You always have repetition, though, and keeping it fresh is a whole other challenge.

DS: *You know every instrument gets numb quickly and deadens to stimulus pretty easily. What do you do when you have actors who are starting to dry up?*

BS: I find that the best help is the scene partner. I tend to pull the scene partner aside and say, "I need your help. Here is what I think he/she will probably be helped by. Just bring them out." This means going off-text, off-book, and improvising within the lines of the scene. This doesn't guarantee the actors won't be thrown, but a switch may be thrown that brings them to life.

DS: *What happens to your continuity?*

BS: I learned a great deal about emotional continuity from director Steven Spielberg. We talked about when an audience is with you because you have created emotional continuity. Picture continuity may then go out the window but nobody will notice. You can ask them later if they saw that mismatch. They say, "What?" Because you've created an emotional through-line, everyone is with you and it gives you confidence.

DS: *What do you do with actors who are really emotionally blocked?*

BS: In the extreme cases, I'll find something else to shoot. I might even come back to it the next morning. That's an extreme example of somebody who is really blocked.

DS: *Of course, they could come back just as blocked. Actors become terrified when that happens, and it only creates more inner tension.*

BS: If it happens again after having the scene partner try to help, I would give ourselves a little bit of time and space to talk about preparation and what else might be of help.

DS: *Can you give me an example?*

BS: Sure. We did a scene in *City of Angels,* which was really tricky because, even though it had a very fantastical premise, it had to feel so grounded that it would be like witnessing a relationship about to fall apart in divorce. It was a betrayal scene. That was what was so interesting about it. You had to forget the fantastical element and really commit to the betrayal: the relationship betrayal. I tried, of course, to be the grand captain saying to the others, "If we just commit to our choices, we shouldn't have to worry about the fact that we could all end up looking like we've got egg on our face." Meg, in particular, knew that it was a really hard scene to play credibly and it was clear there was a level of connection that wasn't happening. We took time out and the discussion was, "I know you have a full life now. You have a marriage of so many years. You have a child. You are a very smart woman. You have to access something important that is going to fit the story needs for yourself." In her case, she was fortunate because she was able to reach something. A switch was thrown on. But, prior to that rehearsal process, there was no truth there.

DS: *By bringing her back to her personal life, you encouraged her to make a link between her own life and the possibility of betrayal.*

BS: On all levels. It was the literal sense memory of the moment that had obviously transpired. She built it herself.

DS: *And it worked.*

BS: In that case it worked really nicely. I think blockage becomes like a record skipping and it's finding a way to take that pressure off. Sometimes, it is literally just taking a moment to let everyone relax. If suddenly somebody is not emotionally connected and they're stuck in a rut, I love to say, "Okay, let's just sit here alone." Everyone's off the set. Again, we get off the text. "Let's just sit and improvise. Let's make sure you know exactly what your objective is here and how you are adjusting your attack. Let's just explore this moment together. You fill in the words. You write it."

DS: *Have you ever tried to have the actor break down emotionally? Sometimes tears, anger, vocalizing, and physical movement helps actors get back in touch with what they are holding back. Have you ever tried that?*

BS: That's interesting. No. That's very smart though. It's a beautiful purge.

DS: *The actor opens up and trusts himself again and reconnects to himself. One can have them hit a couch, scream, or run around and jump. Just making sounds and being very physical helps blast through that wall.*

BS: It makes great sense. That's the hardest thing to do, particularly on film sets. It's not so private. There are 150 people in your face and everyone's looking at their watches.

DS: *What is your least favorite type of actor?*

BS: God, my least favorite: I think there's a vanity that goes hand in hand with not listening. It simply comes to those who, out of insecurity, come into a work situation and don't have the capacity to be themselves, to open their eyes, listen, and join the rhythm of the room. Some actors come in and feel as if they're just here to drop a few pearls. I think it is vanity and insecurity tightly wound together. I've had the most interesting difficulties with actors who are so self-loathing that they take everyone hostage because they are so critical of themselves. They're watching themselves perform and critiquing themselves at the same time so that they are not in the scene; not open to what's coming to them. They are also selfish because they are not there as a scene partner.

DS: *They're not giving anything.*

BS: Correct. In television, I've run into certain male actors who were difficult. It's classic: men who had problems with their dads. You can see it coming. I ran into not a few of these guys but several. They were self-loathing people who, unfortunately, were just not going to be good collaborators.

DS: *What did you do to break them out of it?*

BS: Sadly, what would bring them out is reaching a level and a pitch in our interaction that usually involved yelling and screaming. I think that environment was recognizable to them so that then they could get into it. The only way they could feel engaged is by having somebody get in their face and be a bully. It's the bully mentality. In the end, you have to bark back at a bully so that they'll finally listen. I'm a very easy-going person but when you recognize it you think, "God, this is exhausting but here we go again." That's what would happen. I would end up having to yell at an actor to stay put and listen because it's the other actor's coverage, "Godammit, the camera is rolling. This is not your moment. Fucking sit and listen." That would do it. Finally, he'd be there. I had that a lot in television and I don't know why. There are just a lot of interesting and bitter people who come into the game.

DS: *Do you think these actors are very talented, intuitively?*

BS: What I find is that a number of them are, but they have a very specific and narrow band that they feel safe with.

DS: *Do you believe that narrow band is what made them successful and so now they're afraid to let go?*

BS: That's correct.

DS: *They're afraid to do what they originally hoped to do: be creative.*

BS: I think you're right. I think they've been rewarded for a given stripe they have. And that's exactly it. They're just going to work that thing. Those are the most frustrating, because they're heartbreaking. You see that the root of it is a lot of misery.

DS: *They're trapped as regulars on a series.*

BS: Lead regulars. On top of that, they're carrying a sense of obligation to their role, like, "I'm supposed to act like this." They have their own fixed personal character concepts.

DS: *What type of actor is your favorite?*

BS: The best ones in television and in movies are hungry to play. They're hungry for someone to come in whom they can have confidence in so that they can just let go. I think it's chemical, emotional, and intellectual. You're like little puppies at the dog park. Especially in television, which was great training; it was like being a substitute teacher in their classroom.

DS: *That's a good analogy.*

BS: I would just make it a point to introduce myself and spend a little time with the actors without distracting them from the work at hand so we could find a common language and a certain level of personal comfort. Through that, we could engage in conversation about the work that was coming up in that script. One nice thing that happens is that they might know some of your work and you get to talk about that. So then there's a certain confidence level that's yours to either reinforce or blow. I started to do movies, and on a couple of occasions, have gone back to do a television program. At that point, I had a little bit of a pedigree.

DS: *When you come in as a new director on a long-running show, do the actors resist you? If you talk to them about the role or the emotional arc of a scene and they realize you care about their performances, do they begin to trust you?*

BS: Yes. In reality, these actors know their characters better than you do and the best way to establish contact is to talk intelligently about the story that you're embarking on. Does it relate to each character? They will impart to you what they know about their characters. So, you're not walking in presumptuously saying, "Here's what your character is. Let me tell you." Instead you're saying, "I'm very excited about harnessing that aspect of your character in a story you haven't done yet." Actors are amongst the best storytellers you get to work with. So, to get to engage their story skills inevitably means you will discuss the acting process.

DS: *After directing a feature and then going back to television, what kind of homework did you do to prepare?*

BS: It's funny, after my last movie there were two cases. One involved a friend of mine who created the show. They had shot the pilot and asked me to do their first episode. That was exciting. It was a pilot that was shot and I got to look at the pilot and what was created. I was able to see the universe they created. What's so nice about it is that when you have really smart and lively producers who are excited about continuing to discover their new world. So, my preparation consisted of having an emotional response to the pilot. "Okay, here's what they succeeded in creating. Let me run with that. Here's how I respond." A friend of mine, J.J. Abrams, created the show *Felicity* and was also executive producer. I went in and said, "Here's what I sensed in your pilot and here's what I'd like to do" — whether it would be a new direction for a new character, or pictorially. Then we talked about it. It was nice because it wasn't a matter of trying to reign myself in.

The other case was the pilot for *Judging Amy.* At that point, I had done two of the first ten *NYPD* episodes. Going back to *NYPD*, I felt as though the cement had hardened quite a bit and it just wasn't fun. I thought, "If I'm spoiled now it's because I want to have a really vital process and I want to feel I can really make a contribution. The environment doesn't allow for that, so I can't put myself back in there because it's going to make me worse. I'm going to suffer for it." So, I've been cautious about it.

DS: *Do you feel it's important to understand the actor's language?*

BS: I think it's vital to know the language. I don't know how I could communicate without it. I would feel like I had my tongue cut off or that I was a bull in a china shop. Ever since I left class I, thankfully, get ceaseless compliments about my ability to communicate with actors. It's a respect, an understanding, and a vernacular. I need it to the point that I would feel quite crippled without it.

DS: *You want the actors to know that you understand their instrument and their life. Then they'll eat out of your hands. They know you're on their side.*

BS: They feel protected.

DS: *Whom do you think is the best actor's director?*

BS: It sort of varies in my mind. Obviously, when Marty Ritt was around . . . well, I can't imagine somebody stronger. I gauge it by courage of performances and people who feel safe enough to go out on that limb. I've never seen him work, but there's Peter Weir. I'm amazed at the courage he gets out of people. Look at Robin Williams in *Dead Poets Society*. It was his first serious role and we could forget the zany part of him. I know from all reports that Sydney Pollack is supposed to be wonderful with actors. He used to be an actor.

DS: *And a very good one.*

BS: He's a fine actor. He's amazing. He's actually been acting more the last couple of years. Actor Billy Bob Thornton, who's directed some films, is another. Billy Bob's an actor, and I think that there's a certain sensitivity and honesty that comes out of that. It's amazing how many of the strongest actor's directors . . .

DS: *Are those who have been actors. Marty Ritt was an actor, too.*

BS: Well, I used to grill him about what he was emotionally responsive to and it was so great. He said, "It was weird, but I was a very tactile actor. So I would arrange little sensory stimuli around the set, like a piece of material that is evocative to me. I would put it behind a chair where I knew, due to staging, I would come to rest." He was a tactile responder.

DS: *Do you find your approaches are different, technically, when you direct actors for film or for single-camera television?*

BS: No, but I would say that you have to separate the question from two levels. There are two big differences. One is degree of celebrity and one is time. The celebrity factor is a whole other thing because you may have actors come into the room who believe, not necessarily that they carry a certain weight, but who have a certain sense of pride about their process. They're like, "I don't need much help," or "Here's what I do." Frankly, that exists in television too, on successful shows. If you were to go and direct an episode of a very successful series in its fifth season and try to have a real, engaged conversation with some of those lead actors about their characters and their preparation, I'm sure a trailer door would slam in your face. It's unfortunate.

Setting aside celebrity for the moment, if they are truly open and happy-to-be-at-work actors who are thrilled to show up, then there's not a difference in approach. Then the problem is time. What I find in television is that my most effective and useful time directing and working with an actor is in the audition process.

DS: *Let's talk about the auditioning process.*

BS: Television is a horrible race. You have an hour show and seven or eight days to do it. That means you need to get the scene up on its feet quickly. I will always use the time during the lighting set-up to try to find that day player, that guest actor, to spend time with. I found that, even though it is not a relaxed situation, the audition is my greatest time. You can actually sit, make some adjustments, and find a comfort level with each other. Hopefully, the actor feels protected and you can try to relax him. You lay the foundation in that room for the work you will do. So, when he shows up and has 75 to 150 people around him and is very tense, you're that fellow who was in the room with him that day. He knows you are his friend. You get to bring him back to where you were at the end of your process in that room. That, in television, was always incredibly valuable time. In features, the only blessing you have is more time on a daily basis because you'll shoot two pages instead of eight or nine. This gives you a chance to use the full day in terms of preparation and discussion. There's more room for discovery on a feature day than there is on a television day.

DS: *How do you select your casting director?*

BS: In the world of features, I really do my homework. When looking at a film, I pay attention to the secondary casting as well to see if it's specific and interesting. I want to not only find a kindred spirit, but someone who is really smart about the story because then they will have an approach. Chances are, I've seen two or three films that they've cast and that's how I choose. I loved the casting director I worked with on my last film, David Rubin, but he became a producer. When I knew he was going to produce for Sydney Pollack, I said, "You are going to go produce your first movie. Whom are you going to pick for casting?" I put it to him that way and he said, "Avy Kaufman." I sought out the last three or four of her credits and they were all beautiful, smart, specific casting choices in films that I respected. In television, however, there is often somebody in place. Then it's a matter of establishing your language with the casting director.

DS: *Many actors feel that in an audition they have to come in with a finished performance. Not that they know the lines, but that they've got to give you all the results that they think you are hoping for. Do you believe they should?*

BS: I don't. The sad part is that pressure does exist out there. I try to picture that actor's day and he may be going to read for Steven Bochco's show and then a reading for a McDonald's commercial.

DS: *If they're lucky. Three auditions in one day!*

BS: If it's the McDonald's commercial, he knows he has to deliver a result, because the creative powers that be — an ad agency or a commercial director — are all looking for a result. They have no facility to get to it. All they want to see is what they have in their heads. Depending on who the television director is, that may also be the case. In my case, I want to look for somebody who is really relaxed and loose. I will often, in trying to find the character, play with some divergent adjustments just to see what the instrument is like. How relaxed are they? Can they trust you and take a different path?

DS: *Who reads with them?*

BS: Depends. With *City of Angels,* David Rubin, my casting director, read. In the case of *Moonlight Mile,* I've been reading with them.

DS: *Do you find that better than not?*

BS: Not better or worse. In this case, I wanted to because, if the actor can handle it, I wanted to be in the connected moment. The heart of the story is a romance, but a subtle one.

DS: *You've been reading with the women?*

BS: And the men. Oh yeah. Playing the woman's part. Which, of course, puts them at a disadvantage. I always say, "The good news is you will eventually have a stronger and much more attractive scene partner. Bear with me."

DS: *So you really want to feel what they can give, which will tell you if they're able to give to a love partner. That's really interesting.*

BS: You could call it an experiment. I had this intuitive thought that I wanted to do it and it's been great. It tells me a lot about them, whether they can connect, and if I can end up feeling something.

DS: *Do you ever try to tape auditions?*

BS: For certain secondary roles I might, and that's only for myself to have.

DS: *Do you have actors you are considering for roles read together?*

BS: When it's appropriate. In this case I will because casting for a couple means that the chemistry will be a huge part of this. I look forward to having them read together and getting to know each other.

DS: *What do you think about actors seeing their dailies?*

BS: Generally, I gauge it on the actor. Most of the actors I've worked with haven't wanted to come to dailies. Meg Ryan won't look at herself. She didn't want to be near the monitor if there was something being played back. Conversely, Nick Cage was endlessly fascinated watching himself on the monitor. It wasn't an ego thing. He had a really odd way of being able to sit back and watch his character objectively.

DS: *Do you like pre-production rehearsals? And, for how long do you rehearse?*

BS: I think that's story dependent. There are times when I think, "I'm going to take a flier. I think I want all of these personalities to collide onscreen for the first time." I may spend time with them individually, but I may not. Again, talking about the reality of movie stars and their schedules, Nick was doing back-to-back movies. I essentially had him about two days before production.

DS: *When in the world did he have time to do his own homework?*

BS: You pay a price for that, because you may have someone with a certain degree of physical exhaustion coming into the work, and because they haven't had the time to prepare for the role, there is an anxiety level. The first couple days were really tough, because he felt behind. Meg and I had had time to sit and sift which he didn't have, and he felt robbed. That would translate into a certain degree of rigidity about being open about adjustments and any critique of the work. Finally, he cracked open and we talked about it. He realized it was the price he was paying for going from film to film without having a chance to prepare for the role. Very tough.

DS: *That's not an uncommon situation, especially if you're at the height of your popularity.*

BS: I think the problem is that when actors are at their height, everyone involved — the performer, agent, manager subscribe to the, "Strike while the iron is hot" theory. Ninety-nine point nine percent of these agents and managers have no idea of what their clients' processes are. They don't know what their clients do. Directors' agents never really know what their clients' jobs are. They don't understand the job. They think, "Oh, no problem. We'll get you back on a flight by 9. You'll be on the set in time."

DS: *So, actually you don't make a point of having pre-production rehearsals?*

BS: I love the idea of being able to do it, especially for my next film that is just four performances. It's an evolution of relationships.

DS: *Will you rehearse then?*

BS: Yes, especially because one of the relationships is a marriage that's about 30 years old and all about what's not spoken but exists. Some of it I can indicate in writing, but so much of it will be created between the two performers: all the rituals, all the unspoken habits.

DS: *How much time will you give yourself?*

BS: Ideally, a couple weeks.

DS: *Do you want to direct comedy?*

BS: I do.

DS: *Did I ever work on a comedy scene in class with you? I don't always, you know.*

BS: Yes, we did. I remember, and, obviously it stayed with me through my work. What I remember is truly, truly having to be disciplined about conflict, about finding it, generating it, making sure it's there, and being clear about what it is so that you're not playing for comedy. You're truly addressing the real conflict that leads to comedy. I appreciate broad comedies, but I have no feel for them. I love the comedy that comes out of people who are really playing for high stakes.

DS: *The comedy of life; the human comedy.*

BS: The comedy of life. Exactly.

AUDREY WELLS
Screenwriter/Director

Audrey Wells worked as a radio journalist before obtaining her MFA in film from UCLA. Since then, she has written numerous original screenplays including *The Kid,* starring Bruce Willis; *The Truth About Cats and Dogs,* starring Janeane Garofalo and Uma Thurman; and *George of the Jungle,* on which she is credited as co-writer. In 1999, Audrey wrote and directed the independent feature film *Guinevere,* starring Sarah Polley and Stephen Rea, which received the award for Best Screenplay at the Sundance Film Festival and the Jury Prize from the Deauville Film Festival. At the time of this conversation, she had just completed shooting her adaptation of the best-selling book, *Under the Tuscan Sun,* for Disney.

DS: *You wrote* Guinevere. *It was also the first feature film you directed. Tell me how you chose your casting director.*

AW: I love talking about casting director Linda Lowey because she did an enormous amount of work in shaping *Guinevere* and I trusted her. I chose Linda because she had an understanding of the text of the film. I am first and foremost a writer, and if somebody can't read my script and say intuitive things about it, if it doesn't speak to them from the page, then we probably won't have a good foundation from which to begin. What I look for in a casting director is how deeply they understand the material. It's the same thing you look for in every other person you hire on the movie, from your director of photography to your production designer. You want them to feel the movie. You want them to have a vision of the film.

DS: *What do you mean by, "having a vision of the film?"*

AW: As the writer I make an enormous contribution to any movie that gets made. After that, I'm not insecure about sharing credit. As a director, you are not up there alone. You have actors, a cinematographer who envisions the film and makes suggestions, a production designer, an editor, and a casting director. They are brilliant and I like to acknowledge their contributions. It really doesn't threaten me to say that Linda Lowey did a tremendous amount of work on the casting.

DS: *When you say "vision," do you mean she saw the kinds of people that would flesh out this film, bring it to life, and add a certain depth to it?*

AW: She understood the qualities of each character and brought in actors she respects who embodied those qualities so they could bring something that was truly theirs to the part.

DS: *How did you prepare for your casting? Did you write profiles along with the casting director? Did you give every actor, even the minor and supporting roles, a script ahead of time? Did you give them a character profile before they even read?*

AW: I prefer having actors as informed as possible. I wanted them to read the entire script before they came in because I wanted them to know what they would be a part of — to care, to feel ownership, to feel involved. I wanted them to think that their little part is a really big deal. I wanted them to have a sense of the gestalt of the entire movie. However, some actors didn't get to read all of the script. But those who did were a notch up with me because they were able to talk about the script. That made a difference because I saw a work ethic in the actor.

DS: *Would you describe that?*

AW: Those who prepared for the audition by taking the time to read the entire script made me feel that a supportive actor had just walked through the door.

DS: *When you're watching auditions, what are you looking for and who's reading with the actors?*

AW: One of the assistants.

DS: *Not an actor?*

AW: No.

DS: *And you didn't find that that made any difference? That can be a handicap for an actor.*

AW: Well, one of the most important parts to cast was the role of the mother. I had written virtual monologues for her, so in that instance, it wasn't important to have an actor read with her. Otherwise, when I need to see if someone can banter, I would bring an actor in.

Sarah Polley, who did the lead, didn't audition. She did a table reading with a bunch of actors. That was all she ever did for her audition.

DS: *She was good, though.*

AW: Yes. That was it. She was the only person I ever saw for the part.

DS: *Did you ever tape an audition? Do you think that is helpful?*

AW: Yes. We videotaped them and made compilation tapes for each part.

DS: *Did you ever coach or direct them from the sidelines?*

AW: I really like to have the actor lead the audition. If they wanted to talk before the audition started, I was happy to. If they wanted to stop and start over again, it was fine with me. If they wanted to do it again with input from me, I would give them input.

DS: *But you never offered any input otherwise?*

AW: I would if I was interested in the first reading and thought it could go somewhere, or if I wanted to see it another way. But if I wasn't interested in what I saw, I wouldn't go with it.

DS: *It's interesting that if you saw something you thought was potentially usable, you would then give them some coaching on the side. Many actors would think, "Oh my God. I've done something wrong." They are so insecure. Actors need to understand that when a director gives instructions, it's not because they've done something wrong but because they're doing something right. That's when directors want to see how far the actor can go and whether they can work together.*

AW: Exactly. I think it's a definite positive signal if you're given some direction on your first reading.

DS: *Would you ever have two actors you are considering for a film read together? And, what would you be looking for?*

AW: Their ability to listen to each other and play off of each other. I hate to say it, but you are always balancing a cast and part of what's important is purely visual. If you're trying to create a family, for example, you need to make sure the actors look like they could be related. There are a lot of things that are just awful to actors, but that's how it goes.

DS: *Since* Guinevere *was your first directorial project, how did you feel about directing your own material?*

AW: Fabulous! It was great, absolutely great. Directing your own material is better than anything, and infinitely easier than writing. Infinitely easier. When you write, you are all by yourself. When you direct, you are surrounded by the brilliant people you hired who also want to do the best job they can possibly do.

DS: *So it really becomes a collaborative, family affair?*

AW: Exactly, as long as nobody wants to secretly kill the baby.

DS: *Would they do that?*

AW: I saw an actor do that. Not in *Guinevere* though.

DS: *What happened?*

AW: She became afraid of the part. She absolutely loved it when she was cast. But, when we started shooting, she began misunderstanding the director, which sent her into a free fall of not trusting anything: from every single word that had been written to her interpretation of the character.

DS: *Did she have a good reason for not trusting the director?*

AW: He had told her that he approved of an idea of hers, which he secretly thought was stupid. She found out about that and the relationship was destroyed.

DS: *You mean a character choice she made?*

AW: Yes. He pretended to think they were really good ideas, but actually thought they were really bad. You can understand why that would be hard to combat. She became very toxic and negative, dragged her feet and wanted out. It was a nightmare. I thought that she damaged the film.

DS: *It was your script, right? Were you on the set all the time?*

AW: No, I left.

DS: *Did she trust you?*

AW: Initially we had liked each other, but it became too awkward for her to deal with me. She decided to bring in her own team — a writer and an acting coach — and be her own island of moviemaking. She no longer spoke to the director, nor would she do any of the lines as written. Since it was a comedy, there was a lot of carefully timed banter, so if you change one of your lines, what have you done to the other person's line?

DS: *When a director earns your mistrust, everything is lost.*

AW: It's very important to have actors feel that you will always say what you mean and that you are not trying to manipulate them or dabble in reverse psychology. They need to know that you're being straightforward. That when you say, "That was fantastic," they can really feel great about it. And when you say, "I don't understand what you're doing with this. I want it another way and here's why," they know that you are not secretly trying to punish them or make them look bad in front of somebody else. They know you're just fighting for the material.

DS: *What type of material do you like to work on?*

AW: I look for some kind of summary statement about some aspect of what it is to be alive.

DS: *What you are attracted to?*

AW: I tend to write about people in pain who get well during the course of the movie. I seem to be attracted to that and I write it over and over again.

DS: *Did you rehearse before* Guinevere?

AW: Yes. I had two kinds of rehearsals that were extremely different from each other.

DS: *How much rehearsal did you have?*

AW: It was a low-budget picture and we made it for two-and-a-half million dollars. I had Stephen Rea and Sarah Polley for a week only. Stephen was staying at the Chateau Marmont. Sarah and I would go to Stephen's room at four o'clock and he would order tea. Then they would read the script. They never got out of their chairs, and it was fine with me because we weren't on the set and there is something so artificial about trying to block a scene under those conditions. It wouldn't have been good for them.

DS: *But there was a couch in the hotel room, wasn't there? I remember that couch scene in the film. It was their first night together and it was positively electric. You didn't rehearse that?*

AW: No.

DS: *Was that their choice or just the way it happened?*

AW: It was the way it happened. Being a first time director working with Stephen Rea, I wanted to do what he wanted. It is very important as a young and first-time director to have respect for others. Stephen has rehearsed a million things and he wanted to do it sitting in his chair. Fine. No argument. If that's what he wanted to do, it was fine with me. They were very emotional in the rehearsals. They both cried while they were reading. After a scene I would ask them, "What do you think the scene is about?" Once again, everything was content driven. "What happened in the scene?" I would ask. "What do you feel transpired that brought you to another place?" We would make sure that we understood the function and content of every scene and where the tuning points were. Then I would ask them if anything was hard to say or if there was another way they wanted to say something. If they wanted to change or include something, that was an opportunity for me. They were very focused and wanted to do the script they had read. They didn't want to change anything fundamental. They only wanted to hone the scenes.

Another reason why I didn't want Sarah and Stephen to get up and move around was because they were both very shy people and they would have felt stupid. They barely know each other and yet they were going to have to be lovers in the movie. They just needed to have fun, to laugh, to tell stories, to drink tea, and to order strawberries from room service. They needed to do all the normal life things. The amount of time we spent bullshitting was just as important as the amount of time we spent rehearsing because Stephen and Sarah needed to like each other a lot. They also needed to find out that I wasn't going to be stepping all over them or saying too much. It was really a "get to know you" time. The fact that I wasn't overbearing that first week was really important.

DS: *How many hours were you spending there a day?*

AW: About three.

DS: *Did you rehearse with the rest of the cast at all?*

AW: Yes, my other rehearsal came directly out of your class. I had cast the family members. I was going to have a huge challenge because I was going to have to shoot both dinner table scenes — which included the mother, father, main character (Harper), her sister, and the sister's husband — in one day. To make matters worse, it was the second day of shooting. Clearly, I needed the performances to be there because we would have no time to work on the set. Everybody was going to get a take-and-a-half, and then we were going to have to move on. I needed to have a great rehearsal that would create a relationship between these five actors, both as people and as the characters they were set to play.

First, I invited everyone over to my house and asked them to sit around the dinner table, just as they would in the scenes. I set the table and put food on it, so props were at hand. We read through the scenes and loosely rehearsed them a couple of times, just getting a feel for the words. Then I asked them to do an exercise that came directly from your class. I had each person at the table say something, in character, that spoke the truth about how he/she felt about two other people at the table. What they had to say about each other was absolutely staggering. They got out all of their hostilitiy, their secret loves, and their insecurities. They spoke out the subtext of the family tension to each other. What they had to say helped create the tension they needed. Once Harper, the main character, heard what her sister, Susan, said to their father, she had good reason to feel intimidated and uncomfortable around her.

I remember when the character played by Emily Proctor — the older daughter — said to her father, "I really hope that Mom dies first so that I can finally be with you." When we got on set, they already knew all these awful things about the other characters. It really helped set the stage for that scene. The family tension was there. They weren't just imagining it. They had created it at my dinner table. They had created the alienation and the hurt. The crazy thing is that even though we only had an hour-and-a-half to rehearse that day, nobody forgot it. Because it was so short, it was extremely intense. It was absolutely focused and everybody came out with their innermost secrets, desires, and the resentments they held as characters.

DS: *This technique really helped?*

AW: Absolutely. I explained that we were going to have an extremely challenging day in which we were going to shoot both scenes. I asked them for their help and I told them that I wasn't going to be able to work with them individually on the set. I told them the kinds of feeling I wanted the scene to have. I didn't exclude them from the process. I let them do their thing a couple of times just to get the feeling of things. Then I said, "Okay, I want to do this exercise." This was a little scary for me, because you feel stupid when you have a lot of great actors around and you're leading them through an exercise. You don't want to insult anybody.

DS: *Did you encounter any resistance or any patronization for having made that suggestion?*

AW: None whatsoever. I think what was important about it is that I preceded this exercise by explaining the necessity for it. They didn't just feel as if I was jerking them around because I was a director and I had time to rehearse them. I told them, "We're up against a wall. We're shooting eleven pages in one day. You've never met each other before, so I'd like to suggest a way to bridge this gap in one hour."

DS: *This is the kind of thing that actors long for, this kind of specific attention to their roles and relationships. They rarely get it. In fact, they usually don't even get rehearsals before production.*

AW: I have to say, it was great. And the limited time was a good thing because nobody had a chance to sit and expound for half an hour about their character. They weren't even allowed to say something about every other person at the table. They could only choose two other people. They created the family history because what each person said was fact. They created their backstories and that was it.

I have to say that I never would have thought of that, of the power of blurting out what you're feeling, if I hadn't learned that in your class.

DS: *Did you ever encounter any resistance from your actors, either in rehearsal or on the set?*

AW: Yes. There were times when I would ask for things that were very simple from one of my principal actors, something very technical such as, "Could you please end up one foot to your right" and he would balk. This made me extremely resentful because I was on a low-budget movie schedule and anybody who took an hour of my time to explain why they couldn't move one foot to the right was keeping me from finishing my day.

DS: *That's an important thing for actors to realize.*

AW: True. If actors take too much time out of my day, they are hurting the entire movie because you didn't get all of your shots. They can't possibly grasp everything you need to accomplish that day. Although we always dealt with each other with respect, I would sometimes get resistance that was totally out of proportion to what was at stake. This was really hard for me because I feared for the film. I needed to get so many shots in a day. When he was uncooperative, I sometimes had to redesign the way I was going to shoot the scene because he had eaten up so much time. Actors behave different ways with different directors and that was how he behaved with me. It was a challenge.

DS: *Were you both satisfied with the results?*

AW: He loved the movie and I loved him in the movie. We have good feelings about each other.

DS: *What other problems did you encounter on the set?*

AW: Everyday starts with a creative problem such as, "How will you block the scene?"

DS: *You hadn't done much pre-planning?*

AW: No. I know that sounds shocking, especially for a first time director, not to have storyboarded...

DS: *Why didn't you?*

AW: Because we hadn't been on the set and it just seemed like make-work. It just wasn't going to stick. I would arrive every morning on set with a very strong idea of what I thought the blocking should be. The actors would arrive and I would suggest the blocking. Ninety percent of the time, that's the way it went. Sometimes they would want to do something else or have a different idea and we would try it their way because it was a good idea. That would require different solutions; different motivations to move. What's happening with the props that makes somebody move from here to there? Why are they moving on that line and not the other one? It would require a lot of seat-of-the-pants adjustments. But, you have to be that way. The actors arrive on a set they've never seen before and things start occurring to them. They may have excellent notions and you want to make use of that. Arriving with that degree of looseness is always a little frightening, but it was always the way to go.

DS: *And, ultimately, probably more rewarding.*

AW: I think so. It's not a special effects movie, so I didn't use storyboards. It wasn't created in the editing room. It was a dialogue film. So, we would discover blocking together in the morning. It always went pretty smoothly, but it meant that every day started with a creative problem. Not a problem in the negative sense, but a creative question.

DS: *Did you ever talk about objectives and actions with your actors?*

AW: I only talked about objectives and actions.

DS: *The "why" and "what's" really driving this person? You talked about the subtext as if it's the super objective, right? For example, the actress said, "I hope Mother dies first so that I can finally be with you." She wants to replace her mother. Did you discuss these things?*

AW: We would definitely talk about that kind of thing before we started filming. Once we were talking about objectives and actions in individual scenes, I would use that language in order to break that scene down into beats. I never said, "Be funny," or, "Be warmer." We always talked in terms of objectives and actions and that spared me a lot of humiliation and pain.

DS: *Were they aware of what you were doing with them? Were they aware of your understanding of their instrument and their language? Did they have any appreciation of it?*

AW: I think they did, in that they did not find me irritating. They found me helpful. Sarah has told me that a number of things I said to her really meant a lot.

DS: *For example?*

AW: I remember when she was sitting at the dinner table, I suggested she feel like she could not turn her head to look at either of her parents because there was a sheet of Plexiglas that her cheek would press against if she tried. That gave her a feeling of constriction that was very helpful.

DS: *Jean Smart's monologue performance in a later scene was so unforgettable.*

AW: Yes. I wanted Jean to feel sexual rage and then to conceal that rage so that it only came through her eyes.

DS: *What was the rage coming from?*

AW: Loneliness and indignation that she was undervalued and unloved. The text of the monologue was, "What are you doing with my daughter?" But the subtext was all about, "Why am I so alone?" "Why not me?" Putting a lid on that.

I felt that Jean's performance would be more powerful if she was very, very restrained. Before we had arrived, she had anchored the scene in terms of what her physical behavior would be. And we never changed it. The quieter she was in her performance, the more desperate she was.

DS: *How come she became the villain in that family?*

AW: Because the more passive her husband became, the more aggressive she became until he completely wrote her off and she was on an island by herself. It was a terrible wound to her. And she was so beautiful and sexy. I felt that her cleavage was an important statement for her character and yet she got nothing from this man. He preferred her elder daughter. It's painful.

DS: *Do you block your camera or bring your camera to your actors?*

AW: You don't really know what you'll see until you're on set with the camera. How far away can you get? What lens do you want? What point of view do you use? What kind of shots? There would always be a shot I knew I needed: a poetic shot. Every scene had at least one shot that poetically expressed the scene. Other than that, it was coverage.

DS: *So you envisioned, before you got on the set, that one shot? Please elaborate.*

AW: In the seduction scene on the couch, I always knew there would be a very slow push-in on Sarah as she lay on the couch and that he would enter that shot at the end of it. That entire scene was blocked so that it was a cat-and-mouse game. She creates a distance; he closes it. She starts in a chair and moves to a table, so he moves to the table. She moves to the couch, so he moves to the couch until, at the very end of the scene when she has decided to comply, she closes the distance. I had that concept for the blocking.

DS: *All that time she was creating the distance, she was also inviting him. What about preparation time before a shot? Did you ever have to encourage the actors to take time out?*

AW: Not with this group of actors.

DS: *Did you ever improvise a scene before the shot? The scene before the scene — the scene that has not been written but that would logically have occurred prior to the scene the audience sees.*

AW: Yes. I don't know if you remember when Harper first comes to Connie's loft. He's having a fight with a girl. When action was called they had to be in a fury and she had to be crying and throwing things. They definitely improvised to get into the mood.

DS: *Whose idea was that?*

AW: I think we all knew it had to happen. Clearly, I could not expect her to just be crying on, "Action."

DS: *Sometimes actors prepare on their own because they know they need a handle to get into the scene. Most don't however, because they don't know how.*

AW: Come to think of it, a lot of directors are afraid of emotion, aren't they?

DS: *Did you ever encounter an emotionally blocked actor?*

AW: I did. I tried to prepare for those things by getting to know the actors ahead of time, to know their life story. I would spend as much time alone with them as I could and would ask, "How long have you lived in L.A.?" "Is your family here?" etc. Sometimes, when you ask about the family, you will hear, "I'm a foster child. I haven't seen my family in a really long time." That came up with an actress who had a long crying scene. She was having trouble getting to her emotions and I'm afraid that I went up to her and said, "How did you feel at Christmas when you didn't have a family because you were a foster child?"

DS: *Do you think she hated you for it?*

AW: No. But it was brutal. I told her, "You're all alone at Christmas and nobody loves you." It was harsh, but I did the right thing for the movie. She cried very hard and afterwards, she felt battered and bruised. I know she still likes me, though, because she calls me and comes to screenings. She is proud of her work. I wouldn't have known what to say to her if I hadn't gotten into some personal conversations with her. Even if an actor is only there for a day, getting to know them a little bit can end up being very helpful. Sarah had to do a scene — it actually didn't end up in the movie — where she had to cry hysterically. I knew that Sarah had been a political activist and during a demonstration was beaten with police batons and they knocked out her teeth. The scene was to lock herself in the bathroom and get into the shower with her clothes on because she was crying so hysterically that she was out of her mind. When she was having trouble getting there I said, "He is going to knock the door down and when he gets in, he is going to knock your teeth out with a baton." People tell you things because they think you are kind and compassionate and they can trust you.

DS: *What do you do when an actor is dried up?*

AW: Stop shooting.

DS: *And what then?*

AW: I would give the actor one thing to try and get in each take. Let's say in a scene somebody had four lines and they were completely dried up. I would make a suggestion for each one of those four lines before I would shoot the scene. Then I would know that by the time I had four takes I could fix it in the cutting room because I had the best in different takes. So you start being strategic about it. You start thinking about where else the emotion is in the scene. If the actor really can't come up with it, you can't just bludgeon them to death. You start thinking, "Well, what is the other actor doing? Is there something on the table? Is there something on the wall? The sky? Is there something else I can do to convey the emotionality of the scene?

DS: *You try to solve it visually?*

AW: Yes, or I would give them an action on each line. "Really hurt her feelings this time." "Instill doubt in her." I would try to give them something substantive.

DS: *And that would work?*

AW: Hopefully, but if something is blocked, it doesn't.

DS: *Well, they might translate it into something more personal and active for themselves.*

AW: Don't you feel that when somebody is dried up they have also lost their will to be good? They don't give a shit, in that moment, whether they are any good or not.

DS: *I never thought about it that way.*

AW: I've seen it happen. They're quitting. They want to go home. They don't want to hear anything you say. They hate you in that moment because they think you think they're bad and they don't know what else to do. They can't listen to your stupid suggestions anymore. The relationship isn't always so lovely that you say something to them and they say, "Gee, thanks."

DS: *What do you do when that happens?*

AW: That's when I go line by line and start looking for other ways to express the scene.

DS: *And when they finally hit it?*

AW: That doesn't always happen. These are the scenes that end up unfinished because you have to move on. Actors can be sort of manic. They feel really good or really bad. And if they're depressed and they can't shake it, they don't give a shit. What do you do when you are working with an actor who's your lead and he feels like that? What can you do?

DS: *I would get very personal. "I know you're dried up and you know I have to get this shot. Are you mad at me? Do you want to yell at me? Yell at me."*

AW: Or, sometimes the best thing a director can do is shoot it differently and figure it out later. You rewrite the scene in your head. You start looking for solutions.

Another thing is positive reinforcement, no matter what. I never berate anybody because its counterproductive. You need to give a lot of praise and support. It has to be genuine and if you can find anything to say, say it.

DS: *Did you ever coach from the sidelines?*

AW: Yes. I did.

DS: *Was it helpful?*

AW: Yes, because an actor may get in a groove but forget a line and get off track. They don't know if you want to call cut or keep going. At that point I just say, "That's fantastic," or "Pick it up," or "Get her attention." You can say that kind of thing off camera. Some actors need a ton of it because they can't get through a scene at all without coaching.

DS: *Describe what you are talking about?*

AW: There were a couple of instances where I cast somebody because their essential qualities were perfect but they were not very experienced. There was no way that I was going to get a complete take of anything. They actually benefited by working on a line basis. I would be off camera helping them and they would get to repeat lines and play with them until they got it.

DS: *How important is matching business?*

AW: It has to be secondary to what else is going on and to the spontaneity of the actor. But, actors who do match business well are a gift to the editor and the director. If they don't match business, they can actually make takes unusable. I prefer it if they are consistent.

DS: *What was your average shooting ratio?*

AW: It was really low. About three takes.

DS: *When actors' impulses seem to belie the logic of the character what do you do? An actor does something that is a total surprise and you love it but you have to wonder if the character would do it.*

AW: I would tell the actor that I was absolutely crazy about what they just did. "That was brilliant but I have to think about it because it may not ultimately work. So could we have something else, as well."

DS: *What about dailies? Do you allow it? Do you forbid it?*

AW: If an actor wants to watch dailies, they can.

DS: *Did anybody want to?*

AW: Sarah sometimes did. We didn't really have dailies. We had videos we watched at lunch when actors wanted to go to their trailers. It really depends on the actor. It depends how neurotic and controlling they are. Some are fine with it. Some get stressed out or depressed from watching dailies.

DS: *Do you have any feelings or thoughts about comedy versus drama?*

AW: Except for *Guinevere,* I write nothing but comedies. I wrote *The Truth About Cats and Dogs. The Kid* is a comedy. I rewrote *Runaway Bride.* I wrote a very broad family comedy called *George of the Jungle.* From a writer's standpoint, every word is significant in comedy. There's not a lot of leeway in comedy dialogue unless you come up with something funnier. If you change the sequence of words in a sentence, it can go from funny to unfunny in one second.

DS: *How do you feel about casting people in comedy? What is the essential thing you really need to look for in an actor?*

AW: I look for sincerity because the funniest thing in comedy is always sincere intention. If you start playing something just for laughs, it goes way downhill. I'm always looking for somebody who can really believe in the part and the necessity of saying things. The more dead-on serious somebody is with the lines in a comedy, the more hilarious they are.

DS: *So you're saying not to worry about how you say the line because the line will take care of itself. You have to give me the heart of that moment.*

AW: Why are some people so funny and others are not. I can't explain it. Some people are just funny when they are serious about something.

DS: *Well, we've often heard comics are basically tragic figures who take their pain and make fun of it. Another important element is for actors to have an innate sense of irony about life — a sense of humor about it.*

AW: It also helps if they are coming from a place of low self-esteem and hatred. *(Laughs.)* Self-hatred is a wellspring in comedy.

DS: *Can you see a director saying, "Do you hate yourself? You ought to, you know, because it will help the scene." [laughs]*

DS: *Do you have any advice for directors and actors?*

AW: Practice flexibility, mutual respect, and positive reinforcement. Actors who help the director make the movie are so valuable.

DS: *What do you mean when you say, "Help make the movie?"*

AW: If the director needs you to move two feet to the right to get out of somebody else's key light, just do it. Just do it. There are so many things going on and we can really use the actor's help. Don't fight the small details. Fight the important battles, not the details. Same thing goes for directors. If something is really important to the actor and you can accommodate them, do it.

GEENA DAVIS
Actor

Geena Davis won the Academy Award for Best Supporting Actress for her role as the offbeat dog trainer in *The Accidental Tourist*. She was again nominated for an Academy Award and Golden Globe Award for her performance as Thelma, opposite Susan Sarandon, in Ridley Scott's *Thelma and Louise*. She received more Golden Globe nominations for Best Actress for her portrayals of a political speechwriter in *Speechless*, which she also co-produced, and as a baseball phenomenon in *A League of Their Own*. Davis made her feature film debut in *Tootsie* and went on to star in such films as *The Fly, Beetlejuice, Earth Girls are Easy, Hero, Angie, The Long Kiss Goodnight*, and *Stuart Little*. Davis also starred in three television series, including *The Geena Davis Show*.

DS: *How do you handle working with actors who peak earlier, take forever to create what the scene calls for, or are so nervous they keep flubbing lines?*

GD: My job is to get the best version of my performance into the movie. Because I'm not picking the takes that will be used in the final film, I have to try to get my performance right as many times as possible.

Let's say I'm in a shot with another actor. Maybe I know, from working with this person, that his or her earlier takes are better. My later takes tend to be better. Now because I want my best performance to end up in the film, I have to accommodate the other actor. In such cases, the only thing I can control is myself; I cannot control them. So maybe I'd think, "Is there something different I can do in my preparation to make my earlier takes better?" Maybe I can say, "Let's organize this so I shoot my close-up last," so that I have a chance to get better in a different way. Ultimately, my goal would be to see what I could do to change my approach in order to accommodate the situation.

DS: *Can you be more specific about how you would prepare?*

GD: I like to save it. Save showing other participants what I'm doing until the camera is rolling. I've prepared. I've worked on the script and I've done everything I can to be ready for the filming. But I don't necessarily want to reveal to the other actor what I'm doing early on.

DS: *Because . . .*

GD: Because then I have shown my cards and there's less opportunity for happy accidents. I like the real give and take that happens on film when you throw a surprise to another person, who doesn't know what you're going to do. I've also built in plans to change what I'm doing if they start anticipating and I see that they've figured out what I'm doing. Then I think, "Okay, next take I'm going to change and surprise you so that it can stay fresh."

There are many different ways actors won't be in sync. If the other actor doesn't know his or her lines, that means you aren't going to get a good take until the tenth or twelfth one, so you have to pace yourself. Or, they could have a completely different style. For example, many actors remain in character between takes, or even the whole day. I don't happen to work that way. I like to fool around, tap dance, sing songs, or play cards, do anything in between. Not only set-ups but takes as well. Sometimes that doesn't work with what another person is trying to do, so you have to respect each other's needs. Whatever it takes to get that tiny moment on film is what counts.

There's a philosophy that says, "It's the journey, not the destination that counts," which is a great way to look at things. But for acting on film I do not believe that whatsoever. I don't care if I have the worst experience in the world filming something. If I'm happy with my performance in the movie, that's what I care about. I mean, you could have the most fabulous experience — everyone bonded, lifelong friends — but if the movie didn't come out well, what's the point? Okay, I had a great time but I didn't accomplish the job they hired me to do. What I want to do is get my best acting in the movie. I don't care if it takes putting lighters under my toes if that's going to help get the performance I want in the film.

DS: *Do you like to rehearse before production?*

GD: No, I don't because rehearsal for a film is usually only one or two weeks. I feel that's too short a time to accomplish anything. But it's just enough time to let everyone know what you are going to do for no good reason that I can see. So if the director insists on rehearsing, I deliberately don't show what I'm going to do. I do a sort of fakey version and risk having people think, "Yikes, is she going to do it like that?" I'll pretend that I haven't really had a chance to think about it yet but, of course, I have.

I think it's valuable to meet and read through the script and say, "Does this scene work for you?" or "Shouldn't these be switched?" or "Maybe we should trim this." One hopes the writer is present and he or she can hear the words out loud. I think you can get a lot from that.

DS: *Did you have any pre-production rehearsals for* Thelma and Louise?

GD: Not per se. Susan and I had meetings with the writer and the director. We would talk through the scenes and that was really valuable. We accomplished quite a bit.

DS: *When you started in films, had you had the New York theater experience?*

GD: No. Actually I never did a play in New York. I studied acting in college at Boston University and I did summer stock.

DS: *Do you find that there is a very big difference between acting on film and acting on stage, not only in terms of how you approach a role but how you execute it?*

GD: Yes, very much so. From when I first decided I wanted to act, I knew I wanted it to be in films. It's not that I don't like plays and couldn't enjoy that. It's just that the particular challenge of making a film appeals to me more. You're creating a mosaic. You are creating little pieces of something that are going to add up to a story. You pick out a tiny moment, a two-minute part of the movie that you typically shoot that day only. You try not only to make that the best moment you can, but to have it make sense in the whole picture and know which part of the whole you are trying to serve. That is really fascinating and appealing to me. I love being the custodian of my character's journey and knowing what I want to accomplish. There's something special about the 100 percent focus on that tiny moment. You have a twelve-hour day and how much of it are you acting on film? Maybe a half-hour or an hour altogether. For some reason, for my nature, that gun to my head — the necessity to do it well right now or have something I regret in the film forever — I find stimulating.

DS: *How do you begin working on a role?*

GD: When I approach a role, there are many different facets to examine. The first is to figure out what the movie is trying to say, what the theme of the movie is. I start with that because then I can see how my character fits into it. Then I figure out one sentence that tells my character's journey. If I know that I can approach my theme scene by scene, act by act, and finally, moment by moment, I can ask myself how this scene contributes to the bigger picture. How can I make the tiny parts add up to the big sum? How can I make my arc as big as possible? Can I make it more dramatic? When we break the movie up — and everybody knows movies are shot completely out of sequence — when we break it up into those little parts, I'll still know where each one goes. We may shoot something on day two that goes at the end of the movie. So, what has happened to my character beforehand? How did it get to me and how did I end up in this place? Sometimes, when you start shooting something that goes at the end of the movie and people don't know how you are going to play the beginning of the movie, it can be very confusing for them.

DS: *You mean the director in particular?*

GD: It can be the director or other actors. It's easy to have a picture of a character like, "This character is tough." But if you are doing a scene where you feel that your character should completely fall apart, they'll say, "But I thought this character was tough. It doesn't make sense to me." It's because they haven't seen the other parts. You have to realize always that it's the contradictions of the character that make them who they are.

DS: *That makes them human and unpredictable.*

GD: And that's my job; to make it as complex and three-dimensional as possible. Show all the different colors of the character. Ultimately, I am the only one who knows all these different things that I'm going to do. The vast majority of times, directors can help or, at the very least, not hinder your efforts.

DS: *They will leave you alone . . .*

GD: Ninety-nine percent of the time they will either leave you alone and trust you, or see what you're doing and try to help.

DS: *But the arc of the characters and their many sides are not worked out beforehand?*

GD: There is only so much time to discuss this stuff. Directors usually have so much to be responsible for — from the color of your toenail polish to what country they should shoot the movie in — so you don't end up discussing these details. And they do trust you. They have to think, "Hey, you know what you're doing. You were hired because you know what you're doing."

   If you've hired people you believe in, trusting their instincts is a good thing. As a director, you have a story you want to tell. You have a distinct point of view about it, and you want to make sure that gets across. But movies happen on the set, on that day, at that moment. Whether you've talked about it beforehand or not, you get there and you're faced with a scene that the director and actors have to figure out together.

DS: *Has a director ever given you a piece of direction which seemed contradictory to what you worked out for the scene?*

GD: Disagreements work themselves out. It almost never comes to a conflict. There have been a couple of occasions when the director wanted me to do something that I simply did not want to do, so I would just appear incapable of doing it. I would say, "I have no idea why, but I can't seem to do it." "Oops, I flubbed a line," or whatever. I just want to make sure that nothing gets in the film that I'm not proud of. Whatever happens, I never want to do a take that I would regret later — where the director would choose that particular take in the final edit.

DS: *What do you hope for from a director?*

GD: I love whatever they bring to the part. I don't need them to leave me alone. I love to hear any ideas about the character because I know I will either blend it with what I'm doing or, if it doesn't help me, I won't. I feel comfortable enough to use what I need. If they say something that's helpful, I'm thrilled. I've worked with some really great directors like Sydney Pollack, so you obviously want all the help they can offer.

DS: *You did* Tootsie *with Sydney.*

GD: Yes. My first job. Such an incredible introduction to the business. He has such respect for acting. Here I was, just a kid who had never been on a movie set, wearing only my under-wear in this scene... To be treated with such welcome. He immediately treated me like, "You know what you're doing." And I did, because I was treated that way. I came to it with such a tremendous comfort level and confidence because both he and Dustin were so supportive and accepting. What I most value from directors is their appreciation of acting and an inherent confidence in what actors bring to the role. I find the best quality in directors is when they are really confident about their storytelling, that nothing threatens them. Then whatever happens during the day is not going to make them flip out. "So, the house is pink instead of blue. So the sets blew up or you got sick. I'll find a way to tell my story because I'm a confident storyteller."

DS: *What do you fear most from directors?*

GD: Insecurity causes a lot of problems in a director. It's not good if they are insecure about their talents or what they are trying to accomplish.

Then they're second-guessing everybody else. They're not trusting people and they're closing themselves off to other people's input because they're insecure about their own vision. Therefore, other people's ideas make them very confused and threatened.

DS: *Would you say it's because they didn't do their homework or because they just don't have it in them to think along those terms? Maybe they can only think visually and are not character or story-wise.*

GD: I've worked with people who do seem to have an appreciation for storytelling, but somehow lack the core belief in themselves. If you are coming from insecurity, you are not going to be able to entertain other people's ideas.

I had one situation where the shooting script was in rough shape, but the writer was banned from the set because the director felt so threatened by the comments the writer would make. Ordinarily, to get the writer on the set is the greatest gift you can have because if a problem arises you have the original source to help you out of it.

DS: *What kind of comments was the writer making?*

GD: Offering line changes, which is his territory. Clearly, he was not there to tell the actors to act the scene better, but to say, "This isn't working, so why don't we change the line to such and such?" Insecurity, I believe, is what causes directors to be screamers. I had one experience like that and I don't want to repeat it. It is so unproductive. The least productive way to get what you want is to scream at people, crew, or actors. It is such an immature and non-productive way to approach a problem.

DS: *Did it ever affect your performance?*

GD: Just my mood. I was never personally yelled at, but that kind of atmosphere does not make it conducive to doing your best work. It's just not the way to work.

DS: *It's intimidating, especially for actors who don't have the background that you have or the respect that you have earned. They can actually freeze up.*

GD: How are you going to be creative with your work if somebody is going to yell at you if you risk something? And it's all about taking risks and being in a comfortable environment where you are supported. I don't want to work with people who don't respect actors. For example, I was at a dinner party once where a very famous director was talking about actors. He basically said that you have to treat them like children and trick them into doing what you want because they are so stupid. And I'm thinking, "Boy, you're obviously hoping that I'll never work with you." If I knew a director felt that way, I would never work with him.

DS: *Do you ever ask your fellow actors how they thought the scene went?*

GD: Sometimes. When I've worked with Dustin Hoffman I have, but he's like a mentor to me. We did a movie together called *Hero*. That was ten years after *Tootsie*. I had a more substantial part opposite him in that one, so it was fun to do. Certainly with him it happens and feels natural. Maybe that's because of him.

DS: *Has any actor ever come to you and made a suggestion?*

GD: Yes . . .

DS: *And . . .*

GD: I try to not let it bother me. One time, an actor interrupted to ask me if that was really what I was going to do and . . .

DS: *Was the camera rolling?*

GD: Yes, we were shooting a scene and that didn't sit very well with me. But that's the only time that has happened to me. I made sure I got across the point that I didn't want to be interrupted during a take.

DS: *Do you ever work on a scene with the other actor alone?*

GD: I have talked about possible dialogue changes with the other actor before going on the set, but I wouldn't work on the acting of a scene with him or her.

DS: *It wouldn't go with your way of working anyway, because you prefer not knowing what's going to come at you or what you are going to give them.*

GD: I have asked actors to change their lines when they're off camera if I thought it would give me something. Surprise me, say something different — something that will shock me, if I need to be shocked.

DS: *What's your feeling about close-ups? Marlon Brando talks about saving it for the close-ups. Do you find yourself doing the same thing?*

GD: I try not to save it for the close-up, because that's not fair to the other actors, but I certainly know that I want to make sure what I'm doing is really good in the close-up. It's a really odd phenomenon because everything is off camera except for you. You could tape up a picture of your mother, have your dog sit there, have the actor say something completely different, or even have a different actor there... you can do anything that works to make you feel what you want and need. I once had a great thing happen to me. I had to do a screen test for *Accidental Tourist*. It was the only screen test I had ever done and I knew that there were three other women testing. This was a big deal. This was definitely a part that I was desperate to get. It meant everything to me and I was just beside myself with nerves.

I was preparing for this scene where I had to be very emotional. The character's friend had just died and she's having this heated telephone conversation. I'm preparing like crazy when an assistant comes up and says, "We're ready for you." "Okay, I'm ready," I said. Suddenly they're having problems with the lighting and it's going to be another ten minutes. "Oh my God!" I'm thinking, "How could they do this? It's all ruined. This is the worst thing that has happened to me. I'm ready *now*. How will I ever get ready again? I have to be angry and upset for this scene and . . . Oh, I *am* angry and upset." It sounds crazy but it was literally as if this huge lightbulb went on.

DS: *In other words, you used the emotional reality of your real-life event, which was exactly the same as the character's in that scene. Your story really sheds light on that often-used phrase, "Use it."*

GD: Yes. Now, when I'm working and I feel something, I channel that into the scene. I don't have to manufacture feelings when I am able to feel things in the here and now and use whatever I feel. I can turn it into something interesting to watch. But back to the screen test, then the hairdresser came to see if I was okay and poked me in the eye with a comb. For the first second it was like, "How could you do this on the biggest day of my life?" Then I realized, "No, no, no. That's fabulous. Step on my foot. I don't care anymore." It really changed my life. I try to realize that I'm always experiencing *something*. Even if it's that I can't work it up for this scene, at least I'm feeling that.

DS: *Do you take time — as you described you were doing at that time — to prepare? Do you still do that before a take?*

GD: Less and less. I just want to know what my intention is in the scene. My script is filled with notes by the time I'm going to shoot it. I decide what my goal is for every moment in the scene and then try to remain open as to how I'm going to accomplish the goal.

DS: *You're really talking about your objective.*

GD: I'll look at my notes almost every time before a take just to refresh myself and remember what I'm trying to accomplish in the scene. I don't often have to spend a lot of time before a take to get into character as long as I know where I've just come from.

DS: *Do you concern yourself at all with creating the reality behind the objective? In other words, if you need to get reassurance from somebody, do you work on creating the insecurity that would make you seek reassurance?*

GD: Yes, I do that.

DS: *Which is the kind of preparation that propels you into the objective. But you don't spend a lot of time.*

GD: I don't spend a lot of time on it. As I said, I usually let it go completely and don't make myself stay in some sort of "mood."

DS: *But your focus is on something personal that evokes a strong desire to go into the scene and get what you need. How do you handle multiple takes? You've already said you like many takes because the more you do, the freer you feel . . . the more spontaneous you are.*

GD: I do. I do. I never think, "Okay let's stop," because I always feel there's something else that I might be able to find.

DS: *Do you concern yourself with matching emotional and business continuity?*

GD: As far as matching business, it just absolutely happens without my having to think about it too much. I'm really lucky. There's just some part of my brain that keeps track of it. Sometimes I'll do such complicated things that the script supervisor will say, "You realize that we're printing that take and in that one you picked up a cup and took a half a sip, touched your hair, and then you fixed your shirt." But I don't worry about it. I can almost always remember what I did without having to consciously keep track.

DS: *So matching is just as critical as it ever was?*

GD: Well, I don't want to make an otherwise good take unusable because I leaned back at the wrong time! I like to do a lot of business and, fortunately, I'm able to recall it.

DS: *Do you think directors should take an acting class? Do you think it would be valuable for them?*

GD: You know, I'm not going to recommend what they should do because I've worked with some great, great directors and I have no idea whether they've ever taken an acting class. Probably not, but there didn't seem to be anything lacking in them. I guess I would say that it couldn't hurt.

DS: *Can you give an example of when a director really helped you and how he contributed to your performance?*

GD: On the movie *Stuart Little* I thought that I had a really good understanding of what I wanted to accomplish and how I would play the character. But the director, Rob Minkoff, said something that was incredibly helpful. We were talking about the scene where we first meet Stuart in the orphanage. I asked, "Now when we first see him, should there be a tiny moment where we go, 'Oh, it's a mouse.' Just a tiny moment?" Because the line is, "Oh, hello." My instinct was to have a tiny second to think, "Oh, this is a bit weird," but the director said, "No, I think that this moment is what the whole movie is about. You're setting the tone for the entire movie because your reaction to him will tell people that this is a world where mice talk. This is a world where it's completely accepted and normal that mice talk. You should not react at all. This should be the most normal, 'Oh yes,' and 'Hello.' That will color the audience's acceptance of him right from the beginning." It was incredibly helpful. When I do interviews about the movie, everyone I talk to remarks on that moment: "It's so interesting how you accepted him right from the beginning." I think it was great and it had not occurred to me, but it was the director's view of the world of the movie and it definitely worked.

Directors have the same goal that I do: getting the best performance on film. Sometimes it just takes my saying, "You know, I can't do this scene as a whole. Can we break it down into smaller parts?" From my experience they mostly want to help you and indulge you. I'm always thinking of what might help me. Something like, "Can we do just this part of the scene?" Or, "Can I do this one line over and over again?" Whatever it takes.

DS: *Have you ever had a director coach you from the sidelines?*

GD: Let's see. I can't remember a specific incident, but they are completely welcome to do so. I'm not in any way precious about it. If they want to, they can talk to me. There was a funny incident once when I had quite a long monologue to do and the other actor, as we were shooting the take, spontaneously started saying things in between my lines — things that were incredibly helpful to me.

DS: *He didn't even ask you?*

GD: He didn't ask. He just started doing it. It completely affected me. It threw me, excited me. He never overlapped my lines. He'd just throw in a comment like, "Bullshit." Or he'd say, "You're right." Things like that. Obviously, it had a profound effect on me, helped me.

DS: *Do you like to watch dailies while working on a film?*

GD: Always. It started on *Tootsie,* my first film. Dustin grabbed me at lunchtime and said, "Come with me. You're coming to dailies," and I didn't even know what that was. We watched the stuff that I had shot the day before and he said, "Look at that. You did this but it didn't read well on this take. See how it comes across here?" I had never even seen myself on film and it really taught me how to look at dailies. I learned from the very beginning how to use dailies to my advantage.

I don't go to dailies to see how I look. Well, if I look absolutely horrendous I might say to the director, "Is there something we can do about this?" But that's not what I'm looking for. I go to dailies to check my work. I've learned how to use it as an incredibly valuable tool.

Sometimes, I think a shot will come across great because it just felt so incredible. But then when I see the dailies, I can't tell the difference between that take and the other one where I felt I was faking it! If you watch dailies, you might still have a chance to fix a problem somewhere else. If you missed an important character beat that you wanted to get across, you can say, "Well, I'll put it in another scene." So if I go, I can keep better track of what I want to be accomplishing.

However, some directors are resistant to actors going to dailies. Seven times out of ten, they say yes. Three times out of ten they say, "Oooh, I don't really like that idea." Then, I talk them into it. I've always gone. It's just a part of how I work. Only one time have I encountered a director who absolutely said, "No." They fear you are either going to judge other people's work or you are going to become self-conscious and change your performance because you don't want to look unattractive.

The truth is, I've gone to dailies on every movie and I know how to use it as a tool to my advantage. I'm not going to use it to limit myself. I'm going to use it to expand what I'm trying to do. My feeling is that the director should leave it up to actors to know whether they want to or not.

DS: *On the other hand, an actor can become very self-conscious after viewing the dailies.*

GD: That is the risk. An actor just has to know whether it helps or hurts them. I know many actors who not only don't go to dailies, they don't go to the movie when it's done. They hate watching themselves on film.

Directors are probably worried that I'm going to be checking on their directing — whether or not *they're doing* a good job. But that's not really what I'm worried about. I'm trying to help them by making sure *I do* a good job.

ANTHONY FRANCIOSA
Actor

Anthony Franciosa, a notable Broadway actor, won raves for his leading role in *A Hatful of Rain* and was awarded the Theatre World Award and the Outer Critics Circle Award for his performance. When he reprised the role in the movie version, he won the Best Actor Award at the Venice Film Festival and was nominated for an Academy Award as Best Actor. Two years later, he won the Golden Globe Best Actor in a Drama for the film *Career.* He co-starred in Elia Kazan's *A Face in the Crowd,* as well as in his own television series, *The Name of the Game.* He has starred in 50 films and guest starred on many television series.

DS: Your first film was *A Face in the Crowd,* directed by Elia Kazan. It starred Andy Griffith and Patricia Neal. Did Kazan cast you from New York?

AF: Yes.

DS: *What were the auditions like?*

AF: I didn't audition for it. He just cast me. He had seen me in *A Hatful of Rain* on Broadway and asked me if I'd like to do this role.

DS: *What kind of role was it?*

AF: He was a fella named Joey, a little office boy in Tekid, Arkansas. He sees his chance to glory when he meets a character that charms everyone with his music. He becomes his publicity agent and is rather ruthless. As soon as his client starts losing favor with the public, he moves on. He ends up a very rich and famous person.

DS: *That's not anything like the part in* A Hatful of Rain.

AF: No, it's totally different.

DS: *Do you have any idea why Kazan thought of you for the part?*

AF: I think that because Kazan was an actor himself, his forte was to elicit great performance from actors. He wasn't into type casting. He judged a person's talent and if they had the right age, the right look, and the right energy for a role, that was good enough. He never assumed that an actor could not play another kind of role.

DS: *Did you find him particularly perceptive?*

AF: Always. Always. Kazan was an incredibly charming man and one of the things he had, that you felt most strongly about, was his tremendous respect and affection for the actor. He was completely open to what you wanted to do and never judged you in a negative way or made you feel you couldn't do it. He always encouraged you to do more than you thought you could. He believed in freedom for the actor. He would always say, "Let me see what you can do. Let me see it. Don't talk to me about it." You felt that you had a man who was completely on your side — no qualms about anything you did. He gave you a tremendous sense of confidence.

DS: *Did he ever go up to actors individually and speak to them privately?*

AF: All the time.

DS: *Did he ever give direction to an actor in front of another actor? Or, did he always talk to an actor privately?*

AF: If he wanted to tell the actor something he didn't want the other actor to be aware of, then he would tell the actor very privately. Many times this was the way he directed because he felt that the element of surprise was very important. He would tell an actor to do something that would elicit another reaction from the other actor in the scene. For example, he wanted a particular reaction from Patricia Neal in *A Face in the Crowd*. It was her close-up and he wanted a moment of great surprise and shock. We were doing the takes, one and two, and then he indicated to me that he wanted me to say some things to her.

DS: *Things of a personal nature or things relevant to the character?*

AF: Nothing to do with what was going on. He would sometimes ask you to say something that your character might not say — even to use a word, an expression...

DS: *A naughty word?*

AF: Yes. Well, sometimes it really worked.

DS: *What kind of direction did you get from him that was enlightening?*

AF: This was a movie, not a play, and he had a way of watching an actor's natural behavior off camera. He would notice a particular characteristic of the actor, such as the way the actor moves, cocks his head, or expresses something with his hand. He had a knack for using this idiosyncrasy.

DS: *How would he use it?*

AF: For example, I was using my hand to cool myself on a hot day. He saw me doing this and said, "Tony, keep doing that." He said to someone, "Bring the camera over here," and told me to look off and keep doing what I was doing. He used it.

DS: *What about finding emotional colors?*

AF: Well, during the scene he would talk to you. He would say, "Give him a nice good kiss on the cheek. Just grab him!" while the camera was still rolling, and he would sometimes use it.

DS: *What was the difference for you in terms of working on film as opposed to Broadway?*

AF: Kazan said to me, "I don't care what you do. Don't think in terms of big or small. Just think in terms of the truth." Kazan was a man of very high emotional pitch. He never kept saying, "Give me more," or "Give me less." He just used to say, "Let's try it again." He was so involved in the dynamics of the scene, in terms of the truth. If he felt that it was truthful, he would go along with it.

In one particular scene I ad-libbed a line. He was always one for extemporaneous speech from what I'd heard. This particular movie, though, was written by Budd Schulberg and he made it a point to tell the actors to just stick to the lines. In one scene I ad-libbed a line and it was a kind of important scene in the move. I also ad-libbed some singing and in those two instances, which were quite important, he allowed that. He consulted Schulberg, who was always on the set, and it was okay.

DS: *How did you feel acting for the camera?*

AF: He never made me feel as though I was acting for the camera. Many times, I never even knew where the camera was. Many actors usually know where the camera is and play to it.

DS: *What if he needed to repeat a moment?*

AF: He would just say, "Let's do it again."

DS: *He didn't care about matching?*

AF: No. He never cared.

DS: *Did you experience the problem of matching with other film directors?*

AF: Oh, constantly. I don't find it too often in films today. When I started, the script girl was in charge of seeing that everything matched. There seems to be a more spontaneous way of dealing with it today. There isn't a continuity woman telling you, "Oh, that's where you raised the glass to your lips." You don't see that anymore and I'm not quite sure why.

DS: *But how did having to concern yourself with matching affect you?*

AF: Oh, it affects you in a very negative way because you are constantly aware that you have to do the same thing every time and it makes you very self-conscious.

DS: *What were your experiences with other film directors who were not as generous with actors as Kazan was?*

AF: Generally speaking, most directors don't know anything about acting. They don't quite know what to say to you except, "That was very good," and "Let's try it again." But that's okay. You learn. Actors can't rely on a director to help them. You have to come in fully loaded with your own stuff.

DS: *In working with other directors, did you find that they did you more harm than good?*

AF: Well, sometimes. When I was most ill-prepared to do some work, I could be very negatively affected by a director. I think that it's incumbent upon the actor to take care of himself.

DS: *What happens when you come in with some ideas and the director disagrees completely?*

AF: You're hired to do the film and you either do what he wants or you can walk away from the movie. Usually, though, there's some kind of understanding between the actor and the director about what's required.

I worked with other highly respected and admired directors in the film industry. Martin Ritt was one of my favorites and I found Fred Zinneman to be very sensitive and enjoyable to work with. My work with George Cukor, however, was not particularly constructive. For some reason, our relationship started on the wrong foot and never got better. It proved to me, that, as in all relationships, if people cannot resolve their feelings of negativity — or at least make a good-faith effort to resolve them — its pretty well guaranteed that no good can come of it.

BARRY PRIMUS
Actor

Barry Primus, a notable Broadway actor, was a member of Elia Kazan's original company at the Lincoln Center in New York. He has appeared in some forty films including *The Rose, New York New York, The River, Night and the City*, and many more. He co-wrote and directed the feature film *Mistress*, which starred and was produced by Robert DeNiro. His many television shows include *The Practice, Picket Fences*, and *The X-Files*. He has directed such television shows as *V.I.P.* and *Tribeca*, and has also directed theater, both in New York and Los Angeles.

DS: *When working with Kazan, what were rehearsals like?*

BP: To begin rehearsals, Kazan had his cast just read around the table for about two weeks. They did not get up. In casting, he always knew the actors. He didn't read people. I met him for a movie about a year before I started working with him and he just talked to me about my background. The movie was *America America,* so we talked about my background and he even asked, "Are you a good actor?" I said, "Yes," and he said, "Good." He got a sense of me. He used his intuition. He always said, "People who read are just people who read. Sometimes, they read well. Sometimes, they don't. Sometimes the most talented people don't even read well. Of course, reading is an indication and I, as a director, sometimes use it. It is one of the indications, but not all of the indications. You can't totally rely on it." You have to rely, as he did, on your instincts.

He cast me in a very big part in *The Changling*. I was one of the younger actors in the company at the Lincoln Center in the early 1960s when he introduced me to his wife, Molly Thatcher. He purposely introduced me to her to get her opinion of me because he always respected her insights. He wanted people's ideas about people's qualities, what they projected.

DS: *Would he talk to you about your past? Your personal problems? Your experiences?*

BP: Not in a direct way. He would talk to you about what he was looking for. If he was looking for someone with violence in him, then he might discuss something and see what it could invoke in you. He would sometimes ask you direct questions like, "What was your mother like?" and "What was your father like?" But it was often much less direct than that. He would talk about himself and that would stimulate you to reveal something about yourself. That's how he would cast.

He cast me as a very passionate character that is a rebel, a person who commits murder to get a woman. There were certain aspects of me that he felt were right for it. He also felt that I was very sympathetic. He wanted an actor who had violence in him and yet could have his pain understood. He felt I had a young man's tortured quality, which was projected in an empathetic way.

He would always say, "If you don't already have it in you, you can't get it out of you." The bottom line is that the actor has to have what you are looking for within him. If he doesn't have it, you are never going to get it. You can try to teach acting, but that is very dangerous when you are directing. The actor still has to have the potential. Exciting casting is when the actor has it and nobody else has used it.

When Kazan directed Arthur Miller's *After the Fall,* there were actors he directed that did not work out. He worked subjectively, but they didn't like to work that way, so they didn't particularly enjoy working with him. They found it hard and they didn't trust him either. They were people in very big parts — people he had never used before but that he needed for special qualities (verbal dexterity and tremendous presence). I think he found it harder to work with them. They didn't want to be used in a very personal way, so it wasn't easy.

He never badmouthed actors. He always stood by them and never blamed them for anything. He always took it upon himself. He made a pact with the actor, which was that somehow he would help them and they would help him. They were in this war with him, this dark battle, and that was the excitement of being with him.

After every rehearsal he would sit down and decide what it was you had accomplished or not accomplished. And what you hadn't accomplished was just as valuable to him as what you had. He would say, "What we learned today is that you can't do this, and this, and this," — which is very exciting.

He would have actors sit down for two weeks to read the play, discover what the play was about. After two weeks the actors knew enough about the play to start moving. He would talk about what the play was about, which was a technique he got from Harold Clurman while at the Group Theater. Clurman was great at that. He was best on the first day of rehearsal when he would give a long talk about the play. He would inspire the actors, but wasn't a great stager. He didn't have a lot of ideas about staging, nor did he work with the actors in a highly personalized way. He stayed with the actions of the play and worked very strongly with actors' intentions. He cast very well and his productions were very deliberate and very finely delivered. Harold knew his plays very well and really liked actors, but he was not as experimental as Kazan and didn't improvise a great deal.

You always knew you were in good hands with Kazan. He didn't always know what he was doing, but he would still move ahead and say, "I don't know what to do today but let's try this." He was confident in not knowing. He didn't bullshit you. He would always be open enough to say, "I don't know this." He would always tell us to doubt everything. He followed the theory that actors are a little behind in the first days of rehearsal, but then they catch up. And, since the director is always ahead of the actors at the start, he thought the director should lay back and not give them everything right away or it will swamp them.

I once asked him how long he had rehearsed *Streetcar Named Desire* and he took my breath away when he told me that he opened in Boston after three weeks of rehearsal. When you look at the size of the play, how long it is, how complicated it is, you see what an incredibly skilled director he is. It's not mysterious, though, because he had been a stage manager for Clurman and Lee Strasberg. He was an actor. He studied directing at Yale and at Williams College. He read a lot of books and was able to put things together very quickly, if need be. He once said to me on the first day of rehearsal, "You have to know an awful lot about the play before you start. It's really the opening night for directors."

DS: *Did he work in different ways with different people?*

BP: Yes. He was always looking for ways to help each actor, which had to do with who they were and what they needed. Once, on the first day of rehearsals for *The Changling*, I was extremely nervous and stiff and not able to really listen, talk, or do anything. I was full of ideas but none of them were really happening. I wasn't really there. He saw that I was watching him nervously a lot and after one of the rehearsals he said, "I just want to give you this note. I started this play with you and I will end this play with you. Whatever you do, I will never fire you, so don't be nervous about that."

One time I asked him, at some point, not to direct me. It was in the middle of our rehearsal period, somewhere around three months. I asked him not to give me any notes about what I was doing for awhile. I just wanted to do certain things and be left alone about it. And he said, "That's fine." The big thing I remember about him was that he was able to work slowly, build with blocks. He was able to be very confident when we worked slowly. This play was loaded with violence and sexuality. Sometimes he could hardly hear Barbara Loden and me. We were working on a sexual attraction for each other and had all these secrets we created and shared.

DS: *How did you develop that sexuality?*

BP: We brought that in, he didn't give us that. He was hands-on about the meaning of the play and would connect you with the meaning, what each scene was about. Then he would try to fire you up about your objective in some way. He would also try to connect you with someone in an emotional way. He would say, "Look how beautiful that girl is." Or, "That actor doesn't like you, Barry. He is a tall, waspy kind of guy and he looks down on you because you are more ethnic. I know he does."

DS: *Was he saying this privately?*

BP: Yes. I just assumed that he was trying to encourage me and it was good that he was doing it. It was fine because it was helping me. We all knew Kazan. We knew he had those tactics and we would laugh about it. He was a master manipulator. I remember playing a very flamboyant character that was a Moor. Because it took place in sixteenth-century Spain, I wanted a very certain look. So, I used a lot of pictures of Velasquez and Goya and bullfighting pictures. I would rehearse and just play the bullfighter sometimes. Once, I was working on something and he said, "What exactly are you doing?" I was doing a picture exercise, trying to re-create the photo I had by working with a mirror to bring it to the world of the play, but it was very slow. When I told him he said, "Oh, well, good." It must have looked very odd to the other actors. It might have been annoying to another actor, but he said that it sounded good and thought it was creative and with that he signed off. Even though he didn't really understand it at the moment, he knew I was exploring something.

He was very confident, but he could have been frightened of me. I didn't have very much experience in a part that size and he let me know that right away. If nothing else, I could communicate with Kazan. That was his biggest asset. Even when he was worried about some of the actors, he did not share that. He shared, "We will get there. We had a bad day but tomorrow we will have a better one." He did not take his anxiety out on the actors. He did personal things to make you feel good and that was part of his direction. He showed up at my house once and came blustering in. I lived a few blocks from the theater. At that time, Kazan was a very important person and his coming to my house impressed me. He obviously decided that it would be good for me to have that kind of connection, the kind of confidence created by the director coming over. Sometimes, though, we had very big arguments.

DS: *Was this primarily about interpretation?*

BP: No, it was my own fear. It was the actor's fear. Sometimes we'd argue and sometimes he'd settle me down. The part I was playing was very angry and sometimes it would spill over. I was very young at the time and I didn't really understand. I was very frightened of this big opportunity but he was able to help put that in perspective.

In *The Changling* my role, Deflores, had the run of the castle. He wants to have an affair with the castle owner's daughter, Beatrice, played by Barbara Loden, Kazan's new wife. There was a great deal of secrecy in that play: secret meetings, monologues in secret places, hiding and delivering messages. One day, Kazan set up an improv for Barbara and me. He said that she is involved with a man and I needed to spy on her and her lover. So, I had to find ways to spy. I went up on the roof, down the fire escape, and crawled through things while the lovers took cover upstairs, developing their sexual connection. I was getting a physical experience, which I used throughout the play, feeling what it was like to be an outsider — an outcast — and having to use my ingenuity. This improvisation went on all afternoon. It was a basic improvisation that had to be done, and he allowed us the time to do it. He had a lot of patience. He was experimental. He was a process person; ready to do things that hadn't been done before. For Kazan, the most important thing was the theme: how arbitrary authority represses sexuality and growth and causes outbursts. I believe, for him, that was the theme. He worked the play by making the antagonist almost the protagonist because he sympathized with the underdog. This play touched Kazan's own feelings as an underdog. He spent a lot of time talking about being

Greek and Armenian and what it was like to deal with white America. That was his basic theme — that of the outsider — and this play contained that. My character, Deflores, carried a great part of that theme, so Kazan had a great deal to give to me.

That was what was most inspiring about him. He had a grip. He had a point of view that was highly important to him and communicated that to the actors. They flew with that kind of intention. You have to have that kind of grip on a play to have a vision.

I would try a lot of things in rehearsal and he'd jump to his feet and shout, "I love that. I love that, Barry." I once did an improvisation for him in which I expressed my feelings about being an actor and telling people to go fuck themselves. I was combining my personal rebellion with the character that was a rebel. As I said things about Hollywood, he'd say, "I love you, Barry," and run over and punch me in the arm as a sign of affection. Who doesn't want to work with a director like that?

Working with a good director is always a mystery, because what you are responding to is what he is. Finally, good work is the result of character and personality, and Kazan had a very specific character and personality. He was highly charged and very dynamic.

DS: *You said you had a wonderful experience during the improvisation about spying. How did you manage to re-create that experience during the performance?*

BP: I don't specifically remember, but I don't think I re-created the experience. I think just doing it gave us all a feeling of what we needed to do. Climbing on the roof was so exotic and I had it in me: the experience was in me. It was in my body. One practical thing came out of this improv. Two days later Kazan took me to lunch and we discussed the improv we'd done at rehearsal. He asked me, based on that improv, where I thought my room might be. Of course it was a good idea, but I think the deeper reason for doing this was that my character knows the castle better than anyone else does and this gave me a sense that it was mine. And on a deeper level, it once again was a sign of his confidence in me, which is what every actor needs most.

EPILOGUE

Studying people, digging into scripts and their characters, and humanizing it all has always been an exciting experience for me. Examining and putting together all the pieces of the puzzle until they create a comprehensible and organic whole is like detective work — always new, challenging, and fulfilling.

There is so much to think about as a director — bringing the story to life, pulling together the right cast, getting the best work from them, creating the right atmosphere, and knowing when to step in or get out of the way. My objective here has been to introduce and describe various principles and skills to assist you in your work. Out of necessity, much of what I've covered overlaps so I worry that I may have overlooked an essential point, not explained it sufficiently, or repeated myself. Nonetheless, rest assured that you'll approach your next project better equipped. As a result, your work will be more informed and grounded. Don't expect everything to fall into place automatically though because there are no absolutes in the creative process.

Leave no stone unturned in your quest to create meaningful work. Our mission as directors and actors is to touch people and to awaken their sense of universality. Find the common denominator between yourself and others and bring that sensibility to your work. Go beyond words, plot, and effects and don't let the technology distract you from your greater focus. Technology is meant to help reach your goals. It is the means to an end and should not be the end in itself.

This process is a journey of great surprises, adventures, and risks. The reward will be in the fruition of your vision. Bring your heart and passion to your work and you'll never regret the struggle.

Good luck and enjoy your journey.

— Delia Salvi

APPENDIX

In this Appendix you'll find a useful character analysis chart, a list of action verbs, and Recommended Reading for further study.

APPENDIX A: CHARACTER ANALYSIS CHART

The purpose of this chart is to illustrate, in the simplest way, the logical sequence of your character choices. This happens once you have synthesized your analysis of their background.

Sections A through C are the foundation from which you determine your character's objectives in a scene. Sections D through J deal specifically with their behavior in the scene.

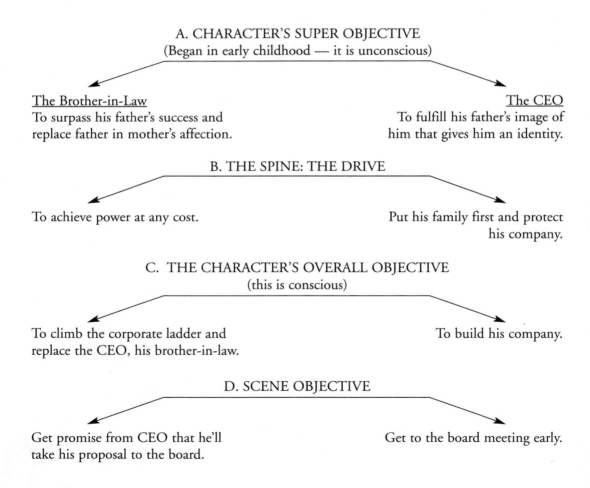

A. CHARACTER'S SUPER OBJECTIVE
(Began in early childhood — it is unconscious)

The Brother-in-Law
To surpass his father's success and replace father in mother's affection.

The CEO
To fulfill his father's image of him that gives him an identity.

B. THE SPINE: THE DRIVE

To achieve power at any cost.

Put his family first and protect his company.

C. THE CHARACTER'S OVERALL OBJECTIVE
(this is conscious)

To climb the corporate ladder and replace the CEO, his brother-in-law.

To build his company.

D. SCENE OBJECTIVE

Get promise from CEO that he'll take his proposal to the board.

Get to the board meeting early.

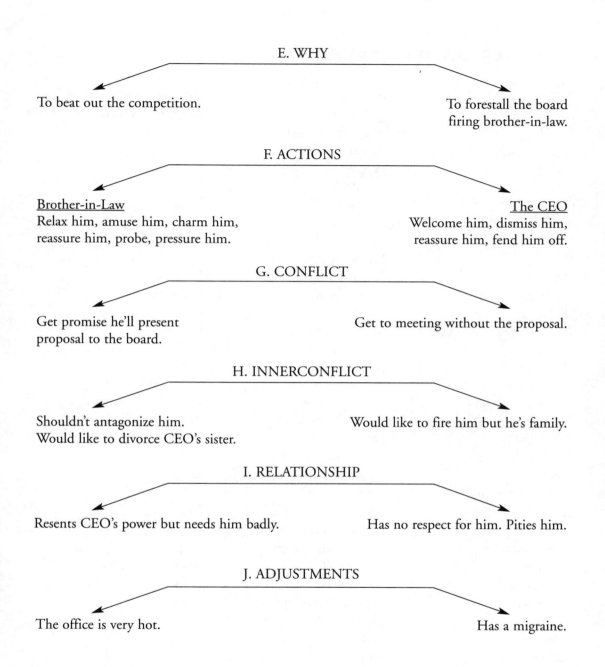

E. WHY

To beat out the competition.

To forestall the board
firing brother-in-law.

F. ACTIONS

Brother-in-Law
Relax him, amuse him, charm him,
reassure him, probe, pressure him.

The CEO
Welcome him, dismiss him,
reassure him, fend him off.

G. CONFLICT

Get promise he'll present
proposal to the board.

Get to meeting without the proposal.

H. INNERCONFLICT

Shouldn't antagonize him.
Would like to divorce CEO's sister.

Would like to fire him but he's family.

I. RELATIONSHIP

Resents CEO's power but needs him badly.

Has no respect for him. Pities him.

J. ADJUSTMENTS

The office is very hot.

Has a migraine.

APPENDIX B: SAMPLE ACTION VERBS

adhere
advise
assail
assert myself
avoid
bait
be on guard
be the center of attention
beat down
beg/plead
blast
bluff my way
bolster up
brighten the atmosphere
bruise
build up
calm down
captivate people
capture
catch the eye
change the mood
charm
check things out
cheer up
cling
come out on top
comfort
command
complain
confound
confront
connect
defend
demand recognition
derail
dismiss
do my work

draw the line
embolden
escape from people
examine
expose
face destiny
fight the lie
figure them out
find protection
find something to do
flatter
flaunt my gifts
flirt
force connection
free myself
get all I can
get along
get consolation
get in everywhere
get love
get on the good side
get rid of someone
get to the point
get the truth
get the upper hand
get through to them
give my all
go against
grab the opportunity
guide
haul over the coals
have fun
heal
help
hide my feelings
hold on to someone
hold onto

hold up
humiliate someone
ignite
ignore
impale
incite
induce
inflame
invite
keep from being destroyed
keep going
lead by the nose
level
live it up
maintain my dignity
make myself alluring
make someone laugh
make them understand
melt into the woodwork
mock
nail
nullify
oblige
overcome
pick up the pieces
please everyone
possess everything
pressure
prevail
probe
protect
prove my innocence
prove my superiority
provoke
pry
pull myself together
pull the strings

push
put on ice
quiet
rationalize
rebel against
refuse
remind
resist
respond
ridicule
rouse
save myself
scar
scorn
seduce
see it through to the end
serve with love
shape
show interest
shut out the world

smash
snatch
sooth
squash
squirm through
stand up to
stir
stop this
straighten them out
subdue
supplicate
surrender
survive
sustain
take over
tantalize
tickle
toy with
urge
wait it out

win back
win my place
win someone over
wound
write off

APPENDIX C: RECOMMENDED READING

There are so many wonderful books on directing, acting, and writing that one would hardly know where begin. Therefore, I have listed those that address themselves most specifically with the goals, values, and processes expressed in this book. These books, in turn, should guide you future reading.

Directing
Dmytryk, Edward, *On Screen Directing,* Focal Press, 1984
Ciment, Michel, *Kazan on Kazan,* Viking Press, 1974
Clurman, Harold, *On Directing,* Macmillan Publ., 1972
Kazan, Elia, *A Life,* Alfred A. Knopf, 1988
Lumet, Sidney, *Making Movies,* Alfred A. Knopf, 1995
Rabiger, Michael, *Directing: Film Technique and Aesthetics,* Focal Press, 1989.
Stevens, Jon, *Actors Turned Directors,* Silman - James Press, 1997
Young, Jeff, *Kazan - The Master Director Discusses His Films,* Newmarket Press, 1999

Acting
Brestoff, Richard, *The Great Acting Teachers,* Smith & Krause, 1995
Easty, Edward Dwight, *On Method Acting,* House of Collectibles, 1966
Hagen, Uta, *Respect for Acting,* Macmillan Publ., 1973
Hethmon, Robert, *Strasberg At the Actors Studio,* Theatre Communications Group, 1991
Hull, Lorrie, *Strasberg's Method As Taught,* Oxbow Publ., 1985
Manso, Peter, *Brando,* Hyperion, 1994
Meisner, Sanford and Dennis Longwell, *Sanford Meisner's On Acting,* Vintage Books, 1987
Stanislavski, Constantin, *An Actor Prepares,* Theatre Arts Books, 1936
Stanislavski, Constantin, *Creating a Role,* Theatre Arts Books, 1961
Strasberg, Lee, *A Dream of Passion,* Little Brown and Co., 1987

Miscellaneous
Aristotle, *The Poetics,* Hill &Wang, Incorporated, 1972
Freud, Sigmund, *Totem and Taboo,* A.A. Brill, Promethus Books, 2000
Egri, Lajos, *The Art of Dramatic Writing,* Simon and Schuster, 1946

INDEX